GUADALUPE
MOUNTAINS
NATIONAL
PARK

GUADALUPE MOUNTAINS NATIONAL PARK

An Environmental History
of the Southwest Borderlands

Jeffrey P. Shepherd

UNIVERSITY OF MASSACHUSETTS PRESS
Amherst and Boston

Copyright © 2019 by University of Massachusetts Press
All rights reserved
Printed in the United States of America

ISBN 978-1-62534-434-2 (paper); 433-5 (hardcover)

Designed by Sally Nichols
Set in Adobe Garamond Pro and ITC Franklin Gothic

Cover design by Rebecca Lown
Cover photo by Anton Foltin, *El Capitan, under storm clouds*, in *Guadalupe Mountains National Park, Texas*. Shutterstock.com.

Library of Congress Cataloging-in-Publication Data
Names: Shepherd, Jeffrey P., 1970– author.
Title: Guadalupe Mountains National Park : an environmental history of the
   Southwest borderlands / Jeffrey P. Shepherd.
Description: Amherst : University of Massachusetts Press, [2019] | Includes
   bibliographical references and index. |
Identifiers: LCCN 2018053115 (print) | LCCN 2018058844 (ebook) | ISBN
   9781613766842 (ebook) | ISBN 9781613766859 (ebook) | ISBN 9781625344335
   (hardcover) | ISBN 9781625344342 (pbk.)
Subjects: LCSH: Guadalupe Mountains National Park (Tex.)—History. |
   Guadalupe Mountains National Park (Tex.)—Environmental
   conditions—History. | Nature—Effect of human beings on—Texas—Guadalupe
   Mountains National Park—History. | Landscape changes—Texas—Guadalupe
   Mountains National Park—History. | National parks and reserves—Texas.
Classification: LCC F392.G86 (ebook) | LCC F392.G86 S54 2019 (print) | DDC
   976.4/94—dc23
LC record available at https://lccn.loc.gov/2018053115

British Library Cataloguing-in-Publication Data
A catalog record for this book is available from the British Library.

Contents

Acknowledgments vii

Introduction 1

CHAPTER ONE
Geology and Environment 11

CHAPTER TWO
Pre-Columbian Indigenous Worlds..................................... 20

CHAPTER THREE
Indigenous Peoples, Spain, and Mexico 36

CHAPTER FOUR
War, Exploration, and Conquest, 1836–1865..................... 58

CHAPTER FIVE
Conflict and Early Community Formation, 1865–1881 84

CHAPTER SIX
The Nature of Economic Development in the
Texas-New Mexico Borderlands, 1880–1915 103

CHAPTER SEVEN
The Interwar Years, 1919–1941 122

CHAPTER EIGHT
The Creation of Guadalupe Mountains National Park 150

CHAPTER NINE
A National Park for the Twenty-First Century 170

CONCLUSION
A National Park in the Southwest Borderlands 197

Notes 203
Index 223

Acknowledgments

This book grew out of a contract with the National Park Service that I received in 2006 (NOA #26-3007-75). When I began the project I knew little about the Guadalupe Mountains, but I had spent a lifetime camping in national parks across the country, so the offer was impossible to turn down. In addition, it afforded a chance to make a contribution to our understanding of the ways in which people interact with their natural environments: how they perceive and misperceive them, try to control and transform them, and in this case, how they ultimately decide to live with and in them. My initial forays into academia began with environmental histories of the intersections between race, labor, and the environment, so this project brought me back to those "intellectual roots," so to speak. Thus, this project was a great combination of long-time scholarly interests in environmental history and a personal affinity for the outdoors. In short, who could turn down an offer to write about the history of a national park? Who wouldn't want to spend time in the Guadalupe Mountains?

I have numerous people to thank for assisting me with this endeavor. Several years ago I received a call from Bob Spude of the National Park Service. After missing each other a few times, Bob and I finally had a chance to talk about the scope and parameters of the project. After a moment of hesitancy, I happily agreed to start. Since that initial phone call, Bob has been a mentor and friend who offered unflagging support.

I would also like to single out several people at the park itself. First, gratitude goes to John Lujan, who served as superintendent of the park for most of the time that I was working on the contract. John's optimism and love for history made this project quite enjoyable. Jan Wobbenhorst was the head park ranger when I began, and until she decided to partake in the joys of retirement, she was an energetic advisor with great knowledge of the community. Like John and Jan, Fred Armstrong, who oversaw cultural and biological resources, was an endless source of information and advice, especially when I was confused about the myriad animals and plants of the park. Finally, nearly a dozen park staff extended a helping hand and a friendly face when I needed assistance.

I relied on people from across New Mexico and Texas as I conducted research into the history of the Guadalupe Mountains and land use throughout the region. Staff at the New Mexico State Library and Archives in Santa Fe helped me navigate materials from the Spanish colonial era through the New Deal programs of the 1930s. Faith Youman was gracious as I grappled with documents pertaining to the Mescalero Apache; and Samuel Sisneros at the State Library of New Mexico and later, at the University of New Mexico, was invaluable in response to my requests. Thomas Jaehn assisted me while conducting research at the Fray Angélico Chávez History Library in Santa Fe; and Ann M. Massman provided assistance with early Spanish colonial records at the Center for Southwest Research at the University of New Mexico.

At New Mexico State University in Las Cruces, I would like to thank the staff of the Zuhl and Branson Libraries and the wonderful people at the Rio Grande Collection. Daniel Smith was a great resource with an extensive knowledge of library materials. Midway into the project I learned that Dr. Dwight Pitcaithley joined the Department of History at New Mexico State University, after serving as the chief historian for the National Park Service from 1995–2005. Dwight has been a great resource and I have enjoyed our conversations about the Guadalupe Mountains. In Alamogordo and Carlsbad, several historians and staff members of the National Forest and Park Services, especially Eric Dillingham, provided me with information on the Guadalupes in New Mexico and Texas. I'd especially like to express my appreciation to David Kayser and Samuel Denman at the Carlsbad Office of the Park Service for assisting with work in the near freezing temperature warehouse that contained great information on the creation of the Guadalupe Park and controversies related to wildlife, natural history, and animal populations.

After several trips back and forth to Austin, Texas, I met many people who provided assistance. At the Dolph Briscoe Center for American History at the University of Texas, I want to thank Margaret Shankley and Stephanie Malmros. At the center I found the only remaining copies of the Van Horn Advocate from the early twentieth century; these are not even available at the newspaper office due to a fire decades ago. The staff at the Texas State General Land Office provided support as I stumbled into the history of Texas land policy. John Molleston, Isabel Alfaro, Kevin Klaus, and Bobby Santiesteban were patient during my crash course in Texas history. The main library at the University of Texas also helped me access books and materials I needed to use while visiting the state capital. The staff at the Texas State Library, especially Donaly E. Brice, senior research assistant, offered useful tips for research, and for using the incredible resource that is known as the Texas Archive Resources Online (TARO). In Van Horn, I'd like to thank the staff at the Van Horn Public Library and the individuals who provided assistance with deeds and records at the Culberson County Court House.

The Department of Special Collections at Sul Ross State University, which also houses the Center for Big Bend Studies, was helpful with my research there. The department and center are wonderful resources that few people have utilized. They have created small treasure trove of materials not only for researchers interested in the long history of west Texas, but the U.S.-Mexico borderlands more broadly. In particular, I would like to thank Melleta Bell and her staff for their assistance with materials in the collection.

Toward the end of the project, I found a cache of sources at the Southwest Special Collections Department at the library of Texas Tech University. After contacting the archives, I was amazed at the alacrity with which Dr. Monte Monroe, senior archivist, came to my rescue. A Formby Fellowship funded research into the papers of Glenn Biggs, a key advocate for the Guadalupe Mountains National Park. Without Monte's extensive knowledge of Trans-Pecos history, I could not have completed this project. Also at Texas Tech, I want to thank Dr. Tai Kreidler; Dr. Diane Warner, and the great staff of the Special Collections Department.

At my home institution, the University of Texas at El Paso, I would like to thank several people. Claudia Rivers has been the head of Special Collections for several years, and her knowledge of the resources for the U.S.-Mexico borderlands is astonishing. My doctoral assistant, now professor at CSU-Northridge, John Paul Nuno, conducted research at the Special Collections Department at UTEP and at the Southwest and Border Collection at the El Paso Public Library. I would like to thank our wonderful department chairs that supported me during the life of the project: Paul Edison, Yolanda Leyva, and Sam Brunk. And finally, as always, I want to express my gratitude to Edith Yanez, departmental administrative assistant, and the real person who kept the department running.

After starting the project, I ran into problems that required specific acknowledgement of one person. Because of its multidisciplinary dimension, I relied heavily on experts in the fields of biology, geology, and archeology. When I finally tackled the chapter on archeology—after skipping over it in favor of others—I turned to David Carmichael in the UTEP Department of Sociology and Anthropology. David's patient and detailed replies to my questions about archeology saved me from certain doom. His knowledge about Southwestern archeology and the ethnohistory of Indigenous peoples such as the Mescalero Apache helped me answer key questions in this report. Although he helped me immeasurably, any mistakes are purely my responsibility.

While working on the final phases of the book, I relied heavily on many people, all of whom helped me think deeply about environmental history. I want to thank Sterling Evans and Flannery Burke for their careful reading of the manuscript ant their insightful suggestions on how to improve it. Everyone at the University of Massachusetts Press has been wonderful, but I would especially like to express my gratitude to Matt Becker, Rachael DeShano, Courtney Andree, and John Berry. I would also like to thank Dr. Ignacio Martinez, my colleague in the History Department. He and I finished our books together, and his friendship and intellectual support helped me through some difficult moments.

And finally, I would like to thank my wife, Dr. Cynthia L. Bejarano, and our son, Joaquin Felix. Cynthia patiently supported my repeated departures for "the park," and confidently defended my junkets to skeptical friends and family who joked that I was surely going on just another camping trip. I have always appreciated your faith in my abilities and your constant encouragement when I doubted myself. And to our son, Joaquin Felix, to whom I hope to impart a love of nature, hiking, and camping in the Guadalupe Mountains and in national parks across the country. This book is as much about the people enjoying the outdoors and negotiating the natural environment in the past as much as it is for your generation appreciating our national treasures in the future.

GUADALUPE
MOUNTAINS
NATIONAL
PARK

Introduction

The sheer rock face of El Capitan, which juts out over the expansive Chihuahuan Desert, is one of the most iconic landmarks of the Texas-New Mexico borderlands region. It has been a crucial component of the sacred landscapes of indigenous peoples, and it has been an important point of reference for the Spanish explorers, westward migrants, military expeditions, and American settlers navigating this vast sea of xeric grasslands, ubiquitous cacti, and breathtaking skies. The stunning feature that has served as a centerpiece for the region's history is the result of millions of years of transformation from a massive ocean, covering most of the Southwest and northern Mexico, to the present-day arid landscape. This deep history, combined with shifts in the regional climate and changes in local flora and fauna, created an environment that is unique yet representative of the northern Chihuahuan and southwestern plains ecosystems.

Understanding this region requires one to slow down, stop, and contemplate the impressive timeframe and the glacial changes that forged the topography. Millions of years passed from what was once an impressive sea to an arid basin and range landscape that proved challenging to even the most resilient hunter-gathering populations. Only the informed hypotheses of geologists can help us grasp the millennia of transformations that produced the towering outcropping known as El Capitan. Indeed, geologists from around the world visit the park to study this astonishing feature.

Scientific expeditions over the twentieth century have yielded speculation on the cultures and peoples that lived in or passed through the Guadalupe Mountains Trans-Pecos region. Due to the characteristics of an arid and rugged landscape, the area has stood at the periphery of the greater Southwest, northern Mexico, and the southern plains. On the one hand it was a marginal place capable of supporting few people within the immediate boundary of the national park. Indeed the greater Guadalupe Mountains Trans-Pecos region was not very welcoming to the peoples and cultures that are associated with it. And yet, the harsh ruggedness of the region was attractive as a refuge from the sporadic violence of human interaction. Native peoples such as the Apache made semipermanent homes in the mountains, in what is referred to as "the Bowl," where water, shade, and small game can be found. The Spaniards saw little that was appealing to them, but they did utilize the salt beds at the foot of the mountains. Explorers, migrants, and settlers moved through the region in the nineteenth century, found water in the springs and languished in the cool breezes and afternoon shade of the eastern side of the mountain. Cattle drives moved northward, and a few families homesteaded in the area. By the early twentieth century, the region remained nearly as quiet as it had been for millennia.

This book narrates the environmental history of the Guadalupe Mountains, the national park, and surrounding borderlands, drawing upon archival documents, published research, and government reports. It begins with the geological and environmental characteristics of the region, and then surveys the precontact cultures associated with the Guadalupe Mountains in New Mexico and Texas, the area between present-day Las Cruces and the Pecos River, and the territory between Roswell and El Paso. Of particular interest are the relationships between the peoples associated with the mountains and the Puebloan, Mogollon, and Hohokam cultures of the Greater Southwest borderlands.

A narrative synthesis of multiple fields opens up new possibilities for understanding the environmental history of the U.S.-Mexico borderlands. Situated at the confluence of different strands of thinking about the past, this book relies on the work of scholars interested in the histories of Native peoples in the American West and the northern Chihuahuan Desert and the Trans-Pecos region, scholars investigating the multicultural history of the U.S.-Mexico borderlands, and those intrigued by the relationships between humans and their environments.[1] Of particular emphasis is the manner in which different groups grappled with a landscape of extremes: the Guadalupe Mountains and the surrounding

FIGURE 1. Guadalupe Mountain region.
—Map by Roger Renteria.

region is hot and dry, with salt beds and cacti seemingly everywhere. Aside from a few springs on the eastern escarpment of the mountains, the only source of water to speak of is the Pecos River, which was mercurial and ornery. The region's soils are mean to farmers and the forests are stingy and thin: not a good combination when trying to grow crops and build a house. Alternately, the mountains explode out of a vast terrain that was once the basin of a large ocean floor, offering a stark reminder that our landscapes are chiseled out of millennia of glacial change punctuated by violent upheaval and transformation. Atop the Guadalupes sits the highest point in Texas, what locals call "the Bowl," with its park-like woodlands reminiscent of the Rocky Mountains. On the west side of the mountains are sun baked slopes and rock outcroppings that crash into the salt beds and the surrounding desert, while on the eastern face one is surprised to find lush canyons, creeks, and stands of trees that are practically stolen from Ohio or Pennsylvania. Indeed, the extremes and contradictions are what simultaneously attracted people to and repelled them from this remote corner of the world.

The focus on a natural topographical feature like a mountain that cuts across several political boundaries such as state and territorial lines poses some real and practical research challenges.[2] The region, though captivating and curious, never attracted vast numbers of people with a penchant for building institutions and producing documentation for historians to use in books like this. Despite a handful of archaeological excavations at important sites throughout the region, the area is not as rich in resources as the Gila Mountains or Chaco Canyon. Whereas the public lands of New Mexico have been conducive to field research, government reports, and archaeological projects, the prevalence of private property in Texas has reduced the amount of fieldwork conducted there. Moreover, the agencies overseeing sites in Texas have had difficulty protecting human remains and material culture. The Antiquities Act and the Native American Graves Protection and Repatriation Act, for instance, generally do not apply to much of Texas as it is nearly all private property. All of this complicates conclusions about the human presence on the Texas side of the mountains.

Despite the gap left in the archaeological record, narratives of Spanish colonization shed light on life in the southern New Mexico and West Texas borderlands. Aided by the lack of immunity to European diseases, Spanish conquistadors subjugated large populations of the Caribbean Basin and

Central Mexico within decades of initial contact in 1492. Spain built upon these conquests by exporting the church, state, and military to accompany colonists as they obtained new lands. As outposts of the Spanish Empire grew into villages, presidios, missions, and sea ports, Spanish explorers penetrated the region between Florida and California.[3] They observed different groups interacting in ways that reflected patterns that had been shaped by customs predating Europeans. Native translators and guides escorted the Spanish, had an extensive knowledge of the resources and topography, engaged other groups through a predetermined protocol, and evinced a working grasp of the cultural geography of the region. We can use the records from these interactions to glean a sense of how these groups struggled to survive an arid climate in a landscape that has remained in the historiographical shadow of the Greater Southwest.[4]

The centuries after Spanish arrival were characterized by periods of silence punctuated by cycles of violence and conflict. Spanish policies during the late eighteenth century shifted to militarization of the northern frontier in an attempt to protect settlements from Indians and European competitors. During the 1700s Spanish outposts such as Presidio del Norte (Ojinaga), El Paso del Norte (Ciudad Juarez), Santa Fe, and communities along the Rio Grande in New Mexico launched campaigns against Apaches in the Sierra Blanca Mountains, the Organ Mountains, the Guadalupe Mountains, and further southeast in the Chisos and Davis Mountains, as well as the present-day Big Bend National Park. These expeditions disrupted Native communities, reduced their numbers, and yielded captives and slaves for Spanish haciendas and mines, as well as new converts for the Church. By 1800, however, the Spanish Empire began its slide toward the independence movements that led to the end of the Empire itself. Indian groups endured these upheavals and faced the nascent Mexican nation with an uncertain future. The finances of Mexico after independence were in a shambles, thousands died in the political violence, and the related emergence of the Republic of Texas further destabilized the Spain's northern frontier.

In the wake of these changes, Hispano communities in New Mexico strengthened their ties with an expanding American economy that sent goods from St. Louis to Santa Fe through El Paso and ultimately to Chihuahua City. Far from Mexico City, and thus able to evade some of its punishing tariffs and taxes limiting international trade, the territory of New Mexico forged unique linkages with Puebloan groups and the more mobile Apaches and Comanches. The distant villages also found it easier and more lucrative to trade with the young and energetic nation to the north. These economic connections were part of unfolding developments in the borderlands that reflected a growing sense of Manifest Destiny in the United States. This ideology—with its derogatory racial views of Mexicans and Indians and its assertion that the American West was a virgin land of untapped wealth and promise—led to the war between the United States and Mexico and the loss of half of Mexico's territory. This pivotal event transformed the lives of Native people by paving the way for the migration of settlers into the Guadalupe Mountains during the late nineteenth century.[5]

Situated along what would become an important migration route between San Antonio and California, the Guadalupe Mountain region became part of the larger historical processes of the nineteenth century: westward expansion, Gold Rush migration, Indian wars, railroad development, and American colonization. Military expeditions led by General John Pope, mapping expeditions led by Randolph B. Marcy, and the Butterfield Overland Mail, Apache wars, the Buffalo Soldiers, and cattle drives along the Goodnight-Loving Trail further anchored the mountains into the epic yet violent history of the American West. These narratives should now be familiar to many readers. But situating the Guadalupe Mountains within this history offers us a deeper understanding of the region, and it offers nuance to our knowledge about humans interaction with the land and the natural resources of the Southwest borderlands.

The decades after the Civil War witnessed new trends and important turning points for the Guadalupe Mountains. Apaches won battles against the U.S. Army, but nearly forty years of warfare with the military forced them onto reservations or deported to Florida and Oklahoma. Some Apaches fled south into Mexico, and a few tried blending into the Mexican population of West Texas and southern New Mexico. As a cause and consequence of Native conquest, new arrivals from across America and Europe tried to transform the borderlands to reflect their varied visions and ideals. Hispanos expelled from the Manzano Mountains in northern New Mexico; ex-Confederates disillusioned with postwar race relations in the South; northerners from Connecticut and Maryland; African Americans escaping Jim Crow; and even Swiss and Italian immigrants tried to carve out a living in this arid landscape. All arrived with preconceptions and myths about the bounty that nature could yield, and their dreams were hampered by the unforgiving lands of the greater Trans-Pecos and the highly charged socio-cultural dynamics of the Southern New Mexico-West Texas borderlands.[6] By 1900 the racial and ethnic lines of towns in the region had been defined by segregation and a dual labor force characterized by extractive industries, the labor of people of color, and the capital of Anglos.[7]

Newcomers and the cultures they imported shaped and were shaped by the arid lands they tried to cultivate. Many of the emigrants from the east coast tried to recreate the lands they had left until they realized that the hard soils of the Southwest borderlands could not bring forth the green pastures they desired. As these communities struggled to establish a foothold, the search for water and stronger economic ties to national markets defined the character of life taking shape in the borderlands. The political economy of water allowed large scale irrigation projects to unfold in tandem with a frenzy to dig personal wells and tap into the vast, though not unlimited, aquifer. The towns of the Guadalupe Mountain region boasted a future as the "bread basket of the nation" as towns such as Carlsbad and Roswell briefly attracted colonists from around the world. These early efforts could not control the mercurial Pecos River as it broke through poorly constructed dams and ruined nearby farms. Unregulated ground well pumping produced sink holes, subsidence, and, astonishingly, fields rotting in swamp-like conditions as artesian wells flowed unabated.[8]

As irrigation and artesian wells sparked expansion, boosters played out their dreams of empire with new railway lines connecting them to national markets. As the dreams were realized across the American West, industrialists, capitalists, developers, and politicians promised a new Eden with the arrival of the railroad and the construction of dams and irrigation districts. Beginning with the Southern Pacific in El Paso in 1880, railroads brought people into the region and initiated a socio-cultural and economic revolution that echoed changes across the west. The railroad was the central reason that towns such as Van Horn and Sierra Blanca grew from dots on a map to towns of potential. This growth demanded water, and in turn, the spike in farming and ranching led to a surplus in goods, which led residents to seek links to markets.

In retrospect, the region seemed to follow a script penned by communities across the West as they battled with uncooperative rivers, arid lands, and capitalist economics. Local farmers tied their futures to export production, but the irrigation districts they created required outside investors to pay for the infrastructure that might bring larger returns on their efforts. As railroads grew they facilitated a kind of dependency seen across much of the arid West: local producers needed railroads to bring new people into the region and export products, but railroads, grain elevators, and processing plants controlled transportation rates for export. By the 1920s the artesian wells began drying up, farms foreclosed, and local merchants left town. When the Great Depression hit, residents of the Guadalupe Mountains Trans-Pecos region faced great scarcity and uncertainty. In sum, the hopes of Hispanos struggling in Missouri Plaza, of Mescaleros trying to remain in the Guadalupes, and even of empire builders such as James J. Hagerman all failed in the lands east of El Capitan.

Despite waves of settlement, the territory within the boundaries of the present-day park was nearly devoid of humans at the onset of the Great Depression. Clusters of homes dotted the vicinity, and a few families eked out a living on the slopes of the mountains. These settlers were an intrepid lot that chose to endure the isolation of what Hal Rothman referred to as the "margin of a periphery."[9] To most Americans this corner of the Southwest borderlands was little more than windswept desert, a dry and brittle void on the national landscape. There was no paved road connecting El Paso with Carlsbad until 1929, for instance. And even after the considerable sums spent during the New Deal to tie together El Paso and Carlsbad, only a few souls followed that asphalt ribbon through endless stands of creosote, mesquite, cholla, and agave. Indeed, to live in the Guadalupe Mountains one had to embrace the expansive sky, blistering heat, mercurial monsoons, hardscrabble soil, and distance from other people.

During the relatively quiet interwar era, the region witnessed oil and gas exploration, the Great Depression, and incipient tourism. Chambers of Commerce in West Texas and southern New Mexico dreamt of ways to connect Ciudad Juarez, El Paso, and the Guadalupe Mountains and Carlsbad Caverns with the popular tourist destinations of Albuquerque, Santa Fe, and Taos. Seeking assistance from the Santa Fe Railway, boosters tried to insert the mountains into the familiar narratives of the epic American West. Their efforts failed to bear fruit as the distance, lack of a romantic Indian past, and insufficient finances hampered tourism. Parallel to these efforts, three of the most important individuals in the history of the national park—J. C. Hunter, J. C. Hunter Jr., and Wallace Pratt—contemplated preserving the mountains. Although they figure most prominently in the postwar history, their relationship with the mountains started in the 1920s, decades before Congress established the national park in 1966.

In addition to tracing the broad environmental history of the mountain region, this book also focuses on the creation of a national park in the Southwest borderlands. This story echoes, but is distinct from, the histories of other parks in the region, the West, and the nation more broadly.[10] The early efforts to protect the mountains set the foundation for boosters such as Glenn Biggs and property owners such as Wallace Pratt and J. C. Hunter Jr. The long-term interest in the park inspired Hunter and Pratt after World War II, planted a seed in the minds of federal employees that the Guadalupes would make a viable park, and provided continuity over generations of politicians in Texas. Moreover, the establishment of the park symbolized a turning point in the policies of the National Park Service (NPS) because Congress used federal funds to purchase private property. Congress typically created parks out of lands it owned, thus the decision to use federal dollars to purchase private land was significant. On the other hand, the park was also one of the last established for very traditional purposes associated with notions of a sublime nature and a romantic landscape of awe-inspiring dimensions. Drawing upon nineteenth century Victorian romanticism and Progressive Era conservation, most parks preserved natural scenery, wilderness, and open space, and the Guadalupes possessed these characteristics in abundance. Creation of the park also reflected the influence of post–World War II scientific assertions about the geological significance of El Capitan, the thousand-foot-tall rock wall that had become a symbol of the mountains. The rock face was a magnificent example of the region's deep history as a Permian Basin landscape and "the Bowl" atop the mountains represented the ecological diversity of the Southwest borderlands. This combination of traditional justifications and newer, scientific rationales facilitated the shift in policy represented by the appropriation of federal monies to preserve private lands.

Each park has its array of interesting characters, and the campaign to create Guadalupe Mountains National Park was no exception. The principals in this case were Wallace Pratt, a petroleum geologist and vice president for Humble Oil, who owned substantial portions of McKittrick Canyon; J. C. Hunter and J. C. Hunter Jr., wealthy oilmen who owned the seventy-two-thousand-acre Guadalupe Mountain Ranch they preserved in near pristine condition; Glenn Biggs, the indefatigable promoter of the park; Joe Pool, a U.S. representative for Texas; and the legendary U.S. senator Ralph Yarborough. The supporting yet crucial cast included Secretary of the Interior Stewart Udall; Chief Justice of the U.S. Supreme Court, William O. Douglas; and President Lyndon Baines Johnson. The political landscape was not simply conservative Texas, but far West Texas where cattle and oil wells outnumbered the human population. Making matters more complicated was the division of the mountain range across Texas and New Mexico. And yet, these characters moved the proposal forward in lightning speed: Congress approved the park six years after J. C. Hunter Jr. decided to sell his ranch. More surprisingly, the park supporters succeeded with their mission while the nation was experiencing great social and political turmoil. Nonetheless, President Johnson signed the bill into law on October 15, 1966.

During the past sixty years, the Guadalupe Mountains National Park and its dedicated employees have struggled to preserve a unique desert and mountain landscape. Initially a small cadre of NPS staff oversaw the park from Carlsbad Caverns, which was an hour's drive to the north. For nearly a decade after creating the park, the staff conducted baseline scientific surveys of flora and fauna, tried to clarify land titles to plots adjacent to the park, and build rapport with the local community. When the NPS finally built the park headquarters, staff housing, and expanded the trail system, the park began to look like a typical national park. Campers rolled up to campsites, hikers went backpacking in "the Bowl," and rangers answered questions about wildlife and local history. Although attendance in the twenty-first century has never approached that seen in Grand Canyon or Yosemite, for instance, the Guadalupe Mountains remain an important part of the Southwest borderlands landscape as a site of tremendous geological transformation and regional history.

CHAPTER ONE

Geology and Environment

The sheer rock face of El Capitan juts out over the Chihuahuan Desert and stands as an iconic landmark of the Greater Southwest borderlands. The striking white façade and the mountains behind it are sacred to Native peoples such as the Apache, and they have been christened by the Spanish who named them after the Virgen de Guadalupe. Westward migrants used the mountains as a point of reference as they navigated what was to them an otherworldly landscape of open desert and expansive skies, and settlers who eventually colonized the region imbued them with a sense of personhood, seeing the mountains as an actor that shaped their lives in a remote corner of the American West. These cultural constructs breathed life into a geologic feature that was the result of millions of years of slow and gradual change. The Guadalupe Mountains encompass more than fifty miles north to south and twenty-five miles east to west, including and surrounding the national park. The mountains are comprised of stratified sedimentary rock such as limestone and gypsum with some sandstone outcroppings, and they are separated from the Sacramento Mountains to the north by a collection of low foothills and the Rio Peñasco. They are divided from the Delaware Mountains to the south by a sheer rock face, a collection of salt beds, and the Chihuahuan Desert. The western side, beaten by the blistering afternoon sun, is much more drastic than the eastern, which contains animals and plants indicative of the shadowed sides of desert mountains. The eastern slope is cut by canyons that funnel rain and snow-pack runoff into the Pecos River. Elevation varies from 2,900 feet at the Pecos River to 8,800 feet at Guadalupe Peak, the highest point in Texas.[1] These geological features, combined with shifts in the climate and transformations in local flora and fauna, created an environment that represents a rare combination of the northern Chihuahua and southwestern plains ecosystems.

Geological Origins

The basic features which have become so iconic in western Texas are the result of millions of years of change. Around 250 million years ago, during the Permian period of the Paleozoic era, the Guadalupe Mountains and Carlsbad Caverns were under water. Part of the vast Permian Sea, the region was covered by the Marfa, Delaware, and Midland Basins and was connected to the great Permian Ocean by a narrow inlet.[2] The Guadalupes grew out of the middle of three arms of water that poked to the edge of land within the Delaware Basin, which was about seventy-five miles wide and one hundred and fifty miles long. The Capitan Reef, now one of the premier aboveground fossil reefs in the world, bulged up from Delaware Basin for hundreds of miles. The reef is the Guadalupe Mountains.[3]

The charismatic sheer rock face known as El Capitan is the limestone remain of an old reef that emerged as a significant feature of the Permian Sea.[4] The sun's heat concentrated the minerals as the water evaporated, and the gypsum and other materials precipitated to the floor of the lagoon. Closer to the shore, the gypsum mixed with sediment that was eroding off the continent. This combination of mud, silt, sand, and gypsum formed tidal flats that rose upward at high tide. When the tide receded, channels winding through mud and tidal pools remained.[5] Ocean currents and waves hit the face of the Capitan Reef and loosened chunks that slid down the front of the reef. The reef grew wider as it expanded on top of its own leftover material. Inverted and resembling an upside-down pyramid, the top-heavy reef collapsed and rolled down to the basin below.[6] These combined processes of erosion downward and larger tectonic shifts that pushed the mountains upward created the basic landscape we see today.

The Paleo-Environment

In the Guadalupe Mountains before the arrival of humans, there were plants and animals whose presence is known only through analysis of fossils and scattered remains. Ninety million years after the Capitan Reef flourished, the lagoons and marshes covering West Texas attracted dinosaurs. Some were pterosaurs, or pterodactyls, and one species, titanopteryx, was the largest animal that ever flew. Although probably warm blooded, and possibly covered with fur, it was a reptile as large as an airplane. In 1971 its remains were discovered in the Javelina deposits of Big Bend National Park, southeast of the Guadalupes. Eventually the size of the animal proved to be a liability and led to a gradual change in the structure and capabilities of the bird.[7]

The climate determined the growth of plant and animal species, and the first humans. Between 13,000 and 6000 BP, when the first humans entered the region, the climate was cooler than it is today. Pollen analysis and radiocarbon dating across the southern plains and Llano Estacado indicate mild steppe characteristics and grasses mixed with boreal woodland, as well as open savannas and occasional playas. The Guadalupe Mountains during this era shifted from the subalpine forests of more than thirteen thousand years ago to the xeric forests of less than eleven thousand years ago. This era witnessed also the decline of large Pleistocene species such as mammoths and *Bison antiquus*.[8] Later periods provide evidence of gradual desiccation of the area. Spruce and pine woodlands disappeared from the lower elevations and Llano Estacado. Nearly all of the playas dried up, except for a few of the largest, most of which were spring-fed by high level aquifers. Desert scrub species in the Guadalupe Mountains completed their colonization of the lower foothills, with woodlands remaining above six thousand feet.[9]

Most of the plants in the mountains originate from the region's moist era, but these plants made important adaptations to the change in climate. The most successful adaptations to desert life have been the cacti, although Chihuahuan vegetation has typically developed the nearly ubiquitous thorns that have allowed these plants to flourish. Cacti have directed more effort toward dealing with the desert climate than toward resisting foragers: the thorns that cover them are there only partly to protect the plant from being eaten. Before cacti made these changes to survive desert life, their spines were leaves that transpired water in a more humid environment. Since plants lose water this way, transforming their leaves into spikes warded off grazing animals and decreased evaporation. The tradeoff involved sacrificing the leaves' wide, photosynthetic layers, which decreased their ability to transform the sun's energy into food. The cacti adapted by changing their stems into a kind of leaf: the skin of their green stems acquired a waxy armor that enlarged to hold water and to offer more chlorophyll-enriched stalk surface to the sun.[10]

While the old forests survived by spreading out across the savannah and mingling with cacti, the age of mammals reached its peak. Evergreen forests grew across the Great Plains in the path of the advancing glaciers, spreading hundreds of miles ahead of the ice. The ice never quite made it to present-day Texas, but the conifer woodland it pushed southward brought arctic animals, such as musk oxen, sabre tooth tigers, zebras, ground sloths, scavenging hyenas, and dire wolves. Although surrounded by desert now, the western face of El Capitan, during the Pleistocene, looked out upon a forest-and-savannah countryside that supported charismatic herbivores such as the North American rhinocerous, mammoths, and strange chalicotheres with their great claws instead of hooves. Herds of long-horned bison grazed across a vast Trans-Pecos, preyed upon by dire wolves and arctodus, the two-thousand-pound Pleistocene grizzly.[11]

As the Pleistocene began to decline, the biggest animals found life tough on the drying prairie. Ground sloths, concentrated in the strips of woodland along rivers and around the waterholes, were the easiest kills for the newly arrived arctic hunters, and were soon too scarce to rely on as game. Remnants of the wetland mammoth herds that fed in marshes stretching from the Gulf Coast to the Rockies retreated to the mountain forests to feed on conifer branches.[12]

The increasingly arid climate indicated a late Pleistocene environment where grasslands covered the Trans-Pecos region. Before the first bands of Paleo-Indians entered the area, the lower level altitudes were covered in juniper, oak, pinyon, and grasses. These plants enjoyed higher rates of moisture and springs that were much more active than today. Tall grasses, such as black gramma and tobosa grass, were uniform cover across the lowlands. Species of dropseed, sacaton, and bushy muhly grew across the Guadalupe Trans-Pecos region. The grasses would have also been highly attractive forage for a variety of grazing animals.[13] By 9000 BC large mammals such as the sloth and mammoth vanished from the Southwest. Drier weather predominated, and the heavy spears and axes that the Clovis hunters used to kill elephants became obsolete with pronghorns and the modern bison. As Clovis hunters sought these smaller animals, they had to follow them to more remote and arid regions where waterholes lay a hundred miles apart and the herds moved opportunistically with the seasons and the rains.[14]

As humans entered the area thirteen thousand years ago, the Southwest had slowly become hotter and drier. The forest plants that dotted the lowlands and mid-level regions shifted upward and only the tops of the Guadalupe Mountains were covered with pinon-juniper forests. The rate of displacement during the Holocene is difficult to determine, but by 5000 BC the lower altitudes supported grassland savannahs mixed with xeric plant species.[15] The shift to a drier environment created the present Chihuahuan Desert around the Guadalupe Mountains. Researchers uncovered evidence of the late Pleistocene environment in and around the mountains. Packrat middens in Williams Cave within the park, dating to 10,000 BC, and middens in Rocky Arroyo and Last Chance Canyon, outside the park, reveal juniper-oak remains indicative of a climate transitioning to a xeric one. Archeologists have also uncovered middens that contain evidence of a drier early Holocene (8000 BC); and other middens indicate that by the late Holocene (3,500 years ago) there had been an increase in succulents and plants similar to modern day cacti.[16]

The Modern Environmental Context

Spaniards crossing through the Guadalupe Trans-Pecos region of far West Texas referred to the rocky, high desert grasslands as "el desplobado," the unpopulated place. The difficulties posed by the sand, cacti, mountains, and rocks, as well as the general lack of water, led Edward L. Hartz, a participant in the Big Bend Camel experiment of the 1850s, to write, "a rougher, more rocky, more mountainous, and rugged country can scarcely be imagined."[17] A travel-worn easterner aboard the Texas and Pacific (T&P) Railway observed in 1883 that the Trans-Pecos region was "so poor that even a crow would have to tote its rations over it."[18] The modern environment of the Guadalupe Mountain Trans-Pecos has indeed posed "obstacles" to human habitation.

Scientists recognize several ecological zones in the Guadalupe Mountains Trans-Pecos region. Today, the Chihuahuan Desert dominates the lower elevations and is characterized by over fifty species of succulents, such as creosote, mesquite, prickly pear cacti, agave, sotol, yucca, cholla, and some palo verde. Ocotillo, barrel and organ pipe cacti, and desert willow can be seen across the region. Several gypsum salt beds stand out like crystalline oceans in a sea of blossoming cacti. Known locally as the salt beds, or salt flats, they are characterized by few flora and fauna, but they have served as catch basins during the occasional violent storm. When the summer monsoons fill the beds with rainwater, they attract animals ranging from the smallest bugs to myriad species of birds, to larger mammals such as coyote and bobcat, seeking out the ephemeral sources of water provided by the cycles of drought and storm.[19]

At the upper Chihuahuan Desert the landscape is a mixture of succulents. Between four thousand and six thousand feet, Texas madrone are one of the most charismatic plants of the mountains. Pinon and juniper cover the canyons and shaded areas of the mountain. In McKittrick Canyon and along the trails to Pratt Lodge and Hunter Line Cabin, one observes a diverse ecosystem.[20] At the higher elevations running from the northern entrance to the park at the Dog Canyon Visitor Center, south into "the Bowl," cacti give way to flora and fauna typical of mountainous regions. Above six thousand feet, the dominant plants become pine and coniferous trees interspersed with hardwoods and oaks. In this landscape, larger mammals can survive, especially near riparian areas and in the shaded canyons. Elk and several deer were and still are predominant. Reports from the Spanish documented the presence of bison on the western side of the Pecos River, but there is scant evidence for bison within the boundaries of the present park.[21]

There are several large drainage systems on the eastern side of the mountains. Dark Canyon had the most complex array of flora and fauna, with the common species being varieties of pine, grasses, juniper, cat claw, deciduous trees, wild grape, agave, and cactus. It drains thirty-five miles eastward to the Pecos River, and drops in elevation from 6,500 to 3,300 feet, although the adjacent ridges reach 7,900 feet. This drainage system is rugged and narrow in places, leading to flash floods during the monsoon.[22] Last Chance Canyon is not as rugged as Dark Canyon and contains less variety of flora, especially below 6,000 feet, where the transitional zone blends into the coniferous-woodland zone at the top of the mountain. Little McKittrick Canyon starts at 4,700 feet and flows eastward for eighteen miles. Rocky Arroyo stretches twenty-five miles across Indian Basin and is an extension of the Chihuahuan Desert along the Pecos River. This connection with the Pecos River region has led to the flora and fauna tied to the high desert grasslands as well as the grasses that bedeviled the Spaniards on the Llano Estacado.[23]

Several physiographic zones surround the area. To the north and east is the Llano Estacado and its flat landscape disturbed only by depressions and playas. Adjacent to the Llano is the northern escarpment, or the Caprock, whose low, sandy hillsides and cliffs extend along the Pecos Valley. As one reaches the Llano, the altitude drops from five thousand to three thousand feet across the Texas Panhandle. The second major zone is the Pecos Valley, which scholars have divided into multiple regions, the most relevant of which is the middle section between the Alamogordo Reservoir and the New Mexico-Texas state line.[24]

With the exception of the higher altitudes of the Guadalupes and some greener pockets in the Chisos and Davis Mountains, most of the region is Chihuahuan desert. Along the mountain slopes and lower elevations, pinyon and pine forests are replaced by desert scrub. Intermittent streams and springs supply water and summer monsoons nourish thirsty plants and animals. At the lower elevations (1,800 to 3,500 feet), across the arid basins there are a variety of desert species, including succulents and semisucculents. The dominant plant of the region is the creosote bush, but Texas persimmon, agave, sotol, and yucca grow along the banks of arroyos or across ridge slopes. Ocotillo and prickly pear also dot the landscape. Mesquite, wild grape, willow, cottonwood, and Carrizo-cane flourish along the riparian regions.[25]

Numerous animals move across different zones and ecosystems, while very few remain restricted to a single locality. Small game such as cottontail and jackrabbits, porcupines, badgers, gophers, skunks, squirrels, an army of reptiles and birds, and a few amphibians can be found depending on the season. Larger animals include whitetail and mule deer, black bear, coyote, pronghorn antelope, and desert bighorn sheep. The most northern and eastern quadrants of the region may have seen bison, but evidence for this is scant.[26]

The animal and plant life of the present-day national park are the result of millennia of climatic change, punctuated by two great eras of human activity: the thousands of years before the arrival of Europeans and the centuries after their colonization of the region. Despite the impact of European plants, animals, forms of land use, and exploitation of natural resources, the park retains considerable biotic diversity. Agaves, inaccurately known as "century plants," dominate the landscape with their unusual stalks that yield flowering platforms for birds and insects. The much shorter lechuguilla is a type of agave that has long, spiny green thorns. They also contain soponin, a naturally occurring surfactant, which Native Americans used as a kind of soap. The cane cholla is another striking cacti, and with its magenta bloom, combines a beautiful flower with a dangerous barbed spine.[27]

As one climbs out of the Chihuahuan Desert lowlands, especially from the eastern face of the mountains, the diversity of plant life is astonishing. The various canyons, depending on altitude and exposure to sunlight, have an array of species that are unique to the region. During the brilliant displays of the "fall colors," the orange of the bigtooth maple, reds of the fragrant and flameleaf sumacs, the yellows of the littleleaf walnut, and the greens of the alligator juniper create a cacophony of color. The summer and spring have their share of spectacular plants. The algerita is a small shrub whose yellow flowers attract bees in the spring, while its red fruit is a delicacy for local animals. The iconic Texas madrone is a resilient survivor of the slow shift toward a drier climate. More populous during the temperate eras, its smooth branches, small white springtime flowers, and red September fruit make it an interesting character on the landscape of the park.[28]

Few visitors hike up the steep incline to what is popularly known as "the Bowl" at the top of the Guadalupes, but those that make the trek are rewarded by a high-altitude forest that looks more like Colorado than Texas. This forest is a remnant of an extensive woodland that covered the lower altitudes thousands of years ago. Today it is one of the few surviving pine and pinyon mountain forests in the state. The dominant trees are limber pine, ponderosa pine, and Douglas fir. Indian paint brush, which grow in the lime rich soils and are attractive forage for mule deer, add a splash of red to the wilderness area. Nodding onion, with its purple flowers and subsurface bulbs, and Mescalero gooseberry, with its small white flowers that attract plenty of birds, are found at these higher elevations.[29]

◀▶

As one drives to the Guadalupe Mountains from the west, the face of El Capitan appears long before the car reaches the park. On clear days when the wind was not whipping up the desert sand, Native people, Spaniards, westward migrants, cowboys, and early settlers would have seen the imposing rock face days before they met the foothills of the mountain. Perhaps the world's best example of an exposed Permian reef, El Capitan has captured the imaginations of geologists, residents, boosters, and environmentalists for more than a century.

The environment that visitors to the national park enjoy is the result of millennia of gradual change punctuated by sharp shifts and extreme transformations. Once a vast sea, the reef we know as the Guadalupe Mountains was home to marine animals that left deposits that built up a hard foundation upon which layers of limestone would rest. Over eons, the temperature changed, continents shifted, and the ocean that covered the Southwest receded. This recession left lakes and playas that provided hydration for animals such as the mammoth. This paleo-environment disappeared as the region became more arid and xeric grasses, cacti, and animals that were adapted to desert conditions replaced the old flora and fauna.

Thirteen thousand years ago "Paleo-Indians" entered this shifting ecosystem and in turn changed the plants and animals. They created shelters, hunted and gathered, and searched for dependable sources of water. They did not, however, alter the environment to the extent that Europeans did when they entered the Southwest in the sixteenth century. After their arrival, and increasing exponentially with the industrial revolution, the environment of the Guadalupe Mountains began to change again. These shifts, however, were less a result of natural changes in the climate or geology than they were of the, perhaps unalterable, impact of an explosive human population.

CHAPTER TWO
Pre-Columbian Indigenous Worlds

The pre-Columbian human history of the Guadalupe Mountains is difficult to narrate because the region never attracted large and permanent concentrations of people as seen in the urban centers of Mesa Verde. This low population density has left behind little evidence from which we can glean an understanding of the cultures in the region. However, the Native inhabitants did utilize the mountains and many considered it a sacred place. Archeologists have found physical evidence of their presence and historians point to a cache of documents from early Spanish explorers demonstrating an indigenous population in the area. Understanding their cultures requires us to consider the peoples in the Guadalupe Mountains Trans-Pecos, Big Bend, Junta de los Rios, and El Paso areas. When focus is then placed within the context and historical patterns of the Puebloan, Mogollon, and Hohokam peoples of the greater Southwest and southern plains, we obtain a clearer picture of the indigenous inhabitants and how they carved a living out of this environment of extremes.

The Paleo-Indian and Archaic Periods

Evidence of human occupation in the mountains dates to the Paleo-Indian era more than ten thousand years ago. Some of the earliest evidence is based on carbon 14 dating of wicker remains in Hermit's Cave in Last Chance Canyon by E. B. Howard in 1933. Within these remnants was a Folsom point. At Blackwater Draw to the northeast of the Guadalupe Mountains, there are several Paleo-Indian sites. At Burnet Cave west of Carlsbad, archeologists found vegetal remains, charred logs, fossilized mammals, and spear points. The site also yielded a Clovis-fluted projectile point alongside bones that were ten thousand years old. Southwest of the Guadalupe Mountains, at Hueco Tanks, a popular state park, and at sites near Van Horn, archeologists uncovered Folsom points evidencing Paleo-Indian peoples.[1]

The Archaic period witnessed some human activity, although the dry conditions made life difficult. The term "Archaic" describes a specific cultural adaptation characterized by gathering plant foods and hunting small to medium size animals, such as deer. The Archaic adaptation was concurrent with the Ceramic and protohistoric periods and has generally been overlooked by archeologists in southeastern New Mexico and West Texas, as these cultures fashioned their lives in accordance with conditions inimical to settlement.[2] With aridity increasing around 6000 BC, declining bison herds forced the Native cultures to supplement their diets with gathering plants and hunting smaller game.[3] Forests began to shrink at high elevations, depriving Natives of sources of subsistence and warmth, and drier plants began to climb in elevation, slowly replacing the woodland trees and shrubs.[4] These changes were dominant by 3000 BC, as people faced greater pressures to adapt to characteristics similar to the modern era.

Objects from caves in and near the Guadalupe Mountains provide some evidence about indigenous life and culture. Archaeologists have found chipped stone tools, large corner-notched projectile points, scrapers, drills, choppers, and cores. Wooden fire drills, digging sticks, atlatls, darts, combs, storage tubes and wands, bone awls, basin mutates, and "woven materials such as yucca mats, basketry, bags, cloth netting, and sandals" have been uncovered. Jewelry from reed and bone beads as well as the shells of fresh water mussels, turtles, and other animals from along the Gulf of California were found in the Guadalupe region.[5]

The peoples of the Archaic era, whom archeologists have included within the regional Jornada culture group, adapted to the harsh environment in creative ways. Settlement sites grew in size and complexity. The first appearance of burned rock rings, often called ring middens or mescal pits, offer glimpses into food patterns and dietary habits. The rings functioned as ovens for roasting plants, suggesting frequent use of the same locale. Some middens were six feet deep. People roasted agave as well as datil and sotol in their middens. Agave was a prime source of nourishment, full of carbohydrates and readily available throughout the region.[6]

A handful of archaeological expeditions in West Texas offer glimpses into the Archaic world. While doing fieldwork during the 1930s, R. M. Burnet found evidence of occupation during the Pleistocene in Burnet Cave. Howard, soon after Burnet, found evidence in Blackwater Draw near Clovis, New Mexico, that humans lived here during the Pleistocene.[7] In 1938 Ferndon conducted fieldwork in Hermit's Cave, and he uncovered sandals similar to those found in Big Bend. Soon thereafter, Henry P. Mera sought to identify relationships between sites on the eastern slopes of the Guadalupe Mountains and the Pecos River Valley. He found open campsites along the river, midden circles, mescal pits, rock-shelters, and cave sites. Some had mutates or grindstones and some "brownware." He found remains of atlatls and bows and arrows, and he also uncovered evidence of "inhumation and cremation," two fairly different burial practices. All evidence led Mera to conclude two cultural traditions lived in the area.[8] In the late 1940s, Donald J. Lehmer claimed that the peoples in the mountains were from the Jornada Mogollon culture because of the brownware sherds there. John A. Corley's research in the 1960s concurred with assertions about the Jornada Mogollon tradition.[9]

Research conducted by Susan M. Applegarth offered more precise conclusions. Her surveys highlighted that rock-shelters with ceramics were associated with triangular arrows, inhumation of infants and adults, bedrock mortar holes, and multiple mescal pits. Shelters and caves that lacked ceramics demonstrated a tie with larger projectiles, baskets, and cremation of adults, and little direct association with mescal pits.[10] Applegarth investigated forty-two cave and shelter sites and found ceramic items in most. Pottery was evident in many of the rock-shelters. Mescal pits existed in some. Most open-air sites contained mescal pits and ceramics. This implies that these groups, especially peoples such as the Apache, constructed mescal pits throughout the region.[11] In a site located in McKittrick Canyon, known to locals as "Honest Injun Cave," Applegarth observed relatively undisturbed evidence for human occupation dating back to 900 BC. The site is within the upper reaches of the Chihuahuan Desert zone, surrounded by cacti and xeric grasses.

Evidence of human occupation in the cave included rudimentary rock walls; debris of fiber, bone, and other materials; and minor depressions in the floor, signaling some kind of pit.[12]

Excavations revealed stratified layers of materials from human occupation, as far down as four feet. Fragments from a sandal were radiocarbon dated at 980 BC and Applegarth uncovered 144 lithic artifacts (metates, grinding stones, and various knives). The discovery of the metates was important because they are not common, compared to grinding stones, in the Guadalupe Mountains. Additional objects uncovered included one hundred flaked stones used as cutting tools, projectile points, seven cooking hearths, and trash piles of animal bones.[13] There were also several shell fragments and shell jewelry within the cave. At least one of the shells was most likely part of a necklace or pendant. The shells were very similar to shells originating from the Gulf of California at the delta of the Colorado River. Other shell fragments originated from the Pecos River. Scant evidence of human remains included a single fragment of a charred human bone situated on top of checkered weave matting. Cremation of human remains was feasible as evidence of this practice existed in Dark Canyon and across the mountains.[14]

Applegarth was not the first to investigate the Dark Canyon Cave site, which has become well known for its paleontological deposits. Some of the most useful information comes from amateur archeologist W. H. Balgemann of Carlsbad, New Mexico. He investigated Dark Canyon Cave, which is a multilevel, multiroom cave, one and a half miles from the junction with Little McKittrick Canyon. Balgemann found Pleistocene faunal material similar to the fluted points found at Burnett Cave by Howard in the 1930s.[15] Below the Pleistocene deposits were remains of mammoth, horse, and camel. At least five different burials were uncovered, and all of the human remains were in the upper level of the cave. Sandal ties and mollusk shells sat in a burial site that contained the remains of an adult humerus. A second site was the only example of inhumation in the cave. It represented the burial of a male youth approximately nine years old, less than a foot beneath the surface. The body was wrapped in netting and probably a fur robe or blanket, in a flexed position, facing east. The other burial sites were adult cremations with a child accompanying one of the adults. Sherds of brownware and lithic materials such as projectile points, knives, flake scrapers, and grinding stones littered the floor. The projectile points and knife dated between 2000 and 1000 BCE, and resembled points found throughout the Trans-Pecos region from the Late Archaic. This supports claims that many of the sites on the eastern side of the mountains point to humans tied to groups of the Trans-Pecos and Greater Big Bend.[16]

One of the best sites for revealing indigenous material culture before European arrival was the Roberts Rockshelter site. The Roberts Rockshelter site is on a side arroyo of Sacahuiste Draw and consists of a shelter sixteen feet wide by eleven feet deep. One of the most important aspects of the shelter is the large midden within fifty feet of the main site, which seems to reveal several separate periods of occupation over a millennium. A limestone basin adjacent to the shelter holds water most of the year and a twenty-foot large mescal pit shows signs of heavy use. The shelter also contained fire hearths and a burned rock circle. Charcoal from one of the hearths is dated to AD 875.[17]

Researchers gathered more than seven hundred artifacts from the site. The lithics were primarily chert artifacts, which separates them from other sites where artifacts were made of limestone. The lithic industry at the Roberts site was more advanced than the other sites. The Roberts site contained shallow slab metate fragments and river cobble stones used for grinding. One hundred and fifty projectile points from the site were similar to the points at Honest Injun Cave. Most of the points were categorized as Livermore, which was common for the Trans-Pecos region, particularly the Davis Mountains.[18] Over one thousand pieces of ceramics were uncovered at the site. The most distinctive were brownware sherds and sherds of Chupadero Black-on-white in the mescal pit. Several of the sherds were El Paso Brown, with an unpolished finish on the surface. A fraction of the ceramics were categorized as El Paso Polychrome, and Applegarth notes that they could have been made by the Apache.[19]

Although burial plots were looted at the Roberts site, human remains beneath the surface yield important information. An adult male was located fourteen inches below the surface. Several ribs, a pelvis, and other bones were recovered. The teeth were worn by possible disease. A second burial contained a child in a flexed position facing northeast. The third site yielded adult sized ribs and scattered pieces of crania. The evidence from the Roberts site indicates a hunting and gathering orientation dating from AD 875 to 1300. The presence of fairly recent projectile points, ceramics, fibers, mescal pits, cooking hearths, remains of deer taken during the hunt, and other material makes it plausible that these were Apache or Jumano peoples.[20]

Radiocarbon dating at the Ellis shelters, northeast of the Roberts site, indicates early occupation during the mid-1100s. The site contained small hearths, a few highly refined lithic remains, manos, projectile points, and ceramics that were Jornada or El Paso Brown. The Richard Brown site, located in a tributary of Little McKittrick, in the park boundaries, had large mescal pits three feet in diameter. The site also contained fire hearths, stone tools, and numerous projectiles, mainly of the Livermore variety, although one was of jasper.[21] A few points contained a double-sided notch that placed them in the Capitan Phase of the Jornada Branch of the Mogollon (AD 1000–1100). This site contained the largest and most complete array of human remains of all sites investigated. Balgemann estimated a range of ages for males and females. One of the youngest children was approximately six months old, while other children ranged from four to twelve years old. Most skeletons were from middle-aged adults, while one seemed to be of an elderly male placed in a sitting position facing the northeast.[22]

Other sites help us understand the cultures living within the orbit of the Guadalupe Mountains. The Brantley site, in Carlsbad along the Pecos River, contained remains from 3000 BC. Artifacts such as chipped stone tools, manos, and metates have been dated to the Post-Archaic, but projectile points have straddled the Post-Archaic, the Late Formative, and protohistoric eras. Twelve hundred ceramic sherds were found at the Brantley Reservoir; and nearly half were located at one site. Most of the ceramics were El Paso Brownware that dated from the mid-700s through the mid-1300s, some were South Pecos Brownware dating from 900 through 1200, a few were Chupadero Black-on-white dating from the mid-1100s through 1400 or Jornada Brownware dating from 900 to the mid-1300s. These samples confirmed association with the cultures throughout the entire region.[23]

Archeologists believe that there is a connection between people of the Brantley site and people associated with the Guadalupe Mountains such as the Apache, especially the site known as Honest Injun Cave. These connections rest on the somewhat confusing series of phases used by archeologists in the region. The Brantley phase (AD 1–750) is based on nearly one dozen sites that have been radiocarbon dated. Rock rings, associated with mescal preparation and stone hearths, and three projectile points offer the most compelling objects for this phase, which continued to be associated with hunting and gathering strategies. The Globe Phase (AD 750–1150) overlaps with the protohistoric that is associated with the greater Guadalupe Trans-Pecos region. This phase has the greatest concentration of materials and constellations of rock rings and stone hearths. The first evidence of ceramics, particularly El Paso Brownware, appear during this phase. These ceramics offer strong evidence for the connection between these sites and sites in the Sierra Blanca and El Paso locales. Variations of arrow points, including Scallorn and Livermore, were associated with the Globe phase. A key piece of evidence is a semisubterranean stone circle situated at an unusual angle.[24]

The last phases for the region bring us into the centuries predating and including Europeans in the sixteenth century. Data implies a declining use of the region, but it also yields the most sophisticated painted pottery to date: El Paso Polychrome, Chupadero Black-on-white, and Three Rivers Red-on-terracotta. Perhaps the most noteworthy finding is evidence of a tipi ring. The Seven Rivers Apache, with their hunting and gathering strategies, may have used the Brantley area east of the mountains. They would be a possible source of an alleged tipi structure tied with a tipi ring, although plains-oriented groups such as the Jumano may have built the tipi. Wickiups in the area have also frequently been associated with many Apachean groups.[25]

The use of ceramics, pottery, stone tools, the bow and arrow, and agriculture were crucial during this era. Between 750 and 1150 the Jornada Mogollon developed sophisticated strategies to survive the desert environment. After 900, their possession of brownware pottery, stone tools, rudimentary agriculture, large storage pits, and above ground dwellings, especially in the region surrounding El Paso, offer evidence of a sedentary lifestyle. The bow and arrow also became central to their livelihood. The presence of some of these materials, along with domesticated plants, and more sophisticated pottery demonstrate trade links between the Guadalupe region and the El Paso-Rio Grande region and with communities of northern Mexico. Archeologists hypothesize that the trade relationships grew across the greater precontact Southwest and southern plains until the middle of the twelfth century.[26]

Analyzing regional history through agriculture highlights the impact of environmental conditions for the development of human economies. Transformation to agriculture in the greater Southwest began before 2000 BC primarily among the Anasazi, Hohokam, and (western) Mogollon. The Gila and Salt River Basins to the west show examples of agriculture around AD 300, while after AD 500, agriculture had fully altered the upper Sonoran Desert. The populations of the Guadalupe Mountain Trans-Pecos did not experience these changes for centuries.[27]

By the end of the thirteenth century, ceramics that anthropologists have categorized as El Paso Polychrome and Three Rivers Red-on-terracotta imply greater integration of the Jornada peoples into a regional trade network. This pottery of the peoples associated with the Guadalupe Mountains Trans-Pecos region illustrates a skill set that incorporated methods used by Rio Grande communities around El Paso.

Anthropologists have debated the "cultural lag" between the groups in the greater Southwest, although the notion of a gap in development assumes a linear progression of cultures. Some argue that Archaic features persisted through European contact, while others point to farming, permanent structures, local trade, and production of ceramics comparable with those exhibited by Rio Grande communities.[28] One might split the difference and accept the reality that the Guadalupe Mountain and Trans-Pecos populations were at the periphery of the Mogollon world and shared, if in a limited fashion, some characteristics of these cultural kin. It seems reasonable that some of the features of Archaic life overlapped with the more ornate features of postcontact era. Regardless, the Mogollon cultures of the fourteenth century experienced life-altering stressors such soil exhaustion, resource depletion, drought, and declining bison.

The drought of the 1300s transformed the cultures of the Southwest. At Chaco Canyon, one form of Anasazi (Ancestral Puebloan) culture reached its "apogee" during the eleventh and twelfth centuries and the drought facilitated its "decline" in the 1300s. Mesa Verde and other high-density sites also lost populations. As these changes unfolded, agriculturalists turned to hunting and gathering as crops yielded less and as food stores diminished. The growing reliance on hunting caused population densities to decline as villagers looked for food in the peripheries of their homelands. This put greater strain on game, which caused tensions between groups competing for those resources. The shift toward a more mobile lifestyle also resulted in a decline in production of pottery and staple crops that sedentary populations used for trade with the more mobile Jornada peoples to the east. The result was a split of the Jornada peoples into a sedentary group and one oriented toward a plains-bison hunting culture, thus the possibility that Jumanos had their ancestral roots in more sedentary populations to the west.[29]

Jumano and Apache Ancestors

The era between 1100 and 1500 reveals several groups of people who may have had ties to the Jornada Mogollon, Puebloan, and southern plains cultural traditions. Discerning the differences between these groups has perplexed archeologists and ethnohistorians. Several groups fit the mold of the semimobile plains people that adopted the horse after the arrival of the Spanish. The groups retained an affinity with the Puebloan peoples of the Rio Grande and northern Pecos River. The similarity of the Pueblo Towa dialect with the plains Kiowa language implies a potential split of the Jornada peoples, who had trading ties with groups between the Rio Grande and Pecos River. The difficulty identifying these peoples is complicated by evidence of traits associated with the southern plains, or "pre-Apachean" peoples. As Jornada cultures possibly retreated from the Guadalupe Mountains Trans-Pecos region, ostensibly toward clusters of villages along the Rio Grande and in a few sites throughout the Sierra Blanca area, anthropologists point to this "new" group, the Jumano, moving into the vacuum.[30]

Although the time of first occupation for the Jumano and Apache is hard to pin down, most archeologists agree that there was very little permanent settlement in the Guadalupe Mountains. Most peoples lived on the eastern fringes and escarpments adjacent to streams and rivers such as the Pecos and Rio Grande, but used the higher elevations for hunting and gathering. Sometimes mobile groups lived atop the mountains on a temporary basis. All of this points to linkages with peoples of the Trans-Pecos and plains, who were primarily hunters and gatherers, utilized caves and rock-shelters in the mountains, and had ties with cultures along the Rio Grande. Sites in the area that have yielded skeletal material of children indicate the use of cradleboard flattening practices of plains cultures. Excavations in the Rustler Hills at Granado Cave, in eastern Culberson County, also reveal occupation between AD 200 and 1450. Fiber materials, baskets, wood, burial materials, and other artifacts from the area point to reoccurring use over a one-thousand-year period, but cultural affiliation remains tentative. The people of Granado Cave may have been Manso, Suma, or Jumano but some scholars argue that they were Hokan speakers that were pushed into this area by more dominant peoples.[31]

Two broad factors limited the use of the mountains and the region eastward to the Pecos River. The slope of the western escarpment, with its extreme aridity, heat, and poor soils limited the impact of Puebloan peoples in the region. Moreover, Puebloan expansion tended to follow river beds, most of which sat on a north-south axis, fairly far away from the Guadalupes. Plains peoples occasionally went to the mountains, but the mercurial river, along with the sand dunes on the bank of the Pecos, minimized migration of bison, and thus plains hunters.[32]

Analysis of the Granado Cave site in the Rustler Hills offers insight into the identities of these groups. Skeletal remains from the cave are similar to the ten-thousand-year-old remains found in Midland, Texas. Pottery strongly resembling that from the Casas Grande area of Chihuahua, the Chupadero and Sierra Blanca regions of New Mexico, the El Paso area, and even shell beads from the Gulf of California and the Pacific Ocean point to vast networks of trade and exchange.[33] Some scholars argue that this culture group was pushed here by another expanding group. The list of possible suspects is relatively short, with the Jumano being at the top of that list.

If the Jumano did marginalize this culture, we are left with several questions, first and foremost being the identity of the Jumanos themselves. The Jumanos are associated with the Jornada Mogollon and have potential links to the Cochise group, which is a term for desert cultures dating as far back as 7000 BC. They may have had a linguistic connection with a Tanoan dialect (Taos, San Juan, Isleta, Jemez, and Pecos Pueblos) and possibly a Caddoan group from the Trinity River in eastern Texas, Arkansas, and the central plains. Tanoan predominated along the Rio Grande and extended southward to its confluence with the Rio Conchos, in Chihuahua. Caddoan languages were spoken across the southern plains and Trans-Pecos region.[34] The linguistic roots of the Jumano are murky, and their ethnic identity is hard to determine.

This collection of attributes and settlement patterns speaks to occupancy by the Jumanos, "proto-Jumanos," or even Apaches in the 700s.

This would make them the contemporaries of the peoples associated with Rustler Hills. But again, these relationships still beg the question of Jumano identity. Use of the term Jumano began with the Spanish entradas in the 1500s, but the Spanish applied it to various groups east of the sedentary Puebloan villages and onto the Llano Estacado. Some scholars argue that they are closely tied to southern plains peoples who were similarly influenced by eastern Pueblo cultures. Best assessments place them as middlemen between plains cultures and the Pueblo, with a homeland around the Concho River.[35]

Nancy Hickerson sees the Jumanos as distinct from the Apaches, and as the people that the Spanish referred to as Teyas. She says they were linguistically close to the Tanoan family and had strong links with the Jornada branch of the Mogollon peoples. They were a mix of agricultural settlements living along the central Rio Grande and semimigratory peoples living north of the Rio Conchos, east of the Rio Grande and across a vast southern plains landscape. The agricultural communities lived much like the Puebloans to the north, while the more migratory bands lived in the *rancheria* mode described by Edward H. Spicer in *Cycles of Conquest*. They were known by the Spanish, hunted buffalo, and traded with the Puebloan peoples to the west.[36]

Their numbers never approximated that of the Puebloans, Apache, or Comanche, but Hickerson claims that they served as intermediaries between these groups for several centuries. Jumanos gained an extensive knowledge of the Trans-Pecos region and exploited the scarce water resources of the Pecos and Canadian Rivers, as well as the playas that accumulated after storms. Some evidence points toward Jumano use of Hueco Tanks northeast of present-day El Paso. Their strategic location gave Jumanos the opportunity to expand their trade in buffalo hides to more sedentary groups in return for corn and other agricultural products. This vast territory and complex economy gave them flexibility to sustain themselves, but it also rested on an ethnic diversity built upon intermarriage with peoples from nations at their periphery.[37]

Jumanos were overwhelmed by the great changes that swept across the Trans-Pecos region between 1400 and 1650. As Apache bands expanded into the region, they formed the western prong of a two-pronged "pincher" movement of which the Comanches were the far eastern prong. When Apaches entered Jumano territory they usurped their position as traders with the peoples along the Rio Grande and forged a different relationship with the Pueblos. Building on their trade in animals and a minor trade in humans stemming from occasional warfare, the Spanish captured Apaches and other Natives and forced them into slavery. Eventually myriad groups, including the Apache, became captors as well as captives in this expanding system. Apaches labeled Mescalero by the Spanish were especially disruptive to the Jumano trade route that extended from La Junta, up through the Davis Mountains, along the eastern face of the Guadalupe Mountains, and into the Tompiro-Piro communities of the Manzano Mountains. Thus, the impact of the Mescalero on the Jumanos had direct relevance for the peoples of the Guadalupe Mountain region.[38]

Bands of Mescalero and the Lipan are clearly associated with the Guadalupe Mountains, but it is hard to determine when Apache peoples entered the region. Two major arguments dominate the literature: one stipulates a migration along the western face of the Rocky Mountains and includes a date of early entrance into the Southwest, while the second argues that Athapaskans came down the eastern slope much later and thus were heavily influenced by plains cultures. Most scholars agree with the latter claim that bands of Apaches entered the region from the eastern route, between the Rio Grande in New Mexico and the Pecos River in Texas, around 1200.[39]

The minority view asserts that Apaches, or the Nde´ as they call themselves, inhabited the region for a much longer period. In fact, researchers such as Jack Forbes, Enrique Madrid, and others argue that Nde´ lived in the area as part of the Jornada Mogollan peoples themselves. In this theory, as the Mogollon groups "dispersed" from their mountain homelands and their riverine pueblos, they experienced a shift in land-use patterns, political organization, and social structure, thereby "becoming Apache" peoples that we recognize after Spanish entry into the region. This stance ties the Nde´ peoples to a wide range of groups stretching across the Greater Southwest borderlands. By the time the Spaniards arrived in the region, the Nde´ groups had experienced enough cultural change from their sibling groups that the Spaniards perceived them as entirely different peoples.

Despite the dispute over their entrance into the region and the pre-contact usage of the mountains, Mescaleros lived over a vast swath of land between the Sierra Blanca Mountains, the heart of their homelands, deep into Chihuahua and from the Rio Grande in the west to the Pecos River in the east. As a culture that combined hunting and gathering with light agriculture, they lived across a landscape accentuated by the salt basins and more lush zones of "the Bowl" atop the Guadalupe Mountains. Their resource base stretched from a horizontal and vertical range that included access to a variety of large and small game such as elk and rabbit, cacti such as sotol and agave, and seasonal camps for warmer and colder weather.[40]

The Mescalero, like all "Apaches," refer to themselves broadly as Nde´, but the Spanish gave them a new name after observing their use of mescal, a drink derived from the agave plant. Agave is a common desert plant and was a staple carbohydrate for peoples in northern Mexico and the American Southwest. Mescaleros harvested the energy-packed roots and baked them in large rock-lined pits, both above and below ground.[41] Mescaleros also used the plant's tough, fibrous leaves for thread and twine that they used to make clothing and to bind together baskets and sacks. They also used the pointed tips as needles. They ground the seeds together with acorn and pinon nuts into "cornmeal" that could be used as a form of tortilla or bread. They fermented the sap into mescal, or pulque, which is still a popular drink in some parts of Mexico. Large clay jugs of mescal and caches of baked agave, bread, and jerky, stored in strong baskets of bear grass and yucca, fended off starvation during the lean times of winter.[42]

Indigenous Settlements in the Paso del Norte Region

In addition to the Nde´, the Sumas, Mansos, and Piros that inhabited missions around Paso del Norte (present-day Ciudad Juarez) after Spanish conquest also had a relationship with the Guadalupe Mountains. These peoples fanned outward from areas such as Casas Grandes before the arrival of the Spanish. These are the groups that likely influenced the plains-oriented peoples and perhaps the Jumanos. The Piro people were a Puebloan group that lived south of the Tiwa villages of Isleta (near Albuquerque), and moved to Paso del Norte with others during the 1680 Pueblo Revolt. Before this migration, most of their villages were situated near Socorro and the confluence of the Rio Puerco, Rio Salado, and Rio Grande. Abo and Quarai, to the east of the Rio Grande, were their centers of religious and economic activity. These towns also interacted with Jumanos that traded with southern Pueblos, and later with Apache bands. Piro Pueblos became a well-used source of exploited labor for colonial governor Lopez as early as the 1650s, though they were somewhat outside the orbit of most Spanish policies of religious conversion, secular taxation, and military pressure. During the revolt, some Piros and Tiwas were swept up in the exodus of Spaniards, where they met the Mansos and Sumas that lived around El Paso.[43]

Less is known about the Manso and Suma people along the Rio Grande near El Paso, Texas, and Ciudad Juarez, Chihuahua, Mexico. Identifying them is complicated by the multiple names that are used to refer to them: Jano, Suma, Jano-Jocome, Conchos, and Suma-Jumano are frequently seen in the Spanish documents. The Spanish were often confused by the myriad bands, villages, and clans that populated the vast region of the present-day tri-state borderland.[44]

As noted above, Jack Forbes examined Spanish sources that referred to peoples bordering the southern Apaches. Forbes stated that the Spanish sources from the sixteenth century confirm that the "Rio Grande between la Junta and El Paso was inhabited in part by the Sumas and Mansos," and he offered a hesitant connection between Mansos, Sumas, and Janos-Jacomes groups with some Apaches. He also stated that "the three accounts [Cabeza de Vaca, the journal of Perez de Lujan, and Espejo] of the early 1580's fail to prove a relationship between the people of the El Paso region and the other Rio Grande groups, however, they also fail to disprove such a relationship." In addition, Forbes cited a 1691 report from Governor de Vargas out of El Paso that the Mansos, Sumas, and Apaches in the vicinity had intermarried, converted, and were speaking in Spanish.[45]

Forbes pointed to other reports to address the Apache relationships with peoples around El Paso. A 1682 journey by Governor Antonio de Otermin into the Organ Mountains in Las Cruces, in pursuit of Apaches, led Otermin to believe that Mansos were related to Apaches. Thus, the Spanish were referring to the Organ Mountains as the "Sierra de los Mansos" by the early 1700s. When the Spanish captured an Apache war chief named Jusepillo in the early 1680s, he referred to his brother, Jusephe, who was a well-known chief of the "El Paso Mansos." Local Indians referred to Jusephe as "Jusephe el Apache." Along with other evidence, this buttresses Forbes's claim that the peoples of the El

Paso region may have been Apachean. Spanish observers and scholars of the region have assumed characteristics for the Apache that did not include more sedentary living such as exhibited by Sumas and Mansos. Rather, they viewed Apaches through a migratory lens that ignored the diversity of Apaches. Forbes implies that prerevolt populations around El Paso were either Apache in origin or their ties with the Apache were strong enough that the Spanish had difficulty differentiating them. At minimum, Forbes argues that intermixture transformed the El Paso populations into Apache peoples.[46]

William B. Griffen, who has written about the Apache and their relationships with Janos, Chihuahua, claims the "entire question of linguistic classification" of these people "remains practically unanswerable."[47] Conchos and Chisos groups living between Big Bend and the Conchos River in Mexico were purportedly Uto-Aztecan speakers, but Griffen is skeptical that the Sumas and Jumano were part of the same language group. He says that the Mansos were more difficult to place in a language group, while the Jano and Jocome to the north of the Sumas and Mansos, were most likely Athapaskan. Griffen argues that into the 1750s the Spanish identified them separately from Apaches in the parish records of the Janos presidio, but he is silent on the classifications utilized in El Paso. Of these groups, the Sumas and Jumano would have lived most closely to the Guadalupe Mountains, but so could have the Mansos.[48]

As the debate over the identities of indigenous peoples in the present-day El Paso and Juarez region illustrates, scholars do not fully understand the precontact cultural history of the region. Lack of a consensus aside, there are some tentative claims that we can make. The first Paleo-Indians entered the region between 13,000 and 11,000 BC. Little is known about them other than that they used crude projectile points, hunted game, and gathered local foods. They were highly mobile and lived in different ecosystems on a seasonal basis. They probably did not remain in the mountains for a significant period of time. Moving into the later eras of the Archaic, thousands of years later, these peoples developed newer technologies to eke out a living from an increasingly xeric environment. Temperatures increased, animals disappeared, and plant regimes adapted to survive with less water. They exploited a larger range of ecosystems, incorporated the mountains and river plains into their cultural landscape, and tried to cultivate plants. In the Formative or Ceramic phases, we see evidence of new technologies in the area. Scholars have found evidence for more rock-shelters, midden rings, and sophisticated projectile points. And finally, during the protohistoric and historic eras, we see the Jumano and early Apachean peoples entering the region. In short, the area including and surrounding the Guadalupe Mountains has been a home, if only temporary, to people for nearly thirteen thousand years.

CHAPTER THREE

Indigenous Peoples, Spain, and Mexico

Spanish colonization of the Americas was part of the long expansion of European power around the globe. Fueled by the desire for trade with Asia, control of the oceans, territorial disputes in Europe, religious zealotry, and the search for labor, Europeans embarked upon an unprecedented wave of imperialism. Aided by Native peoples' lack of immunity to European diseases and divisions between indigenous nations, the Spanish subjugated populations of the Caribbean Basin, the Andes, and Central Mexico during the sixteenth century. Spain solidified these conquests by exporting the church, state, and military to accompany colonists as they exploited the new lands. As outposts of the Spanish Empire grew into villages, presidios, missions, and seaports, Spanish explorers penetrated the vast region between Florida and California, and eventually into southern New Mexico and West Texas.[1]

The Spanish observed groups interacting with each other in ways that reflected specific patterns that had been shaped by customs predating European arrival. Native translators and guides followed well-worn trails, had an extensive knowledge of the land, engaged other indigenous groups through a predetermined protocol, and evinced a working grasp of the cultural geography of the Trans-Pecos region. By combining the historical data that has resulted from Spanish colonization with archaeological evidence, we can paint a portrait of the early interactions between Indians and Europeans. That portrait, however, is muddied by Spanish misinterpretation of the names of Indians, poor understanding of the present-day Southwest borderlands, and disregard for Native political structures. This has resulted in conflicting interpretations found in the journals of Spanish chroniclers. Finally, as diseases decimated Native communities, and as the introduction of horses, weapons, and technologies altered the economies and military capabilities of groups, the interaction between Native peoples accelerated. This new volatility began to drastically transform the indigenous world of the Guadalupe Mountains.

Spanish Entradas and Native Peoples

In 1527 Panfilo de Narvaez led an expedition from Spain that landed in West Florida. Narvaez went west but altered course and followed the Mississippi River south to the Gulf of Mexico, hoping to return to New Spain. Currents diverted them and destroyed one of the four boats, killing Narvaez. Álvar Núñez Cabeza de Vaca, the treasurer for the expedition, survived the dangerous waters and shipwrecked off the coast of Texas. After escaping from captivity by East Texas indigenous peoples, Cabeza de Vaca and a small group meandered across Texas.[2]

Their precise route, however, remains disputed. The two most cited documents—Cabeza de Vaca's *Relacion* and the three Spaniards' *Joint Report*—are vague regarding their travels across Texas and perhaps into New Mexico. One view has the group passing through Big Springs, Texas, along the Concho River where Native groups constructed hundreds of lodges in a village. Cabeza de Vaca's entrada allegedly went west toward the Davis Mountains and turned north following a stream until they encountered women carrying cornmeal. According to this rendition, the stream was actually the Rio Pecos. Nancy Hickerson claims that Cabeza de Vaca followed Jumanos up from the Pecos River and toward the Guadalupe Mountains. After refusing to go west, the Spaniards continued north up the Penasco drainage toward Elk Creek, where they entered a rancheria of forty lodges, maybe in the Sacramento Mountains. They met a Native party, possibly returning from the northern sections of the Guadalupes with deer, quail, and other game. Hickerson alleges that this group could have been Apaches, and as Cabeza de Vaca notes they spoke a different language than the tribes to east. If correct, this confirms the belief that Apaches, especially Mescaleros, inhabited the Guadalupe Mountain region during the 1500s and perhaps earlier.[3]

While Cabeza de Vaca's journey is clouded in uncertainty, ensuing Spanish entradas had a more lasting effect. Based on Cabeza de Vaca's alluring reports of cities of gold, and fueled by the desire for indigenous laborers, a small force led by Marcos de Niza went north from Central Mexico. Although Marcos de Niza received orders not to enslave the Indians, his exploratory work did just that. When he returned with stories of Cibola, a city of golden streets, his contemporaries became hungry for the twin treasures of gold and slaves.[4] In response to the stories of Marcos de Niza, one of the most famous Spanish expeditions began in 1540, when Francisco Vázquez de Coronado received permission from Viceroy Antonio de Mendoza to lead conquistadors north along the Rio Grande. His goal was to find the Seven Cities of Cibola, locate a water passage to the sea, and identify a potential work force for Spanish mines. As Coronado's party proceeded, they concluded that the stories of golden cities were false and that there was no water passage to the sea. Rather than return empty handed, Coronado followed the advice of a Native scout named "The Turk," who claimed that they could find gold in Quivera. Although recent scholarship argues that The Turk fabricated the story to lead the group away from the pueblo, Coronado followed the guide east through Cicuye (Pecos Pueblo), and onto the Llano Estacado and present-day Kansas. Coronado failed to find treasure, and the Crown blamed him for rebellion among the indigenous groups.[5]

Coronado's entire route will not be traced here, but the portions relevant to the Guadalupe region and the local Native peoples are illuminating. Several days after crossing the Pecos River, Coronado encountered Querechoros, "who lived like Arabs" in tents while hunting the "cows" or bison on the southern plains. Coronado noticed the dislike of the Querechoros for the Teyas, who were presumably Jumanos, to the south and east. Although the literature offers contending views—that the Querechoros and Teyas were Apaches, and that the Teyas were Caddoan peoples or Jumanos—there is evidence supporting Coronado. As the Apache usurped territory from the Jumanos and replaced them as a more assertive intermediary between the Puebloans to the west and the plains people to the east, the Jumanos strengthened their alliances with groups such as the Hasinais, Caddos, and Wichitas. As the Apache pushed the Jumanos to the south and east into greater contact with the southern plains groups, the Spanish may have mistook the Jumanos as ethnically related to their longtime trading partners to the east. Coronado's chronicler, Castaneda, noted dog travois, methods of drying meat and preparing pemmican, working with skins, and the ease with which they traded with the Spanish. His observations on facial painting and clothing styles resemble descriptions from the Espejo expedition forty years later, supporting Hickerson's argument that the Teyas were Jumanos.[6]

Spain did not attempt additional excursions into the region for decades, focusing instead on Chihuahua and Sonora. By the late 1500s the Spanish were slowly establishing themselves in Nueva Vizcaya, which included present-day Chihuahua and portions of Coahuilla. By 1567, following trails northward from Durango through Zape, Inde, and Guatimape, Spaniards reached the Parral region and established settlements and mines at Santa Barbara in the San Bartolome Valley on a tributary of the Rio Florido. This town became the staging ground for expeditions further north, especially toward La Junta de los Rios at the convergence of the Conchos and Rio Grande. La Junta de los Rios also witnessed Spanish slave raiding parties that fanned out across the region. Eventually La Junta de los Rios became home to Catholic missions and Spanish presidios, from which expeditions penetrated the Guadalupes.[7]

During the late sixteenth-century Spain commissioned several expeditions that worsened tensions with Natives. The Franciscan priest Agustín Rodríguez convinced Captain Francisco Sánchez Chamuscado to accompany him on a mission to Christianize settlements in 1581. Traversing the Camino Real along the Rio del Norte (the Rio Grande), the small party visited several pueblos, including the Piros and Tewa villages to the north, where Rodríguez remained for a year. Although the Rodríguez-Chamuscado expedition sought the conversion of Natives, it officially claimed New Mexico for the Crown, naming it San Felipe del Nuevo Mexico.[8]

Their incursion provided a pretext for Antonio de Espejo to organize an expedition in 1582 to travel northward. Espejo was under indictment for murder, but he claimed that he had to go north to save Rodríguez from death. Rather than protect the friar, Espejo's real objective was to find new mines and colonize the Indians observed by Rodríguez and Chamuscado. Espejo went through Native villages in and around present-day El Paso and Ciudad Juarez, followed the Rio del Norte northward until he turned westward in search of gold in present-day Arizona, and then reversed course and went eastward toward Cicuye.[9]

The most important element of Espejo's expedition is not its impact on Native people, but the journals of his chief chronicler, Diego Pérez de Luxán. After Espejo abandoned the search for gold in Arizona, he doubled back east and at the Sacramento Mountains turned north to Pecos Pueblo and entered the Llano Estacado. The expedition reached the Pecos River, which they called the Rio de las Vacas for the herds of buffalo on its eastern bank. Pérez de Luxán referred to it as a "medium sized river with exquisite water, surrounded by numerous trees and many vines, roses, rosebush fruit, and many pennyroyal."[10] After four days of travel southward, they encountered no Indians, but they found "goad sticks with which the Indians kill cattle," as well as the tracks and bones of cattle. The party encountered a tributary of the Pecos River; several curves in the Pecos; a brackish, salty, cienega that they named El Salado; and a concentration of cienegas that they termed El Ancon de la Laguna because "a lagoon formed a bay near this river."[11] Within five days the group encountered another mosquito-infested area that they named "El Mosquitero," a stand of mesquite trees that they named "El Mesquital," an "inlet of fresh water with many walnut trees" that contained a fish that they called "mojarra," and a clutch of prickly pear cacti that they termed "El Tunal." An additional day traveling found them at an eastward flowing stream feeding into the Pecos River. At this junction the party "noticed the sierras of the Pataraueyes," possibly the Guadalupe Mountains to the west. They named the place "El Dudoso." Some scholars believe this is when Espejo named the Guadalupe Mountains for la Señora de Guadalupe.[12]

According to Pérez de Luxán, their excursion down the western bank of the Pecos was uneventful until they reached a small rancheria of "Querecheros," as they termed Apaches in the Pecos Valley. Espejo referred to them as "a different nation from those they left behind [the Pueblos]," as he observed them "going to kill cattle for their food," the cattle being buffalo. He noted that "they carried their provisions of maize and dates loaded on dogs which they raise for this purpose," but he apparently did not remain with them for an extended period of time.[13] Espejo continued southward to Toyah Creek, in present-day Texas, where they met Jumanos. In one journal entry Espejo noted, "We met three Jumana Indians, who were out hunting and we were able to understand them through Pedro . . . they said that the Rio de las Bacas came out very far below the Conchos River; that they would take us by good trails to the junction of the Rio del Norte with the Conchos . . . this brought us no little joy, as men who had eaten nothing but pinole. We halted for the night at a large marsh where there were many water holes . . . we called the site La Cienega Salada."[14] They left the site two days later and marched five leagues southward until they found more Jumanos, most of whom were associated with the rancheria from which they had departed. According to Pérez de Luxán, "The Indians, men and women, received us with music and rejoicing. As a sign of peace and happiness there was held a dance between the tents of the Indian men and women. We rested for a day because we had fishing of catfish, mojarra, and sardines, some of which were half a yard in length, a difficult thing to believe. The food was delicious."[15] A day later, the Jumanos led them past the Davis Mountains to where they noticed great forests of mesquite and herds of buffalo north of La Junta de los Rios.[16]

During the next week of their return journey, they encountered more villages. While Pérez de Luxán's journal is ambiguous about their location, they were probably near La Junta de los Rios. On the tenth of August they met the "settled people of this nation, who in their clothing are similar to the Pataragueyes, except in their houses." They saw more cienagas supplied by runoff from nearby mountains, spent days with Native people living in "rancherias," and ate "roasted and raw calabashes and prickly-pears." They traveled over a mountain and stopped "at a valley with many holm-oaks, where there flowed a fine stream of water," which they named El Valle del Encinal.[17] A few days of travel brought them to the "Rio del Norte nine leagues from the pueblo which seems to be San Bernaldino of the Pataragueyes." When they entered the rancheria the people greeted them with a "great reception . . . and gave us quantities of ears of green corn, cooked and raw calabashes, and catfish. They put on great dances and other rejoicings as a sign of peace." When they arrived at the pueblo of San Bernaldino, Pérez de Luxán noted that the "cacique . . . ordered small fish and matelotes brought to us."[18]

On the twenty-second of the month the party followed Native guides to the Conchos River, "at the pueblo of Santo Tomas, where it joins the

Rio del Norte," and waited there for three days as the water level dropped enough to cross over. The party traded with the local Native population, which possessed numerous blankets, bison skins, and "Turkish bows reinforced with sinews." After they forded the river, they encountered an "old Toboso Indian," who told them that people had fled when they heard rumors of Spaniards seeking captives. The "old Toboso Indian" told them that a previous group of Spaniards had enslaved several of his people. During their return, the party encountered Toboso rancherias and some villages inhabited by "Conchos Indians," who Luxán states were friends of the Toboso. The Espejo party ended their expedition in San Barolome in mid-September.[19]

The Espejo expedition of the early 1580s provided valuable information on the Native people, topography, flora and fauna, and resources of the region.[20] Espejo was one of the initial Spaniards to report large herds of buffalo, their migration patterns, and the people who hunted them: the eastern Puebloans, Apaches, and Jumanos. The Spaniards would also popularize the name "ciboleros" for a specialized group of buffalo hunters along the Pueblo-Llano Estacado frontier. Although they initially thought they were Jumano, they later applied the term to multiethnic groups of genizaros that hunted the large beasts. Espejo and Pérez de Luxán observed that the Jumanos lived across a vast region from central-eastern New Mexico south of El Paso del Norte to past the Pecos River in the east. Finally, the expedition confirmed the cultural ties between the people in the Guadalupe Mountains and La Junta de los Rios.[21]

Eight years after Espejo's entrada, in 1590, Gaspar Castaño de Sosa, lieutenant governor and captain general of Nuevo León, led an expedition into New Mexico to establish a colony. Castaño had experience in the region as he was one of an increasing number of Spanish slave traders that went through Paso del Norte and into the southern Pueblos. His slaving ventures were known to many, and it was public knowledge that his commanding officer, Luis de Carvajal y de la Cueva, the former governor of Nuevo León, had instructed him to explore territory in hopes of capturing Indians to sell into slavery.[22]

Despite lacking permission for colonization, one hundred and seventy-five people followed him up the Pecos River. Lacking guides familiar with the territory, the group suffered cold and hunger on a five-month journey that eventually took them to the northern Pueblos. Within a few days of leaving La Junta, Castaño's group entered a well-established rancheria adjacent to a stream feeding the Pecos River. Captain Alonso Jáimez, the second in command, used an interpreter to ask about paths northward. People from the rancheria could communicate with the interpreter because, assuming they were Jumano, they had a trade relationship with the groups around La Junta. Castaño's journal notes an encounter at some salt beds with Apaches, Jumanos, or Piros who had traveled from the Rio Grande near present-day El Paso. He observed that "These people had with them many loaded dogs, as is the custom in those regions."[23] One entry states that they encountered Indians on the bank of the Pecos, and perceiving the Spanish a threat, the "Querecheros" attacked Juan de Vega, an Indian in their group, and threw him in the river. After a brief battle the Spaniards captured and hung four of the "offending individuals."[24]

Castaño's party did not encounter any battles when they entered the villages east of the Guadalupes. This was after they passed the Davis Mountains in November 1592, when they encountered a band of Jumanos or Apaches. An entry in Castaño's journal noted the Guadalupe Mountains in the distance, and on November 30, they observed a river flowing from the mountains to the west, possibly the Rocky Arroyo. Nearby his party found a large corral that Apaches or Jumanos may have used to trap animals. Near Dark Canyon at the northeastern edge of the mountains, the group found a pottery jar and ears of "recently shelled corn."[25] The expedition did not stay long, and they continued past present-day Carlsbad, Artesia, and then to Pecos Pueblo.[26]

More impactful entradas, such as Juan de Oñate's expedition between 1598 and 1601, opened the door to colonization of northern New Mexico. His entrada, clouded in controversy, could be judged as a failure considering he faced resistance by Native communities and mutiny by men in his own colony. Rather than focus on food and shelter for his colonists, Oñate embarked on several missions to search for gold. The Crown recalled and tried him for negligence and incompetence. His initial mission nonetheless led to Pedro de Peralta establishing Santa Fe as the capital of New Mexico. Despite his recognition and legacy in the Spanish borderlands, Oñate's efforts only indirectly impacted the Guadalupe Mountain region. His contact with Jumanos was limited to the bands outside of Santa Fe, and Jumanos near the headwaters of the Red and Brazos Rivers in the Texas Panhandle.[27]

A significant result of Oñate's expedition was the establishment of Paso del Norte as a colony and military garrison. This colony was established south of the Rio Grande, on the "Mexican side" of the present-day international boundary, in modern Ciudad Juarez. The missions were also established on the southern side of the river, but convulsions of the Rio Grande in later centuries, placed them north of the river, on the U.S. side. The shifting river and changes in boundary lines reveals the mercurial nature of the river itself, but also the blurring of national borders and the topographical unity of the Southwest borderlands environment. One hundred miles southwest of the Guadalupes, Paso del Norte became a staging ground for raids up the Rio Grande and Rio Pecos against Jumanos and Mescaleros. In the early 1600s, bands such as the Siete Rios pushed the Jumanos toward the Comanches, and the Apaches of the Guadalupe Mountains became the focus of Spanish aggression.[28] Thus the newly established military garrison would face no lack of pressure from surrounding Native groups.

Accompanying the military was the growth of missionary activity in New Mexico. The Franciscans were the most prominent order along the Camino Real between Chihuahua and Santa Fe. In 1623 Alonso de Benavides became the custodian of the Franciscan order and agent of the inquisition for New Mexico. It fell upon Benavides to establish missions in Native communities and solidify their presence in the borderlands. He initiated the mission Nuestra Señora de Guadalupe de los Mansos near El Paso del Norte and strengthened El Paso as a midway point along the Camino Real. The twelve friars joining Benavides took up posts in New Mexico and West Texas to proselytize the Natives. After a few decades these missions expanded. Benavides founded churches among the Tompiros south of Albuquerque, several of which counted Jumanos as neophytes. The friars boasted seventeen thousand converts in the Pueblos, and by 1630 church records claim that twenty thousand souls had been saved. In 1629 when Benavides received additional staff, he sent Juan de Salas to convert Jumanos in the Trans-Pecos. Flanked by soldiers, Salas and Diego Lopez marched two hundred miles through the lands of the Apaches Vaqueros to what they believed were Jumano villages. Though he lacked evidence to support his claims, Salas reported that the Jumanos and neighboring tribes on the Llano allegedly "fully accepted" the teachings.[29]

The encounters between the Franciscans and Jumanos, though difficult to reconstitute, did not reflect the larger tensions between Pueblo peoples and the missions. The two major centers of activity were Santa Fe and El Paso del Norte, both of which sought Native labor. As Jumanos were caught between Apaches and Comanches, northern bands in the Tompiro region were relocated by Franciscans to El Paso. Many of them assisted with the missionizing efforts in the Pueblos, a response that further angered their onetime trading partners and contributed to their detribalization. Their strategic acquiescence probably saved them from the violence of Spanish colonists and land holders.[30]

The external pressures combined with internal decisions about their own survival led many Jumanos to accept Catholicism, perhaps only superficially, and to "blend" into the Hispanic population. They adopted elements of Christianity, began speaking Spanish, and worked at the lower rungs of the colonial economy. Although it is difficult to confirm the extent of conversion, the friars were generally pleased with what they believed was a successful religious indoctrination within the Jumano groups around the missions of Paso del Norte. Others faced capture by Spanish, Apache, or Comanche slave traders and ended up working in Spanish mines and on haciendas of colonists. Some found refuge with Apache or Comanche families, and a few carved out a life in autonomous communities across West Texas and northern Chihuahua.[31]

During the mid-1600s, the maelstrom of Spanish colonization and the rise of Apache "raids" placed tremendous pressure on the Pueblos of New Mexico. Encomenderos, combined with public taxation, drought, assaults from Apaches, and religious oppression in the form of punishment and the destruction of sacred kivas, led to the Pueblo Revolt of 1680. This event, often known as the Great Northern Rebellion, rearranged the military, religious, economic, and political landscape of the region, and expelled the Spanish from New Mexico for more than a decade. As Antonio de Otermín, the governor of Santa Fe during the rebellion, fled southward, he and the surviving colonists acquired people from the southern Pueblos of Isleta, Laguna, and Piro. Debates rage over whether these refugees willingly followed the Spanish or were enslaved by them, but the end result was the same: they joined Mansos, Sumas, and other Native peoples in the missions around El Paso.[32]

Although the Pueblo Revolt transformed New Mexico, it had an indirect impact on the Guadalupe Mountain region. Facing dwindling options, the dispossessed Tiwas, Piros, and Tompiros settled into the El Paso missions and crafted relationships with Mansos and Sumas that ranged from intermarriage to selective segregation. Most Indians in the mission orbit used the surrounding landscape, which included the Guadalupe Mountains and salt flats, as a source of survival. As these groups exploited natural resources, they came into conflict with Mescaleros. Thus, the revolt may not have directly involved Mescaleros in the Guadalupes, but it fueled population growth in El Paso, which in turn led to greater demands on regional resources. And this exacerbated tensions between the Mescaleros and Spaniards.[33]

Shifting Power Relations in the Shadow of the Guadalupes

The conflicts that triggered the revolt in New Mexico facilitated a shift in power between Apaches, Comanches, Jumanos, Pueblo peoples, and the Spanish associated with the rise of the horse and the gun across the Trans-Pecos region. Whereas the Spanish responded to the Pueblo Revolt with the violent 1692 Reconquista, officials in Nueva Vizcaya turned their attention to the mounted warriors of the Apache and Comanche nations.[34] The ensuing Spanish campaigns against them led to cycles of conflict for most of the 1700s in the Trans-Pecos region. Alternately, the preexisting alliances and conflicts between Apaches, Pueblos, Spanish, and Jumanos were exacerbated by the colonization of a vast part of Texas, New Mexico, and northern Mexico by the increasingly powerful Comanches.[35]

The Comanches entered north Texas from Wyoming via New Mexico between 1650 and 1740, carving out an empire of impressive scope. Comanche origin stories and anthropological research ties them to the Shoshonean peoples of the Rocky Mountains and Great Basin. The majority of Comanche cultural sites were east of the Pecos River, but Daniel Gelo worked with Comanches to map places between the Rio Pecos and Rio Grande. Five of them, starting northwest of the Guadalupe Mountains and going south and east, are: Sierra del Alamo, San Augustine Pass (north of Las Cruces), Las Cornudas (forty-five minutes east of El Paso), Ojo del Cuervo, Guadalupe Peak, and Ojo de San Martin. Gelo identified sites in a string roughly from the Big Bend National

Park northwest up the Rio Grande to San Antonio, New Mexico.³⁶ Additional evidence for Comanche knowledge of sites as far west as the Organ Mountains, comes from Comanche memory and Anglo military expeditions that relied on Comanches. Randolph Marcy, after the U.S.-Mexican War, employed a Comanche guide named Manuel who was "perfectly familiar with almost every stream and water-hole upon the prairies." The guide knew Hueco Tanks and identified Guadalupe Peak for Marcy. Robert Neighbors also used a Comanche guide on his expedition in the early 1850s and noted a cave in Hueco Tanks named after the Comanches. The Butterfield Overland Mail followed a section of Manuel's path south of the Cornudas Mountains and north of Hueco Tanks, down to El Paso.³⁷

The mastery of the horse by the Comanches had lasting effects on all people of the region. Caught between the Apaches in the mountains and the Comanches across the Llano Estacado, the Jumano homelands evaporated. With their access to buffalo reduced, and as the targets of Spanish and Native slave traders, the Jumanos splintered and blended into other tribes. Some were enslaved by the Apache and eventually adopted as kin, while bands around the La Junta and El Paso region became part of the Sumas and Mansos, or the recently arrived Tiwas from Isleta. Jumanos living southeast of the Manzano Mountains even approached the Spanish for protection. One particular group led by Juan Sabeata made a plea in 1682 to the Presidio at El Paso. Sabeata told his patrons that he had visited Jumano rancherias along the Pecos River and found them deserted. Sabeata believed that these villages had been attacked by Mescaleros. Eastern bands turned to their allies, the Hasinai and Caddo. Although a few Jumano communities remained sprinkled across the Trans-Pecos region, by the late 1700s they had been dispersed as a clearly defined group.³⁸

Comanche domination of the southern plains pressured Apaches in New Mexico and West Texas, increasing their role in the slave and horse exchange complex. The targets for this trade were Spanish settlements below Albuquerque, such as Socorro and Belen, all the way to Ojinaga. Villages between present-day Ruidoso and eastward toward present-day Carlsbad and Artesia were also targets of Apaches. Settlers complained, but Crown representatives were restrained because the Apaches served as a buffer against the stronger Comanches. By avoiding preferential treatment toward either group, the Spanish tried to manage hostilities between them. Tentative peace negotiations between the Spanish and Apaches disintegrated in 1738 when the Spanish militia from Paso del Norte captured an Apache leader named Cabellos Colorados and sold captives into slavery.[39]

By middle of the century, relations between the Spanish and Apache had been vacillating between a suspicious détente and outright warfare. Often vilified as "raiders," and blamed for hostilities in New Mexico, the Apache consisted of decentralized bands of extended families. They organized their societies along egalitarian lines and based their economies on a spectrum of light agriculture to seasonal hunting and gathering.[40] This mobility made them especially loathed by the Spanish, who sought to "reduce" Native people to the control of Spanish military or Catholic missions. This tension dated back to the expeditions of Oñate and escalated into outright destruction of Spanish and Apache villages, enslavement, and violence in the region.[41]

Recent scholarship indicates that the Spanish borderlands were not a place of equitable power relations where groups crafted a "middle ground" of cultural hybridity. The area that contextualizes the Guadalupe Mountains was in reality the domain of Comanches, Mescalero Apache, and Lipan Apache. Contrary to the claims of Spanish soldiers and commanders, the Spanish presence in the vast swath of land between the Colorado River Delta and the Gulf of Mexico was the domain of the indigenous people. This reality became clear with the destruction of Spanish missions and settlements during the seventeenth and eighteenth centuries. Presidios lacked funds and weapons and frequently suffered from corrupt military leadership. Spanish colonization stagnated and, in some cases, declined, especially throughout Comancheria.[42]

Compounding these shifts in power was the lack of Spanish knowledge of the Trans-Pecos. Aside from entradas along the Pecos River and the expeditions out of Santa Fe, the region between Pecos Pueblo and El Paso and between Rio Grande (south of Albuquerque) and the Pecos River was a terra incognita.[43] In 1724 Pedro de Rivera inspected the province of New Spain, and his engineer, Francisco Álvarez Barreiro offered one of the first maps of the Guadalupe Mountains. In 1745 Juan Miguel Menchero mapped the area around Carlsbad, but he quickly returned to Santa Fe as Apaches followed his trail. The fact that a Spanish survey mission fled the Trans-Pecos with Apaches close behind illustrates the limits of colonial power in the borderlands.[44]

These expeditions constituted a rough form of ethnographic observation that provides some tentative data on the Apache bands of the region. The so-called Faraones inhabited the mountains between the eastward bend in the Rio Grande (present-day Mesilla to El Paso) all the way to the Pecos River. They were closely related to the Mescaleros from the Sacramento and Guadalupe Mountains through the Big Bend region and into the Bolson de Mapimi. Some scholars claim that they were same bands of people. East of these Mescaleros were the Llaneros, who were subdivided into the Natages, Lipiyanes (Lipanes), and Llaneros. They lived between the Pecos and Colorado Rivers (in Texas), with some overlap with eastern Mescaleros. The easternmost band was the Lipanes, who claimed southern Texas to the Gulf of Mexico and south into Tamaulipas, Coahuilla, and Nuevo Leon. To further complicate matters, some scholars note that the northern Lipan bands were in fact Mescalero, or vice versa.[45]

Given this geopolitical landscape, Spain was virtually paralyzed in the region between the north-south axis of the Rio Grande in New Mexico and the villa de San Antonio in the province of Tejas. Referring to West Texas, eastern New Mexico, and the southern plains as *el desplobado*, the Spanish understood that colonies there would be easy targets for Comanches and Apaches. Comanche destruction of missions along the San Saba River during the 1750s was illustrative of Spanish weakness outside of southern Texas, El Paso, and Santa Fe.[46]

The attacks elicited responses from the military, especially the forces garrisoned in El Paso. By the mid-eighteenth century, El Paso had a vibrant economic life and ties to Santa Fe, Chihuahua, Janos, and settlements along the Rio Grande and Camino Real, and its residents were deeply concerned about their survival in a region surrounded by Native people.[47] In Paso del Norte and across the northern frontier, before the Bourbon Reforms of the 1770s and 1780s reorganized Spanish settlements, most power fell into the hands of the presidio captain, who was also the lieutenant governor of New Mexico. He controlled an area extending from Carrizal to the south, the salt flats at the foot of the Guadalupe Mountains to the east, and Rincon to the north. There were generally between fifty and one hundred military men stationed at the presidio in Paso del Norte, ready to attack Apaches. This, along with the twenty-five hundred Spaniards and mestizos, and numerous "acculturated" Indians, represented a sizeable population.[48]

One example illustrates the role played by the military in Paso del Norte during campaigns against Apache. According to the diary of Pedro José de la Fuente, captain of the presidio, on August 30, 1765, a contingent of men traveled to the salt flats near the Guadalupes in search of an Apache group that allegedly seized cattle from a *vecino*. De la Fuente indicates that the vecinos were following the Indian trail from the Rio Grande northeast to Hueco Tanks, through Cornudas, and between the major salt beds south of Guadalupe Peak. The contingent failed to find the Apaches, but such brief events, like the chance encounter between de la Fuente and an Apache woman, provide scholars with glimpses of what life was like in the region. On November 29, de la Fuente left the presidio a second time to reconnoiter the far eastern boundaries of his jurisdiction. When he returned on December 1, he brought "an Apache Indian woman of the Guadalupe Mountains with two little children." De la Fuente claimed that "she had fled from her people of her own volition and had come determined to live among us." It is difficult to confirm her identity or motivations, but the incident hints at the complex cultural relations in the region.[49]

Spanish Policies and Transformation in the Borderlands

Spain tried to strengthen its position in the late 1760s as King Charles III, a Bourbon reformer, commissioned the Marqués de Rubí to investigate northern presidios. The suggested reforms emerged from global changes in the dynamics between Spain, Britain, and France caused by the fallout from the French and Indian War (Seven Years War). At the Treaty of Paris in 1763, French claims in North America below the present-day U.S.-Canadian border fell into the hands of the Spanish, while Spanish territory in Florida shifted to the British. Spain sent Rubí in 1766 after the acquisition of Louisiana Territory to assess the populations, military and financial resources, and general standing of northern communities. Of relevance was the expedition that he commissioned against the Mescaleros in the Organ and Guadalupe Mountains. These military assaults into Apacheria failed to capture individuals charged with raiding Spanish settlements along the Rio Grande. His inability to capture Apaches proved the need for a greater military presence and to controlling the mobile Apaches in southern New Mexico.[50]

Rubí's recommendations became policy in 1772 and replaced diplomacy with targeted use of force. The implication of this policy, which was central to the Bourbon Reforms, included a series of presidios every one hundred miles from Altar in Sonora to the Gulf of Mexico, approximating the present U.S.-Mexico border.[51] Rubí understood the limitations of this military solution, but an underlying goal of the plan was to take stock of frontier resources, solidify Spain's power, and facilitate the acquisition of more territory and subjects. The plans were a European solution to an American dilemma of powerful Indian nations that understood imperial rivalries and had acquired tremendous stores of guns and horses. The one element of diplomacy in the plan involved seeking peace with the Comanches in alliance against the Apaches, who, though smaller in number, consistently frustrated Spain. Although Spain tried to stabilize trade and military relations with the Comanche, plans to control the southern plains and eastern New Mexico were as unrealistic as they were impractical. Hispano villagers refused to comply with a peace policy, Apache bands did not follow a central leader, and the deeply entrenched trade in captives destabilized the region.[52]

In 1775 Hugo O'Connor became comandante inspector and took control of the Spanish frontier army. Connor approached his position with a zeal and organizational ability that stunned his superiors and shook the frontier armies out of their stupor. And yet O'Connor's skill could not reduce the number of Spanish deaths at the hands of Apaches and Comanches. He launched campaigns against Apaches in the Guadalupe, Sacramento, Sierra Blanca, and Organ Mountains where Spaniards killed one hundred and thirty-eight Mescaleros and captured over one hundred, all of which they impressed into slavery. Spanish forces attacked in 1776 with the aid of Comanches interested in capturing Apaches in the Guadalupes, killing one hundred Apaches. This compelled Sierra Blanca Mescaleros to travel to Paso del Norte for a treaty.[53] O'Connor's campaigns nonetheless failed to subjugate the Apache. For his failures, O'Connor was replaced with Teodoro de Croix in 1777, who tried to negotiate a larger peace with the Mescaleros. That effort also failed because the Apaches simply had an upper hand. The Spanish militia could not track them in the mountains, and they continued to trade and take slaves from the Pueblos and Comanches. The Spanish simply lacked leverage over the Apache.[54]

In the light of the failed military strategy, a revolutionary experiment resulted in the appearance of a "reservation era" in Spanish borderlands history. A royal order in 1779 attempted persuasion and pacification to reduce conflict with Apaches on Spain's northern border. Ostensibly Spain halted internment of Apaches and replaced it with *establecimientos de paz*, or "peace reservations." Several Mescaleros accepted protection by the Spanish, primarily from Comanche warriors, and moved into the reservations. Band leaders approached the Spanish commander of Presidio del Norte, Manuel Muñoz near present-day Ojinaga, Chihuahua. Muñoz met with those Mescalero leaders to establish a new pueblo: Nuestra Señora de la Buena Esperanza, and within a few months, four bands accepted the conditions.[55] The establecimientos de paz were attractive in part because Comanche pressure on the Mescaleros continued unabated. Occasionally groups of Mescaleros came into El Paso and Presidio del Norte in the south. "Apaches de Paz," as the large group entering Presidio del Norte had been labeled in 1787, were supposed to take up farming, convert to Christianity, and assist the Spanish with campaigns against Gila and Chiricahua Apaches near Janos. Within a year, there were allegedly four hundred Apaches, primarily Mescaleros, living in pueblos under the jurisdiction of the Presidio del Norte. These groups were among the many Apaches that moved, if only temporarily, into or near presidios along the frontier.[56]

Apache power briefly waned with developments in New Mexico, western Texas, and northern Chihuahua. First, Teodoro de Croix shifted his treaty-making plans from the Apaches to the Comanches and increased his attacks against Apaches. Second, Comanches understood that their power rested on a balance of "raiding," acquisition of horses, access to bison, and free exchange of goods between the Pueblos and the tribes in Tejas. This power forced the Spanish to negotiate rather than fight with them. Just as the Spaniards began to rethink their use of power and diplomacy, cracks began to emerge within the Comanche empire. The expanse of territory and the wealth of guns, horses, bison, and trade products destabilized Comanche society. This opened up fractures in Comanche bands that made them vulnerable to Spanish military pressure and diplomatic overtures. These changes led to the defeat of Cuerno

Verde, a major Comanche leader, in 1780 by Spanish forces, followed by a surprising treaty that weakened Comanche power in the region.[57]

Pressure on the Apache also quickly grew. In 1787 Governor Juan de Ugalde of Coahuila led four hundred men into the Guadalupe region, where they killed or captured dozens of Mescaleros. They signed another treaty, but multiple attacks by *vecinos* and militias in the 1790s and early 1800s undermined the validity of the agreement.[58] In 1810 another series of attacks ended with a treaty in 1811 with Apaches, and the creation of an establicimiento de paz between El Paso and the Sacramento Mountains. This was a miserable failure due to poorly defined borders, weak enforcement, and attacks by Hispanos and Comanches. This cycle of violence and treaty-making continued for years.[59]

Mexican Independence and Changing Regimes

As noted by the eminent scholar David J. Weber, historians have typically regarded the quarter century of Mexican domination as a "dark age" in the history of the region. Rather than a stagnant backwater, the Mexican frontier was a dynamic place marked by change and upheaval. Indeed, the years between 1821 and 1846 saw economic diversification in the form of trade relations with the United States, liberalization of financial policies, privatization of resources, population growth, and attacks on the Church.[60] More specifically, the opening of the trail between Missouri, Santa Fe, and Chihuahua to legal trade in 1821 pulled New Mexico closer to the U.S. economy. This also increased the flow of guns to Apaches and Comanches, which both used in their expansion across the region. For Apaches in southern New Mexico and West Texas, Mexican independence translated into unchallenged authority along their "raiding" trails between the Guadalupe Mountains and the Pecos River, and south to Chihuahua City.[61]

Other developments brought change for Native peoples in southern New Mexico and West Texas. The financial and administrative crises associated with the challenge to the Spanish government assured that few Hispanos could set down roots in the region. The declining military presence made Hispanos worry about Apache raids. As part and parcel of what Weber terms neocolonialism, the growing inclusion of the frontier into the economic orbit of the United States, Hispano communities lost control of their financial destinies. Combined with the instability of the Mexican government, the distance of the frontier from Mexico City made them easy targets for the expanding American economy. Moreover, transfer of the missions to local parishes during the Mexican era decreased their economic impact on surrounding regions. "Mission Indians" from California to Corpus Christi responded to diminished church power by either taking over the missions, destroying them, or fleeing.[62]

The unpredictability caused by Mexican independence translated into new and unpredictable relationships with Native peoples on the northern frontier. An 1810 treaty with bands of Mescaleros recognized their occupancy of land north of San Elizario, west to the Mesilla Valley, and north to the Sacramento Mountains. José Joaquín Calvo López, the chief of the comandancy general and inspection for Chihuahua and New Mexico, renewed that treaty in 1832, hoping to dissuade Mescaleros from raiding along the Rio Grande. Calvo López reminded them that they needed a license to leave the region stipulated in the treaty, and he encouraged tribal members to remain in or around the establecimientos de paz adjacent to El Paso, San Elizario, and Presidio del Norte.[63]

Mescaleros ignored the treaty and left the establecimientos de paz. These bands returned to the Guadalupe, Davis, and Sacramento Mountains and resumed their tradition of riding deep into Mexico in search of food and supplies. The New Mexico governor Manuel Armijo, perhaps recognizing the desperation of the Hispanos in the territory, agreed to a request from the Mescalero chief José Maria Maria to renew their old peace treaty. The terms of the treaty included a reduction in "raids," an agreement to remain within the boundaries of land recognized by Spain and Mexico, increased rations and a promise of five thousand pesos, and the return of captives. The 1842 treaty garnered the support of several Mescalero leaders, so Maria sent representatives to Chihuahua City that spring. After modifications, Maria sent his approval to the presidio at San Elizario and by the summer Mescaleros under his leadership were at peace. Mescaleros following "General Espejo" also signed a peace agreement with Mexico.[64]

By 1842 Mescaleros in the Guadalupe, Sacramento, and Davis Mountains, many of whom had waged war against Spain and Mexico, were living in relative quiet in or around Paso del Norte. This contrasted sharply with Apache bands to the south and east, where Mescalero leaders Maria, Vueltas, Gomez, and others did not entirely agree with the treaties with Mexico, but nonetheless followed the spirit of the détente. These leaders kept the "raids" to a minimum and sought resolutions to the occasional "theft" of cattle or horses by young men. Peace, if only momentarily, had come to the West Texas borderlands.[65]

Cracks in these agreements emerged as cultural differences and the financial troubles of Mexico pressed down upon Chihuahua and New Mexico. As noted by Mauricio Ugarte in El Paso, Mescalero leaders worried that the departure of governor and general Francisco Garcia Conde, whom the Apaches trusted, would threaten the peace agreements. Conde assured the Mescaleros that the incoming commandant general, José Mariano Monterde, would maintain the status quo and protect Mescaleros from Comanches. Monterde began his tenure in 1843 with a survey of presidios in Sonora, Chihuahua, and southern New Mexico. When he reached the El Paso region, his main concern was with relations between Apaches and the states of Sonora and Chihuahua. Apaches exploited the tensions between the states, took cattle, and returned north. Military units from the states retaliated and further exacerbated the tense situation.[66]

Monterde's stance on the Mescalero may have stemmed from their frustration with daily conditions and the deterioration of the peace agreements. By 1845 the treaties were effectively nullified as Mexican settlers attacked Mescalero encampments seeking revenge for theft of cattle and livestock. Mescalero were angered by the limitations on their movement and restrictions on their livelihood associated with remnants of the establecimientos de paz. Mexican officials reduced the gifts and payments and failed to protect them from rising Comanche hostility. Young Mescalero men were insulted at the assault on gender roles, especially on their masculinity and ability to gain honor and prestige through hunting and customary forms of leadership.[67]

Within the year, international intrigue and the specter of war ushered in violent change across the borderlands. As American president James K. Polk provoked a war against Mexico, relations between Mescalero and the Mexicans completely unraveled. Reports of Mescalero "raids" in northern Chihuahua and southern New Mexico exploded as young men sought out horses, cattle, supplies, and food to replace the decline in provisions offered by the presidios. Pedro Armendariz, from his perspective in Presidio del Norte at La Junta de los Rios, blamed the spike in Mescalero activity on Monterde's shortsighted and inept diplomacy. These failures led Mescaleros to join forces in early 1845 with groups of Lipans to sack villages in Chihuahua. The attacks surprised authorities who had been trying to stop campaigns by Mescaleros from the Sacramento and Guadalupe Mountains against settlements in the Mesilla Valley. Simultaneously, Mescalero chief Jose Largo joined a band of Jicarillas to declare war against the Presidio in El Paso and Mexican villages in the area.[68]

Largo's alliance with the Jicarilla was one of several wrinkles in a complex array of agreements during the U.S.-Mexican War era. Largo did not represent all, or even a significant portion, of the Mescaleros when other band leaders simultaneously sought peace with Paso del Norte. They sought an audience with the governor in Chihuahua and even submitted to an armed escort to declare their peaceful intentions. Mescaleros, aligned with Maria, visited El Paso and declared their allegiance to the presidio while pillaging ranches and farms in Dona Ana. On the other hand, Mexicans had one of their worst fears confirmed in mid-1845: Mescaleros and Comanches met to exchange captives, renew trade, and agree upon an alliance against the state of Chihuahua. This apparent alliance even included groups of Lipans with some of the Comanche bands that had harassed them for generations.[69]

The centuries between the entrance of Spaniards into the Guadalupe Trans-Pecos region and the war between the United States and Mexico left indelible marks on the indigenous peoples. Spanish colonization introduced horses, guns, cattle, Christianity, diseases, foods, and new cultural forms. These imports enabled the Apache and Comanche to increase their dominance over Puebloans, who suffered from European diseases and the proselytizing of the Church. As the Pueblos compressed into fewer settlements, Apaches and Comanches expanded their homelands. In turn, groups such as the Jumano who were caught in the middle faced dwindling options. Once a key player in preconquest regional trade, the Jumanos lost a homeland that stretched from the eastern Pueblos clear across West Texas and south toward Ojinaga. They splintered and merged with other indigenous peoples and barely survived on the margins of a rapidly changing world.

After the Pueblo Revolt of 1680, Spaniards modulated their colonization of the Pueblos, intensified warfare against Apaches, and sought tentative peace with the Comanche empire. Spanish expeditions hunted down Apaches between the Guadalupe Mountains and the Big Bend country, while Hispano communities launched their own ventures against Mescalero warriors. With the exception of a few moments of peace between the two groups, and a relatively small number of Apaches that entered the "peace establishments," tensions continued into the Mexican period. And by the time the United States entered the region, Apaches and Comanches were the dominant powers of the Southwest and Llano Estacado. It took nearly thirty years to conquer the Apache and Comanche and place them onto reservations, and it required a renegotiation of the Treaty of Guadalupe Hidalgo to allow America to drop its promise to stop Indians from crossing the border.

CHAPTER FOUR
War, Exploration, and Conquest, 1836–1865

Mexican independence dramatically shifted the economic and military landscape for Native people in the borderlands. Intimately tied to independence were two additional events: Texas independence and the U.S.-Mexican War. Beginning in the 1830s, Anglos and some Tejanos argued that the western boundary of the Mexican state of Coahuila y Tejas went to the Rio Grande and up through Colorado. This claim encompassed the Guadalupe Mountains. As they argued for the expansive boundary, Texans promoted independence from Mexico. Mexico disputed the exorbitant claims of Texans and sent military forces to subdue the rebellious population. As Texans and Tejanos fought against Santa Ana, and as the insurgents emerged victorious with the Republic of Texas, neither the Mexicans nor the Texans truly controlled the region west of San Antonio. Indeed, most of Texas west to the Rio Grande was the domain of Apaches and Comanches.

Mexican independence, the Texas Rebellion of 1836, the U.S. war with Mexico, and the U.S. Civil War unleashed liberal reforms, nation building, westward expansion, and market transformation that rearranged the social and political landscape of the borderlands at large. The era between Texas independence and the Civil War brought American emigrants, topographical expeditions, military excursions, and new settlements, pulling the Guadalupe Mountain region into the economy of the United States. Situated along an important trading and migration corridor between San Antonio, El Paso, Tucson, Yuma, and San Diego, and by extension, the gold rush regions of California, the Guadalupe Mountains became part of the larger historical processes of conquest, war, immigration, railroad development, and Anglo settlement. The mountains gained notoriety for their geological significance, as a hideout for Apaches, as a site of violent conflict, and an icon of the monumental landscapes of the American West. On a scale smaller than the Rocky Mountains, the Guadalupes have attracted and repelled human groups, but during this volatile era of expansion and war they became a site of intrigue unlike any other time in their history.

War and Upheaval in the Borderland

Texas independence in 1836 had an indirect impact on the Guadalupe region. It was the result of Mexican policy to populate the northern frontier for protection from Comanche and Apache expansion, and to serve as a bulwark against the United States. The Mexican Colonization Laws attracted American families, led by empresarios such as Moses Austin, who immigrated to Coahuila y Tejas and became Mexican citizens. This plan went awry as "undesirable" Americans, ranging from convicts to adventure seekers, streamed into the state with their slaves and transformed the Mexican north. The independence movement that emerged from their claims of oppression, religious discrimination, lack of free speech, and unjust taxation rang hollow as many of those who promoted rebellion migrated only recently to Mexico, of their own free will, and could have easily returned to the United States.[1]

The resulting Republic of Texas claimed a vast tract of land that extended westward along the Rio Grande and included the Guadalupe Mountains. For nearly nine years the Republic of Texas was in a perpetual economic crisis as it tried to settle its debts through selling public lands. Its roots in the American South led to the growth of slavery in the regions where fertile soils nurtured the plantation economy. Racialized labor and privatization of land and natural resources put the slaveholders—and indeed, most Texans—into direct conflict with the Lipan and Comanche, as the slave economy required constant expansion. It also placed the Mexican origin population in a difficult position vis à vis their brethren to the south, as they faced second-class citizenship in Tejas and were branded as traitors by Mexican nationals. This untenable situation pushed Texas into the arms of the United States as it asked Congress for annexation, which it received in 1845. Annexation failed to solve Texas's problems and very quickly America declared war on Mexico.[2]

The contours of the conflict deserve attention because the war shaped events in the Guadalupe Mountains. After Texas declared independence, its boundary with Mexico became a source of dispute. Texas and the United States claimed the Rio Grande as the boundary, while Mexico claimed the northern Rio Nueces. The geographic difference between these boundaries was approximately one hundred miles but the real import lay in the resources that each boundary provided the nation. If Texas could hold the border at the Rio Grande, that gave it a strategic port at the Gulf of Mexico, as well as fertile lands in extreme South Texas. The difference was also symbolic in as much as Mexico did not want to lose more land. When one traveled northward up the Rio Grande, the border dispute also brought into question the ownership of El Paso and Santa Fe.[3]

America inherited this border dispute when it annexed Texas. But rather than deal with the issue diplomatically, it viewed it through the prism of Manifest Destiny as popularized by William O'Sullivan, a newspaper editor and political commentator. The philosophy embraced by nationalists such as Thomas Hart Benton and John C. Calhoun proposed that the nation had been ordained by God to move west, conquer Indians and Mexicans, and transform a "wild" continent into a civilized land for the Anglo-American race. When President James K. Polk sent General Zachary Taylor to south Texas in 1846, he was acting within what he believed was not only the national interest of the United States but its destiny. To him and other proponents of expansion, the shots fired in the contested lands were steps in a natural process.[4]

In less than two years, America had provoked a war, invaded and occupied Mexico City, and forced its southern neighbor to forfeit nearly half of its land. In retrospect it seems shocking that a border dispute transformed into a catastrophic war that left nearly forty thousand dead, destroyed Mexico's economy, and resulted in one of the largest single transfers of land in the hemisphere. And yet, even those who opposed the war ultimately supported it—or at least turned a blind eye to the carnage—when gold was discovered in California in 1848, a land newly wrought from Mexico. The ink on the Treaty of Guadalupe Hidalgo ending the U.S.-Mexican War was barely dry when migrants began streaming across the newly acquired region.[5]

These conflicts had dire consequences for the Guadalupe Mountain region. The elite in Santa Fe had expressed concern about the claims of Texas that it had sovereignty over their territory, but in reality little had changed. Sheer distance compounded the economic and military weakness of a republic that could not reach across the Apache and Comanche empires to dictate policy to Santa Fe. Annexation and war, however, did lead to significant changes in New Mexico. As in California, elites split over allegiance to Mexico or the United States. Some believed that Mexico lacked legitimacy due to its negligence of the frontier, combined with its demands in taxation and regulation of trade with the United States, and thus they expressed hopes that annexation would provide them with protection and access to new markets. This ambivalence shaped the reaction of upper-class New Mexicans to invasion by the American forces and was the main factor behind the "bloodless conquest" of New Mexico during the war.[6] And the "hasty departure" of Governor Manuel Armijo, as observed by historian Anthony Mora, further contributed to the legend that Armijo colluded with the Americans in the takeover of the territory.[7]

As the war between the United States and Mexico raged on, General Steven W. Kearney took control over Santa Fe. The military situation around Santa Fe seemed to be quickly under control, and he ordered Colonel Alexander Doniphan to march southward through the Mesilla Valley and into Paso del Norte. Doniphan planted a military garrison in Dona Ana to subdue the local Mexican population, and he launched raids against Apaches. The garrison took its toll on local residents and several migrated southward to the present-day sites of Las Cruces and Mesilla, the latter of which had a small population living on land grants established earlier in the decade.[8] As it lumbered southward, Colonel Doniphan's Missouri volunteers left a path of destruction behind them. They routed Captain Antonio Ponce de León on Christmas Day in El Brazito, twenty-five miles northwest of the city, and then entered El Paso two days later. This began a month-long occupation of El Paso del Norte, during which Doniphan and his men engaged in drunken violence and destruction of municipal buildings and archives. They left the city in shambles and marched southward to Chihuahua City with orders to conquer the state. After defeating Mexican forces in the Battle of Sacramento, Doniphan entered Chihuahua City in March of 1847. The U.S. troops sacked the city, destroyed churches and municipal buildings, burned crops, and assaulted the citizens. At the end of April, Doniphan left the area, carving another path of destruction to Saltillo.[9]

After Doniphan departed Santa Fe, Kearney appointed Charles Bent as territorial governor and left him in charge of what he believed was a compliant population. Nothing could have been further than the truth. Just a decade earlier, the multiethnic residents of northern New Mexico rose up in opposition to the centralist policies of then governor Albino Pérez, in what is known as the Chimayó Rebellion of 1837. Although Bent may have been aware of the previous uprising, as he and his brother William managed a lucrative trading post in present-day southern Colorado that served what he believed was a docile population. A short while after Kearney's departure, working class Hispanos and a range of Natives collaborated against the New Mexican elite and the American conquerors and orchestrated what essentially amounted to a coup. En route to his home in Taos, Governor Charles Bent was attacked and killed by a group of Hispanos and Indians. Later that winter, other Americans, some of whom had lived in Santa Fe before the war, became targets of the rebellion. The U.S. retaliation resulted in the swift suppression of the insurgents and public executions. The federal government declared martial law and launched violent campaigns against anyone perceived as hostile to Americans.[10]

As the first governors grappled with controlling the vast and disputed lands of New Mexico and Texas, the new territory was buffeted by national debates over slavery and freedom. But more than that, it faced tremendous political challenges when the Texas state legislature gave land to veterans of the U.S.-Mexican War. Some of the most attractive agricultural land was in Mesilla, New Mexico, which straddled the banks of the Rio Grande. Since thousands of acres of farmland were east of the river, Texas claimed it because it argued that the state boundaries followed the Rio Grande up to Colorado. Veterans, many of whom were hostile to the local Mexican population, moved near the town of Dona Ana, and forced residents southward to Mesilla, which was partially in Mexico. Anglo and Hispano leaders met in Santa Fe to determine how they would react to Texan aggression into their territory.[11]

By 1850 the dispute over the New Mexico-Texas boundary was linked to the national question of the expansion of slavery. With support from General Zachary Taylor and Colonel Robert S. Neighbors, New Mexicans voted heavily in favor of organizing as a state, with their eastern boundary cutting through West Texas along a north-south axis. They vehemently opposed the Rio Grande as the north-south border between New Mexico and Texas. Texans, abolitionists, proslavery groups, and anyone with a gun stood poised to fight over the location of this border. Noting the brewing conflict and the potential for international violence that it symbolized, Congress bundled the debate into the Compromise of 1850. And for good measure, it sent a contingent of troops under the command of General Winfield Scott to protect Santa Fe from renewed bloodshed.[12]

The compromise afforded New Mexico Territory the right to decide its slave status with "popular sovereignty," although citizens chose the not all-too-high moral ground of near total exclusion of free blacks. It also turned a blind eye to the old processes of captive taking and slave trading that dated from the Spanish era. The compromise, orchestrated by the ailing Henry Clay, who was a critic of the expansion, rejected the Rio Grande as the border of Texas and New Mexico and set the border at its present location. This deal was made palatable to some Texans because the United States incurred the $10 million debt held by the former republic. The compromise did not, however, end the power of the Comanches and Apaches in the borderlands, especially their ability to traverse the international boundary with impunity, nor did it diminish Texans' appetite for the fertile farmlands of the Mesilla Valley.[13] These two factors, along with the stream of migrants across the continent and the search for a transcontinental railroad route, soon provoked additional tensions over the location of the U.S.-Mexico border.[14]

Immigrants, Surveyors, and the U.S.-Mexico Boundary Commission

The same year that America and Mexico signed the Treaty of Guadalupe Hidalgo, miners in California discovered gold in Sutter's Mill. Ensuing discoveries in Colorado, Nevada, Alaska, and elsewhere brought waves of people to places inhabited by Native Americans. Yet, the newcomers required surveyors and topographical engineers to chart routes across foreign terrain. Assisted by the U.S. military, expeditions into the Southwest included scientists and engineers who mapped the lands the United States had acquired. These expeditions provided crucial information regarding indigenous populations, natural resources, and potential routes for migrants, and, later, railroad lines to unify the nation.[15]

Between 1848 and 1855 the federal government approved numerous expeditions through borderlands region. These surveys were a response to demands for better routes to the West Coast and to assist the army in protecting "settlers" from Indians. However, the first expedition to enter the Guadalupe Trans-Pecos region was not directly tied to the military or the Topographical Corps of Engineers. That 1849 survey was led by Robert Simpson Neighbors, who had traveled to Texas in 1836 and quickly made a name for himself in the young republic. Within a few years he was promoted to major in the army of Texas, and in 1847 U.S. commissioner of Indian Affairs William Medill appointed him as Indian agent for the state of Texas.[16]

In March 1849 Neighbors orchestrated an expedition across West Texas that was comprised of a colorful array of companions: Colonel John S. "Rip" Ford, a former physician, politician, war hero, and Texas Ranger; two Anglos, Daniel Sullivan and Alpheas Neal; and five Native men, John Harry (affiliation unknown), James Shaw (Delaware), Joe Ellis (Shawnee), Tom Coshatee (Shawnee), and Patrick Goin (Choctaw). Neighbors hired a Comanche named Guadalupe who had extensive knowledge of the region.[17] Neighbors left Austin in March 1849 and followed a route that was popular to the Mexican army and Comanche Indians. On the first leg of their trip, they reached the Carrizo Mountains north of Van Horn on April 24, 1849. Most of the group remained there as Neighbors and Sullivan rode west into El Paso to meet Americans and Mexicans familiar with the terrain. Neighbors learned of a well-watered trail from El Paso to the Pecos River. He sent word back to his group and met them in San Elizario, briefly the seat of power in El Paso County, to procure supplies and hire Alvino Zambrano to guide them. Leaving on May 6, the expedition went to Hueco Tanks hoping to find water. From there they crossed over the Texas-New Mexico border to Ojo del Alamo, back down to the Cornudas Mountains, and then east to Crow Springs, or Ojo del Cuervo. After resting at Ojo del Cuervo, the party went through the salt flats below the Guadalupe Mountains. They, like others before and after them, were impressed by El Capitan, thinking it was much closer than it actually was. Ford wrote about "Bold running streams of pure, clear water, whose banks were fringed with trees and shrubbery, presenting the varied appearance of pool, riffle, and lake—now creeping through reeds, grass, and flowers, and anon tumbling from a ledge of rocks, giving to circumscribed spots, scenery of wild and singular beauty, water the slope from the Sierra Guadalupe to the Pecos." Neighbors was less sanguine, noting that the heat, rugged tablelands, and salt beds made the route impractical for wagons.[18]

The Neighbors-Ford expedition helped clarify routes between Texas and California. Neighbors argued that his return route under the Guadalupes was better than his southerly route near El Paso. In response, Francis T. Bryan formally surveyed the return route of the Neighbors-Ford expedition under the Guadalupes. Known as the upper route, the trail near the Guadalupes became popular for emigrants and the military. Combined with the lower route hugging the Rio Grande, by August 1849 nearly four thousand emigrants passed through El Paso to California. One reason for this mass of emigrants was due to a letter that Ford published in the *Texas Democrat*, describing the route via the Guadalupes. This article, part topographical assessment and part self-promotion, gave instructions on how to migrate west.[19]

Westward expansion forced the hand of Congress to approve funds for a massive survey of the newly acquired territories. Missouri senator Thomas Hart Benton, Solon Borland from Arkansas, and Sam Houston petitioned the federal government to fund a survey of Nebraska, California, New Mexico, and West Texas. Congress appropriated finances for Captain Randolph B. Marcy of the U.S. Army Corps of Topographical Engineers to start an expedition across the region.[20] Beginning his trip from Fort Smith, Arkansas, in April 1849, Marcy led a contingent of migrants to Santa Fe. After receiving orders from Washington, he departed the group and his companion James Harvey Simpson—also of the topographical engineers, who went west—on August 14, 1849. Marcy followed the Rio Grande south along the Jornada del Muerto to Dona Ana.[21] From Dona Ana on September 1 he broke east through the San Augustine Pass in the Organ Mountains, turned southeast, and passed the base of the Hueco Mountains.

Marcy had a cursory knowledge of the area, and he relied on a Comanche guide named Manuel who was familiar with the region. Manuel, Marcy wrote, "was born and raised directly in the country over which we desired to pass, and was perfectly familiar with almost every stream and water-hole upon the prairie." Roughly eleven days after leaving Santa Fe his group reached the base of the Guadalupe Mountains, traversed the Guadalupe Pass, and commented on the mountain. He noted bear, bighorn sheep, deer, and great stands of timber, but the salt flats and desert captured his attention. His guide said that the Mexican and Indian populations regularly used the salt beds, which contained a six-inch layer of pure salt. Before they continued their return to the east, Marcy made note of the significant stands of pine, probably the only good source of timber in the region. He also warily commented on Mescalero Apaches, the main reason he did not want to linger in the area. They followed Delaware Creek to the Pecos River, and after difficulty fording that mercurial body of water, arrived at Fort Smith.[22]

Marcy's expeditions were supplemented by several missions across West Texas in the 1850s. Lieutenant Colonel Joseph E. Johnson of the U.S. Corps of Topographical Engineers looked to the work of Marcy, John Coffee Hays, and Captain Samuel Highsmith. In 1848 Highsmith led a party of rangers across West Texas in search of feasible wagon trails. Johnson launched his missions from San Antonio and went across the Edwards Plateau and through the Davis Mountains, hoping to link central Texas with a railhead on the Rio Grande near El Paso. A more northerly trail traversed the Edwards Plateau and crossed the Pecos River at Horsehead Crossing, while another swooped southward toward the Big Bend and up the Pecos to Horsehead Crossing. The first route had been blazed by Neighbors and Ford, while the southern route was cleared in the winter of 1849 by Lieutenant W. H. C. Whiting of the army engineers and Lieutenant W. F. Smith of the topographical corps. The latter route went to Presidio and El Paso, and was the path first taken by Colonel Joseph E. Johnston and Major Jefferson Van Horne years prior to the organized expeditions.[23]

As engineers busily mapped the territories, migrants entered the region with high hopes and a superficial understanding of the land. One such migrant was Cornelius Cox, who went to California in 1849 for gold. Cox was born in Ohio in 1825 and moved to Texas in 1837. After he moved to Harrisburg, he left with a group for California in April 1849. His journal states that they crossed the Pecos River in June, and met Mexican traders returning from Santa Fe. Upon viewing the mountains, he was impressed.[24] He wrote:

> Our camp is situated in what I would term a romantic spot—A beautiful valley surrounded by a continuation of monstrous hills rolling and receding in the distance like billows of the ocean, this is the foreground. A few miles to the northward stands forth the majestic Guadalupe, natures grandest spectacle, a wall as it were extending from the earth to Heaven, grand beautiful, sublime, but we must pass over it. What more could a painter wish, what more could the artist want to call forth the genius of the soul?

The migrant with a knack for literary imagery continued to California and worked in several mines but returned to Texas empty-handed in 1855.[25]

Cox was one of several migrants to write letters to family members back home. An emigrant named John Murchison recalled passing the Guadalupe Mountains and stopping for water at Hueco Tanks. Writing on June 23, 1849, from an encampment on the outskirts of El Paso, Murchison said that his group was the "first to cross them" [the mountains], with forty-five wagons this time, and another one hundred crossing after him.[26] As Murchison's group passed through, Lewis B. Harris was in a wagon train going west. Writing in his journal, Harris was impressed with the mountains and landscape: "These springs run out of the side of a large hill and are situated in a beautiful valley with the most singular beautiful and fantastic hills and mountains scattered over it that anyone could imagine. The Guadalupe Mountains rising perpendicularly thousands of feet are seen at the distance of about 15 miles on the northwest, but the atmosphere is so pure that no one would judge them to be over four or five miles distance." He and his group camped near the mountains for several days under a live oak and next to a spring with "cold and pure water." He eventually traveled up the steep slope of the mountain: "Some of our party ascended the mountain here, and none of them would give up that they had gone less than 2 miles perpendicularly when they were at the summit, then invisible to the naked eye, although we were directly at the base of the mountain." On June 18, they came upon the pass of the mountains, which he thought was a magnificent scene. The group had to tie all of the wagons and horses together to ensure that they did not fall down due to the slope at the base of the mountain. "Here we passed around the Guadalupe cliff which has the appearance of a huge Cathedral. The base of it is I suppose 5000 or 6000 feet high from the valley below . . . in the shape of a steeple." The group stayed at the western base of the mountain, near the salt flat, and the following day broke west to Hueco Tanks and eventually El Paso.[27]

Despite the harsh environment and the popularity of the route via Santa Fe, migrant families followed the trail under the Guadalupe Mountains. Two parties, the Rhines and the McCullochs, made the trek in 1853 and 1854, respectively. They left eastern Texas and crossed the Texas Hill Country, the Llano Estacado, and then traversed the Pecos River and Delaware Creek, neither of which impressed them. While at the base of the Guadalupes, one migrant wrote that they tried drinking sulfurous water from a "boiling spring," but had better luck with Pine Springs, within the present-day park. They described the area as having "pure good water, at the foot of the mountain, with some Pine timber," that might have been a good site for cabins. According to the migrant, the party had left from Grayson County, Texas, and leader of the McCulloch train, a man named Captain Reed, was on his second trip to California. The author believed that the peak was seven thousand feet above its base, and "Indians, Grizzly Bear, Mountain Goat, Antelope, and Black Tailed Dear" inhabited the region.[28]

Most of the emigrants had something to say about the desert landscape and the imposing Guadalupe Mountains, and nearly everyone expressed fear of Indians. Despite their concern, most historians agree that the main causes of death and injury along the trail were standard illnesses, malnutrition, extreme weather, and simple accidents, not attacks by Apaches. Nonetheless, in 1849 one migrant passing through El Paso noted that the Apache "made frequent descents upon El Paso and the settlements near, and the inhabitants are in constant dread of their approach."[29] On July 19, 1849, Lieutenant Colonel L. Thomas had two peaceful interactions with Mescaleros during expeditions in the Sacramento Mountains. In 1854 Lieutenant Commander Daniel T. Chandler went through the same region with one hundred and eighty men seeking Mescaleros who "had been infesting the road leading from El Paso to San Antonio, committing murders and robberies." And in 1852 a "petition from El Paso told how the Apaches were making repeated raids on the ranches of that region."[30]

Reports of alleged attacks spread like wildfire across the nation. One such series of incidents was carried on the *Telegraph and Texas Register*, for January 3, 1850. Titled "Fight with the Apaches," the incident involved Major B. W. Gillock, who received a letter from a wagon train leader named Coons, east of El Paso. As Coons returned to El Paso, he reportedly was attacked by seventy-five Apaches from the Guadalupe Mountains. Hoping that the open space would help him see the Apaches, Coon camped in the salt beds as he sent for assistance from El Paso. Two companies of the Third Infantry out of Fort Bliss escorted Coons back to El Paso. News reports said of the Apaches, "Their great hostility is ascribed to the attacks on them by parties of Americans in the employment of the Frontier states of Mexico, principally those under the command of Chevallie and Glandton, formerly of El Paso."[31]

No encounter invoked greater fear in white men than the possibility of white women being kidnapped. The story of Jane Wilson is illustrative of that fear, though overblown, and particularly relevant for the Guadalupe Mountain region. Born Jane Smith in Alton, Illinois, in 1837, she moved to Missouri and eventually settled near Paris, Texas. She married James Wilson from Hunt County when she was fifteen. James and his father wanted to find gold and joined the Henry Hickman wagon train, consisting of two dozen wagons, which left on April 6, 1853, from Hunt County. The caravan followed the Marcy Trail toward El Paso and camped at the foot of the Guadalupes around June 1. Mescaleros surprised the group at night and rode off the Wilsons' cattle. Men from the group went after the Apaches but found nothing. After the raid, California seemed too risky, and they planned to turn around after restoring supplies in Ysleta. While in Ysleta, the Wilsons claimed that Tiguas took some of their livestock, which the Wilsons replaced by taking cattle from a ranch owned by a Tigua family not associated with the alleged theft. The owners of the ranch proceeded to chase the Wilsons all the way to Hueco Tanks, where they exchanged shots. While fighting over the cattle, the Tiguas apparently killed several of the men and took Jane Wilson back to Ysleta. Martin Hart, an unrelated freighter leaving El Paso for northeast Texas, learned of the fracas, found Jane Wilson, stole her back, and took her with him on his way home. Ironically, Hart's group was attacked by Comanches between the Guadalupes and the Pecos River. Jane Wilson was taken by the Comanches and after months of captivity, escaped. This adventure cured her of whatever interest she had in the West, and she returned home.[32]

Such interactions highlighted the conflicts between immigrant caravans and military surveys, and Apaches, Comanches, and Tiguas, the latter of which moved across the international boundary with ease. These tensions forced America and Mexico to clearly define their mutual border. In the minds of Anglo policymakers, local politicians, the military, and immigrants, the fluidity of the border emboldened Apaches and Comanches to attack migrant trains and flee across the new international boundary. Indeed, conflict between the United States and Mexico over the location and control of the border was tied directly to the cross-border movement of Native people. Although article 11 of the Treaty of Guadalupe Hidalgo stipulated that America was responsible for restraining illegal crossings into Mexico by "raiding Indians," the military had few resources to devote to policing the border. The inadequate military presence was exacerbated by disagreement over the location of the border itself. Conflicting claims, overlapping legal jurisdiction, and other points of contention fueled instability in the region.[33]

As each nation struggled with the political fallout caused by the war and the Treaty of Guadalupe Hidalgo, it became clear that Mexico and the United States had to survey the international boundary. The two nations formed the U.S.-Mexico Boundary Commission to map the border and provide clear lines of territorial separation. This was a difficult prospect considering the surge of people in search of California gold, the crisis over slavery in the West, Texas-New Mexico land disputes, and Apache and Comanche supremacy in the Trans-Pecos. The survey was also complicated by logistical challenges associated with topography, cost, and political differences. The two countries nonetheless organized the commission and began one of the most intriguing chapters in the history of the borderlands.[34]

Both countries had to appease nationalist sentiments and political patronage, while addressing its own particular burdens. Mexico held the most knowledge of the region and offered experienced engineers, but it had to rely on the finances and military strength of its U.S. counterpart. One sign of the peculiarities behind the process was the appointment of John Russell Bartlett, who cofounded the American Ethnological Society in 1842, and by 1847 had authored two books: *Progress of Ethnology* and *Dictionary of Americanisms*. His scientific curiosity and lack of partisanship aside, it is difficult to understand how this naturalist, artist, and ethnographer served as chief boundary commissioner for the United States. Perhaps in an attempt to provide balance to Bartlett's appetite for the humanities, Congress appointed William H. Emory to the expedition. Emory was a leading light of the Army Corps of Topographical Engineers, a West Point graduate, and a veteran of the war with Mexico. Rounding off the trio was Andrew B. Gray, a well-known Texan with an exceptional military background. Gray apparently won his place as a result of pork-barrel politics motivated by the hopes of southerners for a railroad.[35]

The boundary commissioners had the power to determine the international border as stipulated in the Treaty of Guadalupe Hidalgo. Although they went across Texas in 1850, they officially started the survey in El Paso in early 1851. When General Garcia Conde joined Bartlett as his Mexican counterpart, the U.S. contingent had already experienced a murder trial and a few desertions. Rather than begin immediately, Bartlett waited out the winter with an extended excursion into Mexico and a meandering journey to Hueco Tanks and the Guadalupe Mountains. Bartlett was in the Guadalupes during the fall of 1850 as the temperatures cooled and the leaves changed color. After trudging through sandy soils and rocky terrain, he waxed poetic about El Capitan and Guadalupe Peak, both of which he thought were visible from nearly one hundred miles away. He observed that the color "changed to a pure white tinted with buff or light orange, presenting a beautiful contrast with other portions of the range and with the azure blue of the sky beyond." Bartlett watched the sun rise on the snowcapped mountains and he marveled at the changing hues of the trees and surrounding landscape. When they continued west they were surprised by what they believed was a vast lake, when in fact it was an optical illusion created by the sun reflecting off the salt beds. More than a foreboding obstacle and a hideout for Apaches, the Guadalupes were to Bartlett a majestic landscape set in the middle of an expansive desert.[36]

Although Bartlett provides historians with useful descriptions of the mountains and greater borderlands, his artistic and ethnographic tangents exacerbated the controversy that erupted over the confusion about the eastern starting point of the boundary. One view put it eight miles north of Mexican El Paso, while another placed it more than thirty miles northeast. The later point was promoted by the Disturnell map, which had been appended to the Treaty of Guadalupe Hidalgo. Although this starting point for the boundary gave Mexico additional land, Bartlett conceded to Garcia that this was the beginning point for the border. Without approval by Congress, Bartlett and Garcia moved the immense party following the inaccurate map.[37]

The decision to begin the boundary thirty miles northeast of El Paso infuriated Anglos in New Mexico, who protested the loss of territory. If the boundary started here, it would exclude valuable agricultural land in the Mesilla Valley. Led by the territorial governor William Carr Lane, Anglos protested, and Mexican president Santa Anna responded by sending soldiers toward Mesilla. A disagreement that began with lines on a map, and which was compounded by an ill-conceived Bartlett-Conde Agreement, escalated into near war. In response, President Pierce sent James Gadsden, a railroad tycoon from South Carolina, to calm the tensions and negotiate what Americans termed the Gadsden Purchase (Mesilla Treaty) and settle the present boundary. Rather than debate the precision of one map as compared to another, Gadsden offered Mexico a lump sum for an even larger portion of land. They scrapped the old agreement and moved the border south, far below Mesilla, west beneath Tucson, to Yuma. After minor adjustments, the two sides signed the agreement on December 30, 1853, in the town of Mesilla, and the border took its shape.[38]

As the location of the international boundary became clearer, and after the political intrigue and bureaucratic fighting associated with the commission tapered off, topographical expeditions again fanned out across the West. The Pacific Railroad Bill of 1853 authorized the exploration of routes for a transcontinental railroad. Jefferson Davis, a southerner and U.S. secretary of war from 1853 to 1857, supported a path along the Thirty-Second Parallel through the Llano Estacado, the Guadalupe Mountains, El Paso, the new Gadsden Purchase land, Fort Yuma and then to San Diego. The first leg of the expedition in 1853 started from the Pima Villages along the Gila River to present El Paso, led by Lieutenant John Park of the Topographical Corps of Engineers. Park's initial survey provided useful information and was one of the first to suggest drilling for artesian wells for water. Davis ordered the region surveyed, and Park continued west from Dona Ana, New Mexico, to California.[39]

Davis's mandate brought Colonel John Pope into the picture, with a commission to survey the region between Dona Ana and Preston, Texas, on the Red River. Pope was born in Louisville, Kentucky, graduated from West Point, surveyed the boundary between the America and Canada, and served in the U.S.-Mexican War. He came to the Department of New Mexico as chief topographical officer in 1851. On October 7, 1853, Pope traveled from Albuquerque to Dona Ana in preparation for his survey of West Texas. General John Garland of the Ninth Military Department furnished troops and joined him from Fort Bliss in El Paso. The infantry contingent was paired with six officers, a mineralogist, surgeon, naturalist, diarist, and wagon master, totaling a party of seventy-five. After leaving El Paso they stopped at Hueco Tanks, sloughed through the salt flats, and reached the Guadalupe Mountains a few days later. The group moved along the eastern slope of the mountains toward the New Mexico-Texas boundary, crossed the Pecos, and arrived in Preston on May 13, 1854. In his report to Congress, Pope noted that the most expensive section of the proposed railroad line would be near the Pinery and Guadalupe Pass because of the rugged terrain and nearby salt flats.[40]

Pope returned after Congress approved $100,000 to search for artesian wells to supply the railway with water. He had a theory that deep wells were fed by sources far away from the actual drilling sites, and he thought that the Guadalupe Mountains served as a sink that filled wells beneath the plains. Pope left Albuquerque for El Paso in the winter of 1854 to test this theory. He drilled wells between Dona Ana and El Paso but failed to hit water. By March 1855, he had crept eastward until he reached the Pecos River Falls at the mouth of Delaware Creek, near the Texas-New Mexico border. He broke drill bits on the hard earth east of the Guadalupes without reaching any water.[41]

As Pope surveyed the region, Texas Naval Captain Andrew B. Gray from boundary commission fame joined the Texas Western Railroad Company to survey a route into the Gadsden Purchase land. The survey began from San Antonio on January 1, 1854, and continued west across the Pecos River to El Paso. Gray was scouting the Guadalupe route, which he said was "perfectly practicable, yet believed to have fewer advantages than the other," which went fifty miles into New Mexico. He advised against the New Mexico route because the railroad charter was in Texas, but he worried that the route below the Guadalupes would be problematic due to rough terrain, salt flats, and shifting sand. Gray was nonetheless quite interested in Guadalupe Peak:

> The peak can be seen at a great distance, owing to the clear and rarified atmosphere of the country. This stupendous basaltic structure is perpendicular, and looks as if it had been shaped by some sudden and powerful convulsion of nature into the form of a large edifice or church, from which circumstance we gave it the name of Cathedral rock. Viewed from the deep gorge below, it is truly sublime and beautiful—its lofty peak towering to a great altitude, and crowning the terminal point of an extensive range of mountains.

After Gray completed the work, he met with General Garland in Albuquerque to discuss the "Indian Problem," and how it might deter construction, and returned to El Paso.[42]

As these and other expeditions cut trails through the new land, mail services began integrating it into the nation. The Butterfield Overland Mail connected the nation with a series of stage coach lines that have become symbols of the "Wild West." For such an icon of Western Americana, the Butterfield Overland Mail operated briefly from 1859 to 1861. If the surveys, along with the emigrant trains going west, did not point to the national importance of the Guadalupes, the short lived overland mail certainly did, as many of them stopped in the shadow of the imposing mountain. The coaches, known as "celerity wagons" were as recognizable as they were uncomfortable, made out of leather, wood, and metal in an attempt to cushion the shock of driving across rugged terrain. Passengers paid two hundred dollars to be crammed into the coaches, sometimes sleeping on top of each other and the luggage they carried. While they bounced across the West, they stopped at stations dotting the trail for food, water, and supplies.[43]

One of the best accounts of the Guadalupes as seen by passengers along the Butterfield Trail came from Waterman L. Ormsby, a correspondent from the *New York Herald*, who rode west in 1858. Ormsby was definitely out of his element in the borderlands. He was apparently scandalized when, near the head of Delaware Creek, his stagecoach stopped to cook breakfast on a pile of buffalo chips. On September 25, 1858, Ormsby arrived at the Pinery Station, situated at the foot of the Guadalupe Mountains, one mile from the present-day national park headquarters. The Pinery Station was fairly indicative of the stations along the line. It was a sparse place situated alongside an acequia that brought water from Pine Springs.[44] When Ormsby arrived at the Pinery, it was a desolate place. One of the first station-keepers, Henry Ramstein, had recently completed work on the station, but the site was abandoned in 1859 due to a shift in the mail route. After the shift, the Pinery was utilized by occasional migrants, until 1870 when Major Albert Morrow out of Fort Quitman began to employ it during excursions against Mescaleros.[45]

Ormsby's journal helps us understand how the Pinery and other stations made up the fabric of life on the Butterfield Trail. After leaving the Pinery, they began the sixty-mile trip to Cornudas. As he passed directly in front of El Capitan, he noted the "steepest and stoniest hills I had yet seen, studded with inextricable rocks, each one of which seems ready to jolt the wagon into the abyss below. It is enough to make one shudder to look at the perpendicular side of the canyon and think what havoc one mischievous man could make with an emigrant train passing through the canyon." After El Capitan they stopped at Ojo del Cuervo near the salt flats, and then turned toward the station at Cornudas. Continuing westward, they passed through Alamo Springs and Hueco Tanks, the well-known source of water for Tigua Indians. They reached El Paso a few days later, and Ormsby continued west to California, leaving us with a fascinating first-hand account of the region.[46]

Within a year after shifting the trail southward, the Butterfield Overland Mail faced larger changes that ultimately led to its demise. Before the Civil War, the proposed southern route for a transcontinental railroad loomed over the Butterfield Trail like a death sentence, but Butterfield himself was pushed out of his position as president of the company due to internal politics. With Butterfield marginalized and in ill health, the ripple effects of the Civil War and corporate maneuverings allowed competitors to take over the transcontinental mail business. By 1865 the Wells Fargo Express Company became the leader in shipping across the American West.[47]

Native Peoples and American Expansion

The legacy of the U.S.-Mexican War, Treaty of Guadalupe Hidalgo, and the Treaty of Mesilla altered the lives of Native people in the Southwest borderlands. Among many things, the end of the war facilitated a wave of migrants into Apacheria, and in doing so, fueled tremendous pressure on their cultures. This transformation placed several bands, particularly those in the Sierra Blanca and Sacramento Mountain region, such as the Siete Rios Apaches around present-day Ruidoso, into direct conflict with settlers and the military. Their proximity to interracial conflict emanating from the Rio Grande settlements in Socorro, Belen, Mesilla, and Dona Ana, as well as ongoing pressure from Comanches, placed them in a different position compared to their kin in the Guadalupe and Davis Mountains to the south, who had access to escape outlets in the Big Bend region and into Mexico.

In the aftermath of the Treaty of Guadalupe Hidalgo, the trajectory of Indian-white relations seemed uncertain. In 1849 Lieutenant Enoch Steen led troops from Dona Ana into the Sacramento Mountains in retaliation for alleged attacks on settlers north of the Guadalupes. The accused Sierra Blancas rarely participated in the raids, and their leader, Santana, scared the solders by claiming that they had two thousand armed warriors waiting if they continued their advance into the mountains. The bluff caused Steen to relent, and the Sierra Blanca Apaches returned to their homes unscathed.[48] The southern bands associated with the Guadalupe and Davis Mountain region were similarly likely to defend against incursions into their homelands, or, if pressure from the military or the Comanche became unbearable, seek refuge in Mexico. One incident involving the topographical survey into the region highlighted the unpredictable interactions. Lieutenant W. H. C. Whiting of the Corps of Topographical Engineers was surveying a road between San Antonio and El Paso in February 1849. Whiting encountered Apache bands loosely following Chief Gomez. His companions, Cigarrito and Chinonero balanced out the more militant Gomez, and the groups began discussing how to react to the intruders. Cigarrito and Chinonero convinced Gomez to allow Whiting to continue westward, and they even led the expedition to water and shelter in Limpia Canyon in the Davis Mountains. The importance of this encounter was that the Guadalupe and Davis Mountain Apaches enjoyed near total control of the region north and east of El Paso. As long as Apache bands could surprise emigrants and return safely to the mountains, non-Indians felt that the region would remain a forgotten outpost.[49]

Although these two interactions ended peacefully, the Anglo and

Hispanic population between Dona Ana and El Paso demanded military campaigns against the Apache. For instance, General Garland, commander of the Department of New Mexico, attacked Mescaleros in retaliation for cattle thefts in the towns of Socorro and Dona Ana. Such incidents increased as Comanches pressured Apaches and as Mescaleros competed with a growing population for resources. Several Apache leaders expressed these concerns to Captain A. W. Bowman, from Fort Stanton, which was recently established in the heart of Mescalero lands. These brewing conflicts led to the creation in 1849 of Fort Bliss in El Paso and in 1851 of Fort Fillmore, slightly south of Mesilla, as a base of operations from which the military could launch attacks against Apaches. Additional forts served similar purposes. In 1853 Fort Thorn (near present-day Hatch) and a garrison in San Elizario, Texas, convinced some Mescaleros to seek peace treaties.[50]

Owing to their decentralized political structure, some Apaches sought peace while others took a more defiant path. In September 1850 several bands from the Guadalupe and Davis Mountains, led by Simon Manuale and Simon Porode, gathered at San Elizario to discuss the future of the region. They visited the nascent "American" town of Franklin, on the north side of the river, and talked with Major Jefferson Van Horne about the potential for peace. Van Horne understood he was supposed to "cultivate friendly relations with them," but he cautioned his Apache counterparts that his superiors needed assurances they would not "raid" emigrant wagon trains. Although the meeting revealed the possibility for peace, the Davis and Guadalupe Mountain bands did not indicate which direction they favored.[51] The diffused organization of the Apache can also be seen in 1851 when Texas governor Peter Hansborough Bell sent John A. Rogers to make treaties with Indians between the Pecos and Rio Grande. He returned with information that drought had forced some bands to seek assistance from the military in Presidio, Texas, across the river from Ojinaga, where the old presidios had existed. Rogers added that he met other bands of Mescaleros who had joined forces with Lipans and Comanches, at San Saba, Texas, where leaders signed a treaty. In contrast, other Mescaleros continued to attack wagon trains and assault Mexicans below the Rio Grande.[52]

After Garland's excursion against Apaches in 1851, some bands traveled to Santa Fe in 1852 to discuss peace with the New Mexico superintendent for Indian Affairs, John Grenier. This meeting resulted in a treaty with the Apache, approved by Congress and ratified by President Fillmore. The 1852 treaty stipulated that Apaches would maintain peace with Americans, abide by the laws of the United States, and refrain from attacking migrants. It also required the end of excursions into Mexico and Mescaleros' participation in the human slave trade. The treaty delayed the creation of a reservation but approved the allocation of stock and supplies out of Fort Stanton. This tentative reconciliation unraveled as non-Indians around the Sacramento and White Mountains appropriated Apache land and resources. Alternately, a band not participating in the peace negotiations in Santa Fe attacked a wagon train in Hueco Tanks. The newly elected governor of New Mexico, David Meriwether, reacted by further stoking the non-Indians' fears of Indian raids and used it as an excuse to wring more troops from the federal government.[53]

Mescaleros' perspectives on this cycle revealed suspicions that characterized cross-cultural interaction. Mescalero band leader Josecito told Governor William Car Lane that their new peace treaty did not cover all Apaches in the area because only a few Mescalero bands considered Josecito their headman. Lane's treaty did not specify which bands it covered; indeed, he made promises to Mescaleros that he lacked the authority to enforce.[54] Other bands rejected the treaty and continued their resistance to non-Indian encroachment onto their homelands.

The unravelling of the Apache treaty of 1852 and confusion surrounding a second treaty not approved by Congress led to conflicts in the region. In August 1853 a Mescalero band attacked and killed ten emigrants and took one hundred and fifty cattle in Dog Canyon, along the Texas-New Mexico border, within the present-day park boundary. Garland retaliated with a major military expedition against the Mescalero and ordered Lieutenant Colonel Daniel T. Chandler, Third Infantry, from Fort Conrad, into the White Mountains. Chandler left Fort Conrad and stumbled into Dog Canyon, where they found only abandoned campsites. Garland persisted with his goal of finding those responsible for the Dog Canyon incident, and in June 1854, he ordered another punitive expedition from Fort Craig and Fort Fillmore. Carrying a white flag, Garland met with Mescalero leaders Negrito, Jose, and Pluma, all of whom claimed innocence. They told the military that they lacked influence over the other bands, but the military continued searching.[55]

As tensions in the Texas-New Mexico borderlands increased, the Army continued seeking information about the Mescaleros. In late fall 1854, Major D. Miles convened a meeting of Mescaleros near present-day Las Cruces. Miles reported that chiefs Palanco and Santos, who claimed territory from the Sacramento to the Manzano Mountains, attended, but that the "hostile" chief Santa Ana, whose lands ranged from the Sacramento to the Guadalupe Mountains, refused to join. Nothing concrete came of the meeting but in early 1855 the region exploded into full-scale war as Meriwether and Garland launched a major assault against all Apaches.[56] Garland ordered Captain Richard S. Ewell and Captain Henry Stanton to search for Mescaleros between Anton Chico and El Paso, including a sweep through the Guadalupe Mountains. Several engagements resulted in dozens of Apaches dead. One battle killed Captain Stanton. Ewell's troops retaliated, and combat continued for weeks.[57]

Garland sent Major James Longstreet and fifty-four men out of Fort Bliss to attack Apaches between the Guadalupe Mountains and Hueco Tanks. Longstreet enlisted José María Polanco as a guide. Following Polanco, who was familiar with the region northeast of El Paso, Longstreet went northeast from Hueco Tanks past Cerro Alto Mountain. In January 1855 they found several Apaches and followed them into the Guadalupes, but due to a lack of water and inadequate supplies, they were unable to keep up with the more skilled warriors they tracked. After several failed days pursuing the group, they woke one morning to find Polanco killed by Apaches. Defeated and despondent, they returned to the fort empty-handed.[58]

The increased military pressure convinced a Mescalero delegation led by Josecito and Barranquito to approach the Indian agent for the Mescalero, Michael Steck, at Fort Thorn. This meeting led to a larger conference in June 1855, during which Meriwether concluded another peace treaty at Fort Thorn with Mescalero leaders. Under its terms, the military recognized as Mescalero territory the lands between the mouth of the Delaware Creek, running north along the Pecos to Bosque Grande, then west to the western slope of Sierra Blanca, across to San Nicolas Spring, then to Hueco Pass, and along the boundary between Texas and New Mexico. This was not a small chunk of land, but once again, the Senate rejected the agreement.[59]

Apache resistance incensed territorial politicians and the military, but the decentralized sociopolitical organization of the bands made it difficult to formulate appropriate policies. Only a handful of Americans comprehended that mobile "tribes" lacked a centralized structure and that an agreement between one band did not include an agreement with all bands. Individuals such as Steck at Fort Thorn and Fort Stanton during the first years of its operations divided Mescalero under his jurisdiction into two categories: those interested in "settling down" at the fort followed Cadete and those further to the south who were more attuned to "raiding" in Chihuahua. Steck did not hold much hope for the latter group, so he focused efforts on the former near the fort.[60]

Regardless of Mescaleros' orientation toward peace or war, by 1856 the U.S. military was increasing its pressure upon all of the bands. In an overt gesture of diplomacy, Mescalero chief Barranquito (or Blanquito) visited Captain Van Horne at Fort Stanton to share concerns about the declining game resources near his camp at Dog Canyon and asked permission to hunt deer around the fort. Conversely, others continued raiding between Dona Ana and El Paso and south into Mexico. In correspondence with Governor Meriwether in June 1856, Steck stated that he believed Gomez and Matteo, who were frequently spotted in Chihuahua, were responsible for the incidents. T. H. Holmes, successor to Van Horne at Fort Stanton, confirmed this; more bands were moving to the fort while a few remained holed up in the Guadalupe Mountains, and launched attacks to the south.[61]

The campaign of William B. Hazen illustrates these increased pressures. Following on the heels of Anglo and Hispano groups seeking retaliation against Apaches, in 1858 Lieutenant William B. Hazen of the Eight Infantry Army of the West led a punitive expedition into the Guadalupe Mountains after Mescaleros had allegedly taken cattle near Fort Davis. Hazen took troops to the mountains and launched a failed surprise attack upon fifteen Mescalero lodges. Mescaleros fought back, killed several troops, and Hazen fled back to Fort Davis. An incident the following year prompted a similar response. Mescaleros allegedly took cattle from San Elizario in March 1859. With troops from Fort Bliss, Lieutenant H. M. Lazalle chased Apaches into the Guadalupes, and the results mirrored Hazen's expedition, numerous deaths on both sides.[62]

Although the Civil War began to overshadow Indian-white relations in the Southwest, tensions remained. More Mescaleros settled near Fort

Stanton, but in January 1860 a band reportedly riding out of the Guadalupe Mountains stole cattle from Mexican and Anglo ranches along the Rio Hondo. Captain Thomas Claiborne followed their trail out of the Sacramento Mountains and along the Penasco River but failed to find them. Rumor had it that the cattle thieves had found refuge in the Guadalupe Mountains. By the summer, most Mescalero bands north of the Guadalupes had agreed to try farming on plots adjacent to the fort. Those residing in and around the Guadalupes continued their forays across the Rio Grande into Chihuahua.

The Civil War

The Guadalupe Mountains saw a brief respite from violence as the Civil War drew troops away to fight in a conflict that wrought destruction upon the southern states. Apache groups were surprised at what they thought was the flight of soldiers from their homelands, rather than a federal crisis and brief demilitarization of southern New Mexico for the sake of slavery and national reunification. Although the federal government recalled some troops to fight for the union in the east, the Civil War also unleashed violence in the West. Moreover, troops from southern states fighting in New Mexico Territory sided with the Confederacy. This brief "demilitarization" ended quickly, and by 1865 nearly twenty thousand soldiers were stationed in the West, more than double the 1860 levels.[63]

In the Southwest during the Civil War, many soldiers served under General James Carleton and his "California Column" whose mission it was to stop a Confederate invasion of New Mexico. This conflict brought some unrest to the Guadalupes, which extended across the New Mexico border into Confederate Texas. To make matters worse, southern New Mexico had Confederate sympathies stoked by southerners such as James Magoffin in El Paso. Seeing the potential for a railroad route that he would profit from, Magoffin helped Colonel John R. Baylor seize Fort Bliss and organize a filibuster into New Mexico under the guise of a buffalo hunt. Baylor led troops into New Mexico and declared the creation of the Confederate Territory of Arizona, with Mesilla as the capital. By the end of the summer in 1861, the Confederate flag flew over Fort Fillmore near Mesilla.[64] The pronouncement did not carry much weight and Union troops, Colorado Volunteers, and the Californian Column recaptured New Mexico. Although Confederate general Henry Sibley occupied Santa Fe briefly, the exploits of John M. Chivington from Colorado and the pivotal battles at Glorieta Pass pushed the Confederate troops back into Texas.[65]

These confrontations, building upon events tied to the Taos Rebellion and the murder of Charles Bent, precipitated a permanent military presence in New Mexico, and this had dire consequences for Native people. Republican governor Henry Connelly enlisted James Carleton and Kit Carson to force all Navajos and Apaches onto reservations and Carleton initiated a program to march Navajos and Apaches to Fort Sumner at Bosque Redondo in northeast New Mexico. With Carson commanding five companies from Fort Stanton, forced relocation began in 1862. Carson had orders to kill all Mescalero men that refused to come into the fort, and he used that authority against the Apaches in the Sierra Blancas and Guadalupe Mountains. Such violence led to the tragic deaths of another group of Mescaleros traveling from the Guadalupes and Sierra Blancas to meet with Governor Connelly in Santa Fe to discuss peace. Shots by the troops of Captain James Grayden of Fort Stanton killed ten Mescaleros, including chiefs Jose Largo and Manuelito. Thus began another campaign to clear the Trans-Pecos of Apaches.[66]

To implement the policy, Major William McCleave took two companies of Californians through the Sacramento Mountains and into the Guadalupes, while Captain Thomas Roberts took two companies through Hueco Tanks and into the Guadalupes. McCleave surprised a camp of Mescaleros in Dog Canyon at night and killed several men. The survivors fled in an attempt to seek protection under Carson at Fort Stanton. Such casualties exacerbated the ultimatum given to a yet another group of Apache diplomats making the trip to Santa Fe that month: go to Fort Sumner or face certain death. This contingent included Chief Cadete and Lorenzo Labadie, their military escort and Indian agent. Within a year, four hundred Mescaleros had made the trek to Bosque Redondo.[67]

The idea of remaining at such a desolate place was terrifying. Indeed, numerous tribal members hid in the Guadalupe and Davis Mountains or fled into Mexico. Those that did go north did not stay for long, and by 1865 most of the Mescaleros had returned south to their homelands.

Whether they fled internment or simply refused it all together, after 1865 they were in the same boat again: pressured by the military, despised by the Anglo and Mexican settlers, dying of diseases and malnutrition, and fighting to hold on to their way of life.[68]

The end of the Civil War marked a turning point for the Mescalero in the Guadalupes and the region more generally. The postwar era saw a wave of migrants moving west, veterans from the Union and Confederacy seeking land under provisions of the Homestead Act. The efforts of the federal government to reconstruct the South also involved policies that sought unification of the nation as a whole. Railroads soon crept across the Southwest, tying together remote regions and previously distant markets. These efforts at integrating the Southwest into the political and economic mainstream of the United States drew to a close the boundary disputes and conflicts over slavery that destabilized the region around the Guadalupe Mountains. The Army of the West redoubled its excursions against Apaches and Comanches, the two groups that continued to cross the international boundary and harass migrants and new arrivals to the borderlands. As long as these bands were independent, the Guadalupe Mountains Trans-Pecos region remained a so-called frontier, a space that was peripheral to the sources of power and wealth emanating from burgeoning urban areas. It would take an additional conquest to force the Apaches onto reservations. The conquest that finally led to their concentration onto these limited lands was led less by guns and cannons, and more by the pressure of growth facilitated by the railroads. What military men failed to accomplish, the steady expansion of farmers, ranchers, and immigrants finalized by the 1880s.

CHAPTER FIVE
Conflict and Early Community Formation, 1865–1881

The post–Civil War years witnessed new trends and turning points for the Guadalupe Mountains. As Apaches and Comanches resisted the military, Texas Rangers, and vigilante groups, Hispanos and Anglos moved into the region around the Guadalupes. Prewar labor and subsistence patterns collided with postwar economic trends, and communal forms of land tenure faced a capitalist revolution. New arrivals from across America and Europe tried to transform the Southwest to reflect their varied visions and objectives. Hispanos from the Manzano Mountains in northern New Mexico, ex-Confederates disgusted with Reconstruction, northerners from Connecticut and Vermont, African Americans escaping Jim Crow segregation, and even Swiss and Italian immigrants all tried to carve out a living in this arid landscape.[1]

Newcomers' success depended on access to water, proximity to transportation routes, their ability to navigate the land laws of Texas and New Mexico, and sheer skill and luck. Most believed that the presence of Apaches and Comanches served as a barrier to settlement, but cases of Indian and non-Indian coexistence occasionally emerged. The federal government forced most Apaches onto reservations, but a few of them remained in Mexico or slid into the sociocultural shadows of West Texas. Hispanos that put roots down around Roswell and Lincoln faced vigilante gangs and racial violence. African Americans lived briefly in Blackdom, New Mexico, but soon fled in search of new opportunities. Within a generation, the racial and ethnic lines of towns in the Guadalupe Mountain region had been set, with de facto segregation and a dual-segmented labor force as the norm.[2]

Just as race influenced socioeconomic relations, environmental conditions limited settlement around the mountains. Emigrants tried to recreate the homelands they left, but the hard soils of the Chihuahuan Desert and the greater Trans-Pecos could not yield the green pastures they desired. Aridity, saline waters, unpredictable river flow, and a shallow aquifer confounded development. Drawing upon a combination of ingenuity, hope, persistence, and new technologies, these ranchers, businessmen, and developers dug deeper wells, organized irrigation companies, and adapted to the climate. But, lacking railroad access to national markets, these first communities faced the arid high desert in near total isolation.[3]

Texas and New Mexico after the Civil War

The tendency of historians to tell a linear story of progress from exploration and expansion, through Indian wars, frontier towns and cowboys, the arrival of the railroads and community stability does not apply to this part of the U.S.-Mexico borderlands. Rather, the region developed in a series of fits and starts, setbacks, collapse, and divergent trajectories. There was no heroic narrative as argued by Frederick Jackson Turner, one of the most well-known historians and advocates of the frontier myth and progressive development.[4]

Several factors caused the uneven growth, particularly the divergent historical arcs of West Texas and southern New Mexico. These differences are important to consider because the Guadalupe Mountains span the Texas-New Mexico state line. Although Texas and New Mexico differed in many ways, the relative lack of Spanish or Mexican land grants in this area reduced the confusion over the land systems and water regimes.[5] By the twentieth century, the federal land policies in New Mexico Territory favored settlers who could afford allotments on public land. In contrast, the General Land Office of Texas sold its public land to railroads, which then sold land to settlers and ranchers. New Mexicans in this regard benefited from territorial status and the agencies that stabilized land values and protected public resources, while Texas sold land quickly to pay off its debt.[6]

Differences over land policy and use of resources were rooted in different histories and political legacies. Despite the lack of land grants and the presence of Natives, Hispanos displaced from northern New Mexico by new land laws, higher taxes, ballooning debt, and racism brought with them the traditions of communal land use and collective water rights. Hispanos from northern New Mexico tried to recreate this system in Carlsbad and Roswell, but Anglo settlers embraced private property and individual rights. They attacked land grants and notions of communal use that accompanied them and devised complex schemes to defraud Hispanos of their homesteads.[7]

The competing land use practices of New Mexico and Texas existed uneasily within a larger national conversation about property rights and citizenship in the nineteenth century. The federal government tried to create a system that embodied the ideals of Jefferson's yeoman farmer, which sought to promote individual liberties and expansion through "settlement." In reaction to failed land laws, and in an effort to incentivize northerners to join the Civil War, in 1862 Congress passed the Homestead Act allowing anyone over the age of twenty-one to acquire one hundred and sixty acres of land. This system was also abused by wealthy individuals and corporations that paid "dummies" to file claims and sell the land to them. Again, attempting to improve its land policies, Congress passed the Desert Land Act of 1877 and the Enlarged Homestead Act of 1909 to make it easier to farm arid land, but the legislation failed to curtail abuses.[8]

The allotment of parcels carved out from public lands greatly benefited New Mexicans over Texans, but both faced the limits imposed by the climate and topography. Farming in West Texas and eastern New Mexico was difficult because the Pecos River was brackish and saline, its banks were sandy, and it occasionally changed course. During most of the twentieth century, Texas and New Mexico fought a bitter battle over allocation and rights to dam and utilize it for irrigation. The streams and rivers feeding the Pecos in New Mexico were a lifeline for communities, but as the Pecos enters Texas it cuts eastward away from the Guadalupes. Thus, the settlements at the foot of the Guadalupes in Texas relied on limited rainfall, meager mountain springs, and occasional snowpack runoff.[9]

Despite the difficulties facing agriculture, a few homesteads gave rise to an isolated and small population in the Texas-New Mexico borderlands. In New Mexico, four land regimes dominated this territory dedicated primarily to ranching and farming: one tied to Spanish and

Mexican land grants (and the controversies epitomized in the Santa Fe Ring and the Maxwell Land Grant), federal lands in the form of Indian reservations, public lands administered by the Department of the Interior, and lands held in private property. The latter two characterized southeast New Mexico and debates over consolidation of landholdings.[10] Although ranching in New Mexico and Texas dates back to the Spanish colonial era, the first ranching outfits in southeastern New Mexico stem from Hispano settlers and the long-range cattle drives across the Southwest. The Texas cattle industry boomed during the Civil War as hunters decimated the herds of bison. Public lands stretching into the Trans-Pecos appropriated Indian lands, and politicians and ranchers saw great opportunity by further concentrating the Indians and settling their lands. And as the war ended, ranchers looked to the vast swaths of land across West Texas and eastern New Mexico to grow their operations.[11]

Millions of acres of grasslands were useless for ranching without a market, and military forts and Indian reservations first met that need. Fort Sumner, Fort Stanton, and Fort Davis were large consumers of beef in far western Texas and southeastern New Mexico. Charles Goodnight is commonly credited with establishing the regional cattle trails that brought beef to the forts from Abiline, Texas, and north to Colorado via New Mexico. In 1866 Goodnight partnered with Oliver Loving to drive cattle to Fort Sumner, where the military imprisoned Navajos and Apaches. Forts and Indian reservations quickly became targets for ranchers selling cattle under government contracts at inflated prices. The booming mine towns of Colorado were also prodigious consumers of beef.[12]

The efforts of cattlemen such as Goodnight and Loving shaped the Guadalupe Mountain region in important ways.[13] John Chisum followed Goodnight and Loving to bring stock to Bosque Grande between 1868 and 1871. He initially received grants to deliver beef to Fort Stanton, and in 1875 he moved his ranch headquarters to the South Spring River near the fort and Mescalero Reservation. More than seventy thousand of his cattle grazed the land between Fort Sumner and Seven Rivers. His cattle fanned out across Mescalero lands in the Guadalupe Mountains, and Mescaleros frequently took the cattle into their shelters in the mountains. Chisum, despite his previous successes, lost his contract to sell beef to Fort Stanton and the Mescalero Agency when he was outbid by Lawrence G. Murphy and Emil C. Fritz, both members of the old Civil War California Column and protagonists in the Lincoln County War. He also continued to lose cattle to Mescaleros, who suffered from rotten meat sold to the agency by Murphy and Fritz at inflated prices. The impact of cattle ranching, the Santa Fe Indian Ring, and the Lincoln County War had dire consequences for Mescaleros.[14]

Although cattle rustling is stuff of legend in the American West, only a few stories about the Guadalupe Mountains survive. A series of recollections from Ben Gilmore now sit in the archives of the national park headquarters in Pine Springs. Gilmore is a well-known individual who came to Salt Flat in 1937 and spent a lot of time talking with locals about regional history. He refers to a place called Devil's Den, eight miles north of Crow Springs. It was a popular site for cattle rustlers and was part of a trail from Carlsbad to El Paso. In 1887 rustlers killed a man named William McCarthy at Crow Springs while delivering cattle to Dud Richardson in New Mexico. With his seventeen-year-old son, McCarthy drove eight hundred cattle from Johnson City, came across the Pecos, rested at Fort Stockton, and then went to Crow Springs. They stopped in the Guadalupe Mountains for a week, went through Guadalupe Pass, and curved around the mountain to Crow Spring. After McCarthy's death at Crow Springs, Richardson caught the thieves, killed some of the rustlers, and helped McCarthy's son, Paul, drive the herd through Crow Springs toward Las Cruces. Years later, the son and his family built a ranch eight miles north of Crow Springs.[15]

The efforts of Chisum, Goodnight, and Loving planted the seeds for colonization of the region. Cowhands they employed left the industry and relocated to villages and towns such as Roswell, Hope, Loving, Queen, and Eddy. Felix McKittrick (for whom the canyon in the park is named) was an associate of Goodnight and Loving, and perhaps John Chisum. Although scant evidence of his life exists, he was a Confederate veteran and one of many men working on the cattle drives of the postwar era. After first viewing the Guadalupe Mountains in the 1860s on a cattle drive to Colorado, he settled in the canyon that now bears his name. Following a similar trajectory, in 1876 the Rader brothers built a portion of the ranch house at Frijole Springs. The Raders filed a claim to the property and purchased the land, but it is unclear what happened to them before the Smith family moved in by the mid-1890s.[16]

These early ranching efforts remained fairly limited, despite the mythical status of Goodnight, Loving, and the Chisholm Trail.[17] During the 1870s and early 1880s the majority of cattle ranching, and the emergence of towns associated with it, occurred in eastern New Mexico. A cattle outfit run by two men known as Pearce and Paxton established a "cow camp" in Seven Rivers in 1873. The Diamond-A Ranch began in the early 1880s near Seven Rivers, and on the eastern side of the river was the Halagueno Ranch, purchased by the Eddy and Bissell Livestock Company in 1881. Lincoln County (present-day Eddy, Chaves, and Lea Counties) had three hundred thousand cattle in the late 1870s.[18] Most of the ranches began roundups in April and continued through August, with some ranches bringing fifteen thousand cattle to railroad shipping points such as Roswell. The shift from open range to fenced ranches began in the late 1880s across southeastern New Mexico. Overgrazing and conflicts over water resources compounded drought, all of which led to the fencing process. A drought in 1885 killed thousands of cattle, but severe blizzards the next season and an outbreak of screwworm crippled the industry.[19]

Drift fences, barbed wire, selective breeding, railroads, well drilling, irrigation, and the larger process of consolidation began in the 1890s. Organizations such as the Southeastern New Mexico Stock Growers Association coordinated the industry, lobbied legislatures, and promoted modernization. Public land surveys and homesteading in New Mexico decreased the likelihood of squatting and open-range grazing. Southeastern New Mexico was the last major region on the plains to have railroads integrating it into the national economy. By the early 1890s, outside capital began purchasing many of the local outfits, competition for land and water increased, and cattle operations became larger, centralized, and nationally integrated.[20]

Anglo and Hispano Settlement Patterns

Although ranching frequently preceded the establishment of permanent towns, there were a few Anglo and Hispano communities that emerged during the early days of the cattle industry. Many of these settlements were established by Hispano farmers and ranchers seeking water between the Pecos and Rio Grande rivers. By the mid-1800s, most Hispanos in the region lived in El Paso del Norte (present-day Juarez) and Mesilla, both important junctions of trade. Towns beyond the Guadalupes, in Albuquerque, Socorro, and Belen, were tied to economic, social, and political networks of families and trading companies that were in turn linked to Santa Fe in the north, Chihuahua in the south, and St. Louis and Austin in the east.

The Spanish-speaking people of southern New Mexico shared traits with their northern relatives, but there were also distinct differences. Southerners around Mesilla and Dona Ana lived in tight networks of families that shared responsibilities for farming, maintaining acequias, and protecting common resources. Most of them were tied to land grants recently established in the mid-1800s and nurtured ties with Paso del Norte and Chihuahua City while the northern communities had lived there for centuries. Southern Hispano communities differed from those to the north because they primarily interacted with Apaches, rather than Navajos, Utes, and Puebloan people. Whereas northern Hispanos endured freezing temperatures and mountainous terrain, southern Hispanos suffered the heat of the desert. Northerners had access to streams fed by mountain snowmelt, while southerners remained dependent on sporadic rains and the floodplain of the Rio Grande. Thus, the human geography of the region was shaped by ecological characteristics.[21]

This combination of difference and similarity continued when the conflict between America and Mexico resulted in the new international border. The war split the loyalties of some Hispanos and left a legacy of resentment toward both protagonists. Like their northern relatives, who faced the brunt of invasion in 1846 by Stephen W. Kearney and, later, the Confederate forces, southern New Mexicans had an equally conflicted relationship with changes sweeping through the borderlands. For instance, many of these communities remained in Mexico after the war, and only became U.S. citizens when the Gadsden Purchase rearranged the boundary and brought them into the United States. This stood in contrast to some of the political elite in the north, who sought annexation into the United States. Moreover, southern New Mexico became, if only briefly, a southern state under the control of an occupying force of Confederate soldiers. And yet, the fate of both communities remained intertwined in post–Civil War developments such as political corruption, legal chicanery, disenfranchisement, and social marginalization.[22]

This historical sketch helps us understand Hispano life in New

Mexico, but the early settlement of the Guadalupe Mountain region is difficult to fully flesh out. Hispanos from northern New Mexico likely began settling between the Sacramento and Guadalupe Mountains and the Pecos River in the early 1800s. As families moved south, New Mexican ciboleros, or buffalo hunters, continued their expeditions onto the Llano Estacado. Settlements in southeastern New Mexico emerged when Anglo ranching and farming operations pushed sheepherders down the Pecos River along the fringe of the Llano Estacado. Families staked out the tributary drainages of the Pecos River east of the Guadalupe Mountains. Settlements benefited from Fort Stanton, which served as a market for Hispano farmers and protected them from Apaches.[23]

As Anglos usurped power in northern New Mexico, Hispanos established communities along river valleys between the New Mexico mountain ranges and the Pecos River. Las Placitas, later known as Lincoln, was one of the first towns in the 1850s. When Lincoln became a county in 1869, Hispanos outnumbered Anglos according to the 1870 census.[24] Andricus Trujillo may have been the first Hispano of La Placita, which was located east of the fort. In 1862 and 1863, several Hispano families fled as Mescaleros regained control of the mountains during the Civil War, when soldiers left the fort. When Kit Carson reclaimed the fort from Confederates, the Hispano settlers returned to Las Placitas. The town attracted Anglos, many of them from the California Column, who were interested in usurping trade with the military. In 1869 Anglos changed the name to Lincoln and it served as the county seat.[25]

Hispanos from the Manzano Mountains also established the Plaza of San Jose in the 1860s near present-day Roswell. They brought thirty-five families to the juncture of the Hondo Valley and the Pecos River where the floodplain widened enough for agriculture. They built adobe houses, a corral, and irrigation ditches carrying water from the Rio Hondo to their fields. A federal government survey in 1867 noted its existence, but it did not provide much information on the settlement. Colonel Francisco Chavez passed through the town that year and later recalled in an interview with the *Roswell Register* in 1901 that the residents were Hispanos from the Manzano Mountains. The only English speakers at that time were a few Confederate soldiers who ran a supply store, two unidentified Anglo families, a Frenchman, and a man named John Newcomb. The name San Jose changed to Missouri Plaza because many of the men who participated in trade networks to St. Joseph, Missouri, such as Felipe and Jose Miranda, were freighters along the trail, and they renamed the town to honor the origination point of the trail.[26] Families moved away in the 1880s as the military forts closed, racial conflicts escalated, and communities upstream diverted water with dams. The small community known as Missouri Plaza, and later as Chihuahuita, remained a segregated barrio in Roswell.[27] Berrendo and El Redepente emerged in the mid-1860s northeast of Roswell. The villages used traditional irrigation, raised livestock, and sometimes traded with Mescalero Apaches, as well as sold goods to military forts in the region. Most families grew wheat, oats, chiles, corn, beans, cabbage, potatoes, watermelons, and beets, and they raised goats, cattle, and sheep.[28]

Texans tended to change the Spanish names of towns by substituting them with the names of Anglo pioneers. For example, references to the site as "Rio Hondo" appeared in the *Santa Fe New Mexican* in 1870, but one of the first Anglo settlers, Van C. Smith of Omaha, Nebraska, changed the name to Roswell in 1873, to honor his father. Smith sold his holdings to Captain Joseph C. Lea, a Civil War veteran and rancher from Colfax County. A budding land developer, Lea was credited with the official platting of Roswell. Thus, rather than recognize the Hispano roots of San Jose, the name Roswell became permanent. Renaming Hispano settlements worked in tandem with land policies, segregation, and a dual-wage labor force to push the non-Anglo history of the region into the shadows.[29]

The economic options for Hispanos declined at the end of the nineteenth century as they lost contracts and trade with military forts.[30] Of the few Hispanos that maintained their independence, many of them relied on the sale of sheep wool for their survival. Early sheep ranchers imported the partido system as they migrated from the northern mountains. This was a contract system in which an owner of a large herd supplied a smaller breeding herd to the shepherd, and the shepherd gave back a percentage of profits in lambs and wool for every hundred ewes in the herd at the end of the year. The shepherd was responsible for expenses and losses and gained excess wool and lambs as he grazed his sheep on the owner's land. Sometimes shepherds could purchase their own herd and land. In 1878 a group of Anglo cowhands even displaced Mexican shepherds from the North Spring River area.[31]

The changing economic circumstances reflected shifting social relationships. It is difficult to determine the precise nature of the racial tension that led many Hispano residents of Missouri Plaza to flee, but the anti-Hispano sentiments of Texans frequently led to harassment. One such conflict stemmed from the vigilantism of the Harrell family from Lampasas, Texas. The five Harrell brothers and their families settled along the Rio Ruidoso on what later became the Coe Ranch. In late 1875 a brother sparked a gunfight with several other men and shot deputy sheriff Juan Martinez. Before dying from his wounds, Martinez managed to kill the drinking partner of Harrell. The local Mexican community evidently attacked Harrell and his associate. The Harrell family took revenge and killed or injured several men and women at a Mexican wedding. As the Harrells fled to Roswell, they killed the Mexican wife of Joe Haskins, an Anglo, and when they reached Missouri Plaza, killed another five Mexicans. Before returning to Texas, they stole livestock from Roswell residents, who in return chased them all the way to Hueco Tanks. Finding them asleep, the group killed several of the brothers. The surviving Harrells disappeared into Texas.[32]

The mountains yielded interesting stories that firmly situated the Guadalupes in the "frontier" narrative of cowboys, rustlers, and lawmen. There was a site near Crow Springs called "The Den," which may have been built by a man named Hart. For unknown reasons Hart was chased by the Texas Rangers out of Ysleta and all the way into the Guadalupe Mountains. Hart was hiding at The Den near Crow Springs, which was a popular spring for Mescaleros. In his recollections, Guadalupe resident Ben Gilmore states that the spring was "almost like a fort" to protect Anglos from Indians as early as 1858. He added that the spring was a popular site for other stage coaches until 1881, presumably due to the railroad. Gilmore believed that it was a kind of "country motel, or a safe place to spend the night." The Texas Rangers also used the site while chasing men such as Hart. He even recalled a story about a group of engineers in 1880 from Colorado who went through Crow Flats on their way to San Antonio. The group almost died on the west side of the mountain, walked south of the Guadalupe Peak, turned north to the springs, and then returned south to a ranger station in Ysleta.[33]

Settlement in southern New Mexico counties remained relatively low for decades. In 1873 there were no official homestead claims on record, but by 1881 that number grew to ninety. By 1883 settlers filed roughly two hundred claims. That number doubled by 1900. Even though these numbers increased, the high rates of failed claims destabilized the population. In 1892 approximately 50 percent of homestead entries were in irrigable locations, but most of the claims failed. Records from the General Land Office (GLO) in Austin, Texas, paint a similar picture of failed land claims and foreclosures due to the difficulty of surviving in an arid environment.[34]

Comparing records in the General Land Office with popular historical sites within the Guadalupe Mountains confirms the slow growth after the Civil War.[35] The area that constitutes the national park covers a relatively small region in the context of West Texas. For instance, in northwestern Culberson County the park encompasses approximately blocks 65 and 66 in township 1, block 65 in township 2, and block 121 of public school lands, and in Hudspeth County block 67 of Texas and Pacific Railway lands. These blocks are a fraction of the land in the two fairly large counties. When one looks at the sections with permanent human occupation, the fraction is smaller.[36] The Hudspeth and Culberson County archives confirm that little of the land in the Guadalupes was covered by patents or claimed by non-Indians as early as the 1870s, but a few non-Indians squatted there. With the exception of McKittrick Canyon, Dog Canyon near the state line, and sections around Pine and Manzanita Springs, the mountains remained vacant. The GLO documents note that an individual filed a claim in May 1879 on section 41, block 65, township 1, which contained Pine Springs. The T&P Railway was the original grantee of this section, but the GLO does not note the name of the individual who filed. This section eventually encompassed the present headquarters of the national park. The state granted land in section 33, block 65, township 1 to the T&P Railway in 1876. The railway surveyed it in 1878 and filed claim to it in 1879. This section contained Smith Springs, which is a short walk north of Frijole Ranch and Manzanita Springs, but the GLO documents are silent about the owners of the land. These brief snapshots are illustrative of life in the Guadalupes.[37]

Regional Transformation and the End of an Era

By 1881 much had changed in West Texas and southern New Mexico, even if few people settled permanently in the area eventually declared a park. First, the creation of the Mescalero Apache Reservation in 1874 signified an important transition in the life of Apaches. With the promise of agricultural assistance and the more problematic plan to assimilate them, Apaches faced the difficult choice to live on the reservation or remain subject to arrest off the reservation. Second, the Salt War of 1877 brought new racial, legal, and economic realities to West Texas and spelled the decline of Mexican financial stability as Anglos rose in power. Third, the Compromise of 1877 ended federal occupation of the southern states that seceded from the Union and placed the control of race relations back into the hands of whites. This led to an exodus of African Americans, some of whom moved to New Mexico. Finally, the Southern Pacific Railway entered El Paso in 1881 and transformed the borderlands.[38]

Of all the pivotal events mentioned above, one stands out as especially important. The entrance of the railroad ended Native military resistance to American expansion. Before this, Mescaleros tried to repel incursions into their homelands. Beginning anew after the end of the Civil War, troops from Fort Stanton, Fort Davis, Fort Bliss, and other military bases attempted to force them onto a few reservations in Arizona and New Mexico. This coordinated series of attacks represented the final attempt of the U.S. military to conquer the most defiant bands of Apaches and Comanches.

Fort Davis housed one of the largest contingents of soldiers in the Southwest borderlands. Situated near the international boundary and the trails used by Apaches and Comanches going into Mexico, the fort played a key role in the conquest of the remaining Indians. Although several officers followed after him, during the year that Colonel Edward Hatch served as commanding officer of Fort Davis, he ordered three excursions into the Guadalupes. On January 20, 1870, Captain F. S. Dodge surprised an Apache rancheria, killed twenty-five warriors and their families, captured their stock, and burned their belongings. During summer 1871, Colonel William R. Shafter initiated an expedition through the Guadalupe Mountains and onto the Llano Estacado. He failed to encounter any Mescaleros or Comanches, but he believed that this show of force in the heart of Native land was just as important as a military battle. "My experience," he recalled of the 1871 tour, "has been that Indians will not stay where they consider themselves liable to attacks." He built upon this theory in an expedition the following year through the Big Bend, where he found Apaches.[39]

The policy of surrounding the Mescaleros and launching attacks on their homelands from forts across the region had begun to take a heavy toll. While troops from Fort Davis required days to reach Apache camps, soldiers at Fort Stanton could reach the Guadalupes quickly. On November 14, 1869, Fort Stanton was notified of an Apache raid on the Casey Ranch along the Rio Hondo that resulted in the loss of cattle for the Anglo ranchers. Four days later Lieutenant Howard B. Cushing with the Third Cavalry attacked the Mescaleros in the Guadalupes. Sources dispute whether or not any Apaches died, but the cavalry captured an Indian or Mexican boy, retrieved most of the cattle, and took Mescalero horses. Mescaleros, of course, retaliated.[40]

The cycle of violence was hard to stop, and in October 1873 Major William Redwood Price, with experience killing Hualapai Indians in Arizona, met with his superiors in Black River, north of the Guadalupes, to share his plans for the Mescalero. Previously he met with the superintendent of Indian Affairs for New Mexico, L. Edwin Dudley, who was still frustrated by Mescaleros who refused to remain near Fort Stanton. Dudley acknowledged at least two groups of Mescaleros: those north of the Guadalupes, including the Sierra Blancas, and those in and south of the Guadalupes. The former had been amenable to a reservation, while the latter, especially those inhabiting the Davis Mountains, resisted. The northern group owned cattle and horses, but according to the non-Indians, they blocked settlement of Anglo farmers in the region. Fearing punishment for the alleged crimes of bands to the south, Mescaleros around the Sierra Blancas called into Fort Stanton Agency for protection from Major Price after he tried seizing members during a meeting. These and some of the bands from the south trickled into the reservation, but hundreds fled Fort Stanton and crossed into Texas where they joined their kin. Price pursued them into the Guadalupes and killed three before returning to Fort Stanton.[41]

The mixed signals sent by the military and Indian Bureau contributed to the confusion and fear that kept most Mescaleros away from the reservation and in hideouts like the Guadalupe and Davis Mountains. Several bands lived as far east as Del Rio, Texas, and far south toward Chihuahua City, and continued to move across the border. A band leader named

Alsate, fleeing from Lieutenant George Bullis in 1877, crossed into Mexico and found refuge in the Sierra Carmel.[42] Even as some bands moved to the reservation, the intratribal diversity bewildered the Indian agents. Cadete, successor to Barranquito, was the most influential around the fort, but he died in 1872 and was followed by San Juan. Another leader, Natsili, did not come to the reservation until 1876, and he became prominent after San Juan died in 1886.[43]

In early 1876 tensions flared again and Mescaleros were blamed for shooting Mexicans within a stone's throw of Fort Davis. Similar violence was revealed in 1877 as corpses dotted the road from Fort Davis to El Paso. Fort Davis and Fort Stockton emptied their armories as nearly every soldier chased after Mescaleros and Comanches in the Trans-Pecos region. Brigadier General Edward O. C. Ord placed Colonel Benjamin H. Grierson, a famed Civil War officer and commander of the Tenth Cavalry, in charge of the district of the Pecos. Grierson covered the region to watch watering holes, Indian trails, and other areas occupied by Apaches and Comanches. Fort Davis had outposts at Eagle Springs and Pine Springs at the southern tip of the Guadalupe Mountains.[44]

Many of the troops chasing Apaches were Buffalo Soldiers, Black Seminoles, and Indian Scouts. Although there are some historical ties between them, there were several differences. Indian Scouts were common in American westward expansion and were hired for their knowledge of the land and cultural geography of a region.[45] Black Seminoles arose from the specific relationships between Indian nations, Europeans, and African slaves in the Southeast during the colonial era and the early U.S. national period. Black Seminoles were the result of marriage between Seminoles and free blacks or escaped slaves. They developed semiseparate communities, and during the 1830s some Black Seminoles aligned themselves with Wildcat, or Coacoochee, who waged a guerilla campaign against the United States. Some of these Black Seminoles joined the U.S. military as scouts after the Civil War, while others followed the post-1877 exodus from the American South.[46]

The Buffalo Soldiers grew out of an 1866 act of Congress expanding the regular army and allowing African Americans to enlist in "colored units," known as the Ninth and Tenth U.S. Cavalry Regiments, and several infantry regiments. In 1867 four companies of the Ninth, led by Lieutenant Colonel Wesley Merritt, reoccupied Fort Davis in far West

Texas. Their main objective was the protection of civilian travelers and the mail on the road between San Antonio and El Paso. Additional companies were at Fort Stockton, northeast of Fort Davis along the Pecos River, and Fort Quitman, where they were charged with essentially the same tasks. When both groups were not positioned along the road, they went on extended missions throughout the Big Bend and Guadalupe Mountains. The Ninth Cavalry remained at Fort Davis briefly and was moved in 1875 to New Mexico. As the Ninth left, the Tenth Cavalry arrived in Fort Davis under the command of Colonel Grierson. Five Companies landed in Fort Davis in 1873, and in 1875 all of Company H arrived at the fort.[47]

Immediately after the arrival of the Ninth at Fort Stockton and Fort Davis, they launched expeditions against Kiowas, Comanches, Lipans, and Mescaleros. In December 1867 a band of Mescaleros from the Guadalupe Mountains descended upon soldiers escorting the mail from Camp Hudson to Fort Stockton en route to El Paso. A fight ensued and the Mescaleros caused the cavalry and mail carriers to retreat until they reached the Eagle Springs Station where troopers were camped. Company F retaliated and the Mescaleros returned to the Guadalupes.[48] A more violent encounter occurred in September 1868 as hundreds of Mescaleros from the mountains, joined by Kiowas and Lipans, attacked a wagon train leaving Fort Stockton, grabbed the cattle, and fled toward the border. Under orders from Lieutenant Colonel Wesley Merritt, Lieutenant Patrick Cusack mustered Company A and pursued the bands into the Santiago Mountains south of Fort Stockton. They caught them, killed two dozen Mescaleros, secured the livestock, and rescued two captive Mexican children. The survivors dispersed in all directions, especially into Mexico.[49]

In 1869 Merritt's replacement, Colonel Hatch, dispatched expeditions into the Guadalupes.[50] In January 1870 Hatch sent Francis Dodge of Company D with two hundred men to pursue Mescaleros northwest of the Fort. They followed old Indian trails into the Guadalupe Mountains and encountered Mescalero camps in the high-altitude forests. A battle ensued and nearly a dozen Apaches died in the gunfight. An unknown number escaped, but they left behind horses, robes, and other supplies.[51]

The most noteworthy battle of the Tenth was against Victorio, a resilient Apache leader who had evaded the military for years. Like his predecessors and contemporaries, Victorio confounded the efforts to capture him because he crossed the international border and moved across reservation boundaries with relative ease. The flaunting of national space by Kickapoos, Comanches, and Apaches appalled President Grant, who had secretly approved a raid by Colonel Ranald Mackenzie into Mexico to pursue "Indian marauders" who had sacked towns in Texas. The invasion caught the attention of General Ord, who commanded the Department of Texas in April 1875. He dispatched Colonel Shafter, who oversaw the work of Lieutenant John Lapham Bullis and the Buffalo Soldiers Bullis commanded. Meanwhile, Victorio launched forays from hideouts in the Candelaria Mountains as far south as Chihuahua City. Victorio's attack upon Carrizal angered Mariano Samaniego, a member of the Chihuahuan political elite living in Paso del Norte, who organized a citizen militia to root out Victorio's band on the Mescalero reservation and the Guadalupe Mountains. Samaniego failed to capture Victorio, who continued to move across the borderlands.[52] In late 1877 and early 1878, the United States and Mexico coordinated efforts to capture Victorio. General Ord ordered Colonel Grierson and his Buffalo Soldiers of the Tenth Cavalry to work with Samaniego, who shared intelligence on Victorio's band to General Geronimo Trevinio in Mexico. These binational efforts were short lived as Trevinio became occupied with political unrest in Chihihuaha City, and Victorio moved into New Mexico. This brought him squarely into the sights of Grierson and three hundred Buffalo Soldiers.[53]

After Victorio and his followers fled the Mescalero reservation, the military gathered the largest concentration of soldiers ever assembled in the Trans-Pecos region. Victorio evaded capture for nearly a year, sacking towns in the borderlands until six companies of the Tenth Cavalry and several companies of infantry patrolled water holes and springs that Victorio used. This tactic proved effective. Confrontations at Tinaja de las Palmas (near Sierra Blanca) and at Rattlesnake Springs (north of Van Horn) weakened Victorio. These engagements forced him to cross the border again where he was shot by Mexican troops in October 1880.[54] Some of his survivors went back into Texas, only to encounter rangers that chased them back into Mexico where several were killed. Survivors recrossed the border near Zaragosa, south of El Paso, until the military allowed them to go to the reservation in 1904.[55]

As the military waged its last series of wars against the Mescaleros, Anglos in El Paso had begun the process of legally incorporating land and resources into the regional economy. Ranchers felt increasingly comfortable fanning out across the West Texas borderlands, grazing their herds on rangeland once controlled by Apache. With this new wave of conquest came an interest in privatizing the regional salt beds. Although the Salt War of 1877 has entered historical consciousness as a moment of local ethnic conflict, it had precursors that illustrated the cross-cultural tensions between Anglos, Mexicans, and Native peoples in the wake of the Treaty of Guadalupe Hidalgo. Townspeople along the Rio Grande between San Elizario, Texas, and Socorro, New Mexico, used salt from numerous beds to cure beef, sell to traders, and employ in religious ceremonies. Suma and Manso Indians, and later Tiguas, orchestrated pilgrimages to acquire this valuable resource. After the U.S.-Mexican War, Mexicans and Indians went to the salt beds at San Andres, near the Sacramento Mountains, the Sierra Blancas, and present-day White Sands National Monument. After the so-called Magoffin Salt War of 1854 over beds near Lake Salinas, New Mexicans gained control over the salt, but people north of Paso del Norte continued to negotiate for San Andres. The Guadalupe salt beds thus became valuable for people in the lower valley and attracted the attention of newly arrived Anglos.[56]

Interethnic tensions increased as salt became an especially valuable commodity. In 1863 residents of San Elizario built a road to the salt beds at the Guadalupes. After the Civil War, Texas adopted Section 39 of Article VII of the Constitution of 1866 that released all mines and minerals to the owner of the soil, thus altering the way resources were allocated and controlled. Rather than recognizing the rights of communities, Anglo property law enabled an individual to claim once common resources. Using this new system of ownership, Samuel A. Maverick of San Antonio secured the location of two Texas land certificates covering nine hundred and sixty acres of land that included some of the Guadalupe salt flats.[57]

When Charles H. Howard filed a claim on adjacent beds, he precipitated the El Paso Salt War of 1877. The spark for the war began when Howard tried to take barrels of salt in San Elizario, obtained from a lake he claimed. Fearing a reprisal and perhaps in retaliation for previous aggression, Mexicans from both sides of the border attacked the Texas

Ranger camp that housed most of the Anglos in the town, and thus protected their new claim to the salt beds. The five day siege of the camp ended when civilians and soldiers surrendered. Howard and two others were executed in return for appropriating the beds.[58] Although Mexicans struck a blow in a war over communal resources, the long term impact of the Salt War was significant. The Salt War ended with the triumph of American property law and the loss of a valuable resource to the Mexican and indigenous people of the region. The war also reignited interest in the claims to the Salinas de San Andres in New Mexico, and Texas representative Gustave Schleicher submitted a bill to Congress recognizing the right to the salt beds in the name of Benjamin Edwards. After a survey of the land, President Chester Arthur signed the bill into law in 1881, but the family defaulted on the payment of $681 for surveying fees. They lost the land and the title remained in the hands of the territory of New Mexico, not the hands of Hispanos in the area.[59]

The most influential development of the era was the entrance of the Southern Pacific Railroad into El Paso in 1881. As a system of transportation that revolutionized America, the railroad "brought the world" to the borderlands. Although tracks did not directly enter the Guadalupe Mountains, they surrounded the region and connected Van Horn and Sierra Blanca to Austin, El Paso, and southern California, and later spur lines from Albuquerque entered Artesia and Carlsbad. The railroad occluded the old trails used by cattle ranchers and westward migrants, and the trade routes of merchants plying the dusty roads from St. Louis to Santa Fe to Chihuahua. Mass-produced goods from around the world flooded local markets and undercut the small business that serviced isolated communities. With these products came new people who did not understand—or care about—the relationships forged by peoples of the borderlands. Their misconceptions about Indians and Mexicans had dire consequences because these newcomers dismantled local social norms, expressed hostility to the idea of reservations, and wanted to assimilate people of color into the lower rungs of the racial and economic hierarchies of America. Finally, railroads helped transport raw materials such as copper, timber, and coal out of the Southwest to the industrial centers of the Northeast, where it literally fueled the growth of the United States. The export of resources contributed to what some historians have termed the "colonial" status of the West vis-à-vis the East. Taken together, these changes brought more people into the region, stimulated a new search for resources, and raised awareness of the region's potential.[60]

Between the end of the Civil War and the early 1880s, the Guadalupe Mountain Trans-Pecos region witnessed important changes. In some ways this change mirrored those seen across the borderlands and the American West. The U.S. military tracked down Apaches and forced most of them onto the Mescalero reservation, giving non-Indians greater access to resources. But this moment in the region's history unfolded somewhat differently. Hispanos from northern New Mexico who were forced from their land established new towns such as Las Placitas, San Jose, and El Berrendo. These families were freighters with ties to Fort Sumner and Fort Stanton and brought goods from Las Vegas and towns east of the Pecos. As these Hispanos put roots down, ex-Confederates, many from central Texas, moved into southeastern New Mexico. These Anglos had particular views about their Hispano neighbors. They were conditioned by their experiences with African Americans and Mexicans during a war that many of them were familiar with, if they had not fought in it personally. By 1881 power changed hands from Indian and Hispano to Anglo, and the region became characterized by subsistence agriculture, limited exports, and a labor system segmented by race. Small towns dotted the landscape northeast of El Paso, but their presence on the periphery of most western growth ensured a future limited by the resources they could exploit from an arid environment. It would take the arrival of the railroads in the 1880s to spur the transformation of the Guadalupe Mountain region.

CHAPTER SIX

The Nature of Economic Development in the Texas-New Mexico Borderlands, 1880–1915

The search for water in this arid environment and the desire for stronger economic ties to national markets defined the character of communities in the shadows of the Guadalupe Mountains. While Mescaleros struggled to survive on the reservation, Hispano farmers lost access to local sources of water because Anglo ranchers, developers, and government officials monopolized it. African American refugees from the Jim Crow South tried to create new lives for themselves in the Chihuahuan borderlands but experienced the racism of ex-Confederates. The political economy of water allowed large scale irrigation projects to unfold in tandem with a frenzy to dig individual wells and tap into the aquifer. Early reclamation efforts could not control the Pecos River as it broke through dams, overpumping by homesteaders caused sink holes, and once productive fields became veritable swamps. Despite this peculiar combination of drought, flood, man-made swamp, and sink holes, boosters dreamed of a breadbasket capable of feeding the nation. Much of this dream relied on the major railroad lines to connect them to markets. The entrance of the railroad in El Paso initiated a transformation that echoed changes across the west. This growth demanded more water, and in turn, the spike in farming and ranching led to a surplus in goods, which led residents to seek links to markets.[1]

In sum, the hopes of Hispanos struggling in Missouri Plaza, of Mescaleros trying to remain in the Guadalupes, and even of empire builders such as

James Hagerman who hoped to irrigate the region, all failed in the lands between the Guadalupes and the Pecos River. By the early twentieth century, the government tried allotting the Mescalero reservation, Hispanos had lost most of their farms and competed for wage labor jobs, floods breached the Pecos River, and artesian wells dried up. The new U.S. Reclamation Service took over the irrigation networks along the Pecos, the U.S. Forest Service controlled most land in the New Mexico Guadalupes, and the homesteaders in El Paso County continued to endure the vast landscapes they had chosen to live in. When the First World War began, regional development, large scale irrigation, municipal incorporation, and railroad lines connecting the Guadalupes to the national economy brought new people and products into the region, but it remained isolated from the rest of the western United States.

Desert Communities and Mountain Families

The drive for irrigation and the ensuing dependency characterized communities in the Texas-New Mexico borderlands at the turn of century. Despite the distance between families and towns, there was a fairly coherent region that crossed the boundaries separating territory and state, but it was not a tightly defined identity. Even after the railroads entered, communities remained linked together in their shared distance from the larger cities of Lubbock, El Paso, and Albuquerque—urban areas which were relatively isolated in their own right. Old-timers and newcomers continued to move across the Texas-New Mexico line, where they traded and sold goods, intermarried, and shared cultural beliefs.[2]

After trying to farm close to the Pecos, many moved west of Roswell, along the Rio Hondo and Berrendo River. Drought hit the town and the barrio of Missouri Plaza hard, so Anglo and Hispano settlers moved to North Spring River, hoping for more water. As these towns took root in the 1870s and early 1880s, they had an ambiguous relationship with the rise of John Chisum and larger ranchers, like Joseph C. Leah, who bought thirteen thousand acres of land along the Rio Hondo drainage. Leah bought the town of Roswell from Van C. Smith, who owned it under its previous name, Rio Hondo, which Smith hoped would provide a haven from the burgeoning vice industries in the region.[3] Despite the claims of boosters, it was not until the 1890s that new railroad lines and the discovery of artesian water that Roswell began to grow.[4]

Roswell became one of the more important towns east of the Guadalupe Mountains. Leah managed to avoid the political and extralegal violence of the Lincoln County War and was an ardent advocate of modernization and financial conservatism based on agriculture and ties to national markets through railroad lines to metropolitan centers such as El Paso. Leah was elected to the territorial legislature in 1888 and was pivotal in establishing Chavez County in 1889, with Roswell as its seat. This move tied him to Pat Garrett as well as Charles B. Eddy, an important "mover and shaker" in southeast New Mexico and its tortured history of irrigation. Eddy came to New Mexico from New York via Colorado and devised ways to manipulate the 1877 Desert Land Act and acquire vast tracts of land in the region.[5]

Several small towns cropped up west of Roswell and Eddy, along the banks of rivers and ravines feeding the Pecos River. From the short-lived town of Lincoln, established by Hispanos, to Hope, Seven Rivers, and Queen, these settlements were tied to the mountains in the west and the Pecos to the east. The towns formed a network of families, ranching operations, businesses, and shared interests. Many of the residents moved from Texas and oscillated between the Guadalupe Mountains in New Mexico and Roswell and Eddy in the east, and they relied on larger towns such as El Paso, Las Cruces, and Albuquerque. Some were teachers, ranchers, cowboys, engineers, politicians, and law officers. Some did all of these things within their lifetime. Charting their histories is important because it reveals the sociocultural fabric of life as this remote region of the desert sat at the cusp of industrialization.[6]

Villages like Seven Rivers and Hope had ephemeral existences. Sometime between 1866 and 1868 Robert M. Gilbert settled in the Seven Rivers area at the confluence of the Rio Penasco and Pecos River. Dick Reid established a trading post in 1867, and as more Anglo settlers came, the site was known as Dogtown and then as Seven Rivers in 1878. Seven Rivers found itself caught up in the larger whirlwind of violence known as the Lincoln County War, but the conflict soon dissipated and the town slid into obscurity. The community of Hope was an irrigation settlement founded in the early 1880s on the Rio Penasco, twenty miles west of present-day Artesia. Initially named Badgerville for the partial dugouts of the settlers, residents changed the name to Hope in 1888. They founded an irrigation company in 1893 and boasted fourteen thousand acres under cultivation by 1919. Low rainfall and sinkholes due to overpumping of the aquifer along the Rio Penasco hurt farming and led to the decline of the community.[7]

One of the smaller settlements was Queen, New Mexico. Situated along the old trail leading to Dog Canyon on the Texas-New Mexico border, Queen was just north of the state line and the present-day Guadalupe Mountains National Park. The first Anglos moved there within years of the final campaigns against the Mescaleros, and some reported ongoing occupation of the mountains by Apaches.[8] Several families constituted this small community in Queen. John T. Plowman brought his family to New Mexico in 1884, and they initially settled south of Carlsbad. In 1899 his daughter Frances Plowman married John C. Queen, who came to the area in the 1890s. Queen's parents, Elias Gibson Queen and Martha Bowen Queen, had moved from Williamson County in Texas, initially to Ysleta. After going back and forth between Ysleta and California in the late 1890s, the Queens settled in the Guadalupes. John Queen had brothers named Victor and Hillman, and Hillman married Abbie Tulk, the daughter of J. W. Tulk, who came to the area from Kimble, Texas. The Queens established themselves quickly and Hillman became one of the first allotment holders in what would become the Lincoln National Forest.[9]

J. W. Tulk and the Queens struck a deal to supply water to Tulk's store from the Elias Queen ranch. Tulk opened his store and secured a post office permit in 1905, thus founding a town, which he named Queen in honor of the family's generosity. Queen was a few days west, following a trail through Dark Canyon, of Eddy (now Carlsbad). Not everyone lived there year round because they needed money to supplement their subsistence efforts, so they worked in Carlsbad or Roswell or as ranch hands on farms throughout the area. They sometimes owned cattle operations or homesteaded in other parts of the region. John C. Queen ran cattle at his homestead, and he sometimes worked on the Robinson Ranch. By 1909 he owned ranches around Carlsbad, acquired Red Bluff Ranch south of Malaga, and played a central role in the construction of the Willow Lake Reservoir in 1922.[10]

Families in Queen and elsewhere came to New Mexico after exceptional life experiences. Captain John S. Shattuck's father took his family from Connecticut to Tennessee and then beneath Cape Horn to California during the gold rush. The elder Shattuck became a judge in California and his son, John S. Shattuck, joined the Confederate army after moving to Texas. After the war he stayed in Texas where he married Julia P. Lyon from Tennessee. Going back and forth between California and Texas, he had crossed the Guadalupe Mountains frequently and on one trip, decided to settle his family at Dark Canyon. He moved to New Mexico in 1885, and he and his wife had several children: Edwin, Dolph, and Ollie.[11] The land they homesteaded was still occupied by Mescalero Apaches, as evidenced by the teepees on the plot. Dolph Shattuck recalled, "It was pretty wild country when he located in Queen," referring to his father, John. "There were Indian teepees on the ranch and a small band of Mescalero Indians were camped at the spot where McKittrick and Dog Canyon join. I can remember my father talking to the Indians and feeling relieved when they told him they would cause him no trouble. They remained for a while then returned to the Mescalero reservation."[12]

Living in the shadow of the Guadalupe Mountains, the family became central figures in the history of the region. John Shattuck became Superintendent of Schools of Eddy County in 1890, after Eddy was carved out of Lincoln County. The son, Edwin, married Sally Middleton from Rising Star, Texas, and they returned to New Mexico and lived nearby at Robinson Draw. They had several children, and in 1901 the family started a ranch known as Bar Four X, near Queen in the Guadalupe Mountains, using land in the Lincoln National Forest, which was established in 1902. Shattuck also served as sheriff for several decades.[13]

Other families lived nearby and did business with settlers like the Shattucks. Walter Thayer was nineteen when he left Maryland in 1871 for a new life in the West. He worked for John Chisum as a cowhand and traversed the Goodnight-Loving Trail for years, becoming familiar with the Guadalupe Mountains. He settled in the Seven Rivers–Rocky Arroyo area and built corrals for his stock. Thayer married Julia Shattuck in 1892 in Carlsbad. He took his family to Dark Canyon in the Guadalupes in 1898 and remained there until 1930. He bought the ranch from F. E. Downs for $1,200 and built several small houses for his growing family.[14] The Thayers enjoyed a rich family life in the mountains. Virginia Thayer

Lucas recalled that the round trip to Pecos, Texas, for supplies took weeks. After a few years of hard work, they boasted orchards that yielded apples, peaches, pears, plums, oranges, prunes, apricots, walnuts, pecans, and grapes. She also noted a "time when the Indians stole a bunch of horses from the ranchers, and all the men formed a posse and chased the Indians all the way to the Guadalupes and got the horses back." She said that her father and the men almost died of dehydration because only the Mescaleros knew where the water was. The father built another log house for a school, and children from around the region went there.[15]

Pearl Cochran Middleton was born in Seven Rivers in 1893. Her parents were William Franklin Cochran and Mary Caroline White, both born in 1862 in Missouri. They moved to Carlsbad and her father was the first treasurer of Eddy County and then county tax assessor. Unlike other families who moved to the mountains and then went to the towns for work, the Middletons went from the town to the Guadalupe Mountains and lived there until Pearl was seventeen. They raised cattle, kept gardens, and rode horses. They attended the Boad Tree School house, operated by a teacher named Lucy Rush. In reference to life and people in the Guadalupes, Lucy Rush stated that "Later many people were there, but would learn they couldn't make a living there just on a 160 acre claim and would sell to someone who lived nearby and would move away. In later years, the ranchers started selling and moving away until there are very few people living in the mountains. Many people have come and gone." She added that the lack of water was one of the biggest limitations to living there, and "the roads had gotten almost impassable in places until the WPA worked on them."[16]

Opal Green McCollaum was born in Crow Flats, New Mexico, to J. M. and Ola Merrill Green in 1898. Crow Flats was on the west side of the Guadalupe Mountains, close to the Texas-New Mexico border. Her father was a goat herder and unlike most women of her time, Opal went to college in Silver City and returned home to teach. She married John McCollaum, whose grandfather was a Texas Ranger in Menard County. John's father settled in southeastern New Mexico after he came to the region on a cattle drive. Opal remembered a man named Aubrey Gist from a nearby ranch who was one of the first to raise Angora goats. John McCollaum worked for him on "a ranch in the extremely rough country on the southern end of the Guadalupe Mountains. They herded goats and marketed very fine mole hair, both in America and abroad." David, son of John McCollaum, worked on ranches between El Paso and Carlsbad, such as the Helms Ranch. His family ran five thousand goats and frequently went to the salt flats in Texas, shoveling salt into wagons. The McCollaum family had a good relationship with the U.S. Forest Service, leasing numerous allotments for cattle.[17]

Slightly north of Queen, homesteads spread out across the mountains in New Mexico. Many of these became large allotments that the Lincoln National Forest preserved after it established the Guadalupe District in 1906. One of the largest landholders in the area was Ruben Segrest. In 1842 Segrest emigrated from Switzerland to Missouri and then to Texas. Several years later he and his countrymen coordinated a colonization endeavor to the Trans-Pecos region. After working on various cattle ranches in West Texas, Segrest moved to northern New Mexico in the 1870s. In 1880 he relocated to Seven Rivers and established the S Cross Ranch, where Indian Creek, now Rocky Arroyo, ran down from the Guadalupes. After several decades Segrest owned nearly half of the land that became the Guadalupe Ranger District.[18]

One of the lesser known families was the Holmesley family. In a 1973 interview conducted by Paul Patterson, Tom Holmesley recalls how his father brought the family from Comanche County, Texas, in 1902 to settle in the Guadalupe Mountains. After stopping in Synder, Texas, to pick up relatives, Holmesley took the caravan to Hope and Weed, New Mexico, the two settlements where his extended family lived. Their life was difficult and required constant adaptation and ingenuity. After practicing medicine for a few years in the Weed and Hope region, Holmesley moved his family south of the state line to Crow Flat, where he built a home and opened a general store. His brother also made a move further southwest to the area around the Cornudas Mountains on the road to El Paso.[19]

This shift led to additional family members moving to the Guadalupe Mountain area. One part of the family migrated to the small settlement that became Dell City, Texas, while the other part moved to Orange, New Mexico. In 1912 Holmesley sold the house and general store and moved back to Comanche, Texas, but returned to El Paso in 1917.[20] While in Crow Flats, Holmesley tried cattle ranching, but the poor soil and lack of irrigation limited his herds. Tom Holmesley recalled the ten-day round trip into El Paso for supplies, which they carried on a wagon drawn by four horses. The children attended a school in Van Horn, and returned home during the summer and spent the school year with family friends. When the Holmesley family moved to El Paso in 1917, they encountered Mexican revolutionaries near the Eagle Mountains, but the revolutionaries were captured by Anglo ranchers until the military arrived from Fort Bliss. Tom Holmesley said that most of the residents of Van Horn were Mexican. They even built a Mexican school in the 1930s on the south side of the tracks, separate from the school for Anglos.[21]

One of the most interesting stories of settlement in the Guadalupe Mountains is of the Iribarne family, who immigrated to the America in 1877 from the Basque region of France. Joame Iribarne and his family went to New York, but a son named Michel settled in Bakersfield, California. For two decades he raised sheep in California until he moved to southeastern New Mexico in 1904. Michel filed a squatter's claim in the Guadalupe Mountains and amassed a considerable amount of land between 1908 and 1924. He ran eight thousand head of sheep and hired Hispanic workers to help him with his operations. Several Basque families followed in his footsteps, coming to New Mexico via the sheep and wine industries in California. By the 1920s there were a half-dozen Basque families herding sheep in the Guadalupe region.[22]

Very few families enjoyed the successes of the Iribarne family. Lack of water, the ruggedness of the terrain, distance from markets, and other factors made settlement in the Guadalupes very difficult.[23] When Felix McKittrick finished working as a cowhand on the Goodnight-Loving Trail, he decided that the eastern foothills of the Guadalupes held promise for a solitary life. In 1869 McKittrick settled in the canyon that now bears his name, a few miles north of Pine Springs. His story is addressed later, but little is known about him.

The cattle industry brought other settlers like McKittrick to the Guadalupe Mountains. Perhaps inspired by the successes of John Chisum, Henry Belcher established a ranch on the western side of the Guadalupes. Belcher arrived in 1905 and brought Herefords to graze on sections of land that he claimed. Aridity was the first and most daunting obstacle confronting him. Rather than drill a deep well, Belcher built an elaborate system of pipes and tanks to divert water from a spring in Bone Canyon. The system worked fairly well and provided Belcher's cattle with water.

With this problem solved, he decided to build a more permanent home, having grown tired of living in a tent for several years.[24]

The story of Belcher constructing a home for his wife, and his wife's reaction to life in the rugged Guadalupe Mountains, has become part of local folklore. Although the stories vary slightly, in 1890 Belcher apparently contracted John Smith to build him a steeply gabled house looking out over the valley to the west. The materials had to be hauled in by mule from Van Horn. Sitting at an altitude of approximately five thousand feet, Belcher believed the new house would be a wonderful home for his wife, Rena, and their child, Bernice. Although he modeled it after east coast architecture, his wife was not pleased with the remote location, and after one day in the mountains, she returned home.[25] Belcher stayed at the house for a short time until he gave the entire ranch to his brother, Henry, who tried to turn a profit on the enterprise. Henry Belcher did fairly well for seven years. A drought in 1915 caused him to concentrate his three thousand head of cattle on less and less land, and soon he overgrazed his ranch. Despite the ingenious watering system designed by his brother, and Henry's persistence as a rancher, the Belchers fell victim to the aridity, heat, and dry soils of the west side of the mountains.[26]

On the eastern side of the mountains sits the present-day Frijole Ranch museum in an old house that has a long and varied history. By 1876 John and Cade Rader had arrived at the mountains and decided to homestead alongside Manzanita and Frijole Springs. Cade Rader built a rock home, the two started ranching cattle, and they seemed to thrive.[27] After the Raders, came an ex-Confederate named Calvin Herring, who left North Carolina after the Civil War and migrated to Texas, where he stopped at the Guadalupe Mountains. Herring's daughter, Ida, married George W. Wolcott in 1888, and they built a home at the location of the soon-to-be Frijole Ranch. Walcott, his wife, and three daughters lived in the two-room house attached to a dugout until 1895, when the Walcotts moved to Midland, Texas.[28]

Ownership and occupation remains cloudy until 1906, when Joe T. Smith filed an application to purchase land within the Frijole Ranch area. Smith was born in Wisconsin in 1866 to Scottish parents and moved to Sherman, Texas, where in 1899 he met his wife, Nella Mae Car. After his application to purchase the ranch, he and his family migrated to the mountains. His application indicates that he owned one hundred and sixty acres in Van Horn when he was working at the Jackson Hotel. Presumably he traveled to the site, known as the Spring Hill Ranch, and thus became interested in the area. Later entries through 1908 document purchases totaling 3,890 acres between Van Horn and the Frijole Ranch.[29]

The Smiths transformed the house into a productive homestead, with gardens, orchards, and fields for grazing livestock. Their wide range of fruits and vegetables fed the family and other homesteads dispersed across the eastern face of the Guadalupes. Smith was so ingenious with his gardening methods that he supported the entire family primarily through truck farming, supplemented by his small livestock endeavors. Smith took produce to Van Horn, Sierra Blanca, Carlsbad, and communities in the region. Although Frijole Ranch would have seemed like an oasis in the Trans-Pecos, the Smiths struggled with drought, illness, and predators such as bears and mountain lions. The Smith family called it the Spring Hill Ranch until they submitted a request for a post office by that name. The name was taken elsewhere, and the family submitted "Frijole" as a joke but the postal service accepted it.[30] Mrs. Smith was post mistress after approval of the office in 1916. Although the ranch remained isolated, the post office marked Smith's determination to strengthen their ties with the outside world.[31]

Anglos began to slowly move to the region after Texas altered its land policies to allow ranchers to own more land, and as railroads tied the region to El Paso and Albuquerque. Towns such as Van Horn and Sierra Blanca owe their existence to the railroad and the links it provided.[32] Van Horn had its roots in the iconic themes of western U.S. history. The town is named after Union Lieutenant James Judson Van Horn, who commanded a garrison at Van Horn Wells, from 1859 to 1861, when Confederate forces captured the wells and took him prisoner. Van Horn Wells bore the name of an unrelated Major Jefferson Van Horne who commanded Fort Bliss in El Paso in 1849, but the city bears the lieutenant's name.[33]

After 1881 Van Horn had an impact on the Guadalupe Mountains in various ways. As they had for a generation, new settlers sometimes stopped in Van Horn before making the fifty-mile trip to the mountains. Many ranchers who bought grazing sections in the mountains lived in Van Horn and based their headquarters in the town. R. P. Bean arrived in Van Horn from Lampasas, Texas, in 1883 and homesteaded the 2 Ranch north of town. In 1883 John Formwalt bought the Moon Ranch, hoping to capitalize on the arrival of the railway. Early settlers, such as Jack Veats, Thomas Owen, Ed Hamm, and A. A. Gus Cox, were part of a community that included Van Horn, the Guadalupes, and the salt flats within its economic orbit.[34]

Newcomers to Van Horn engaged in typical pursuits: ranching, small scale farming, mining, and professions such as carpentry, engineering, and teaching, all of which are necessary for town survival. Residents in Van Horn relied on the Texas and Pacific Railway to facilitate economic transactions with the region, and as new lines connected El Paso to Roswell, the community had a north-south economic tie to complement the east-west linkages. Small cattle trails, sometimes in conflict with giant ranches using drift fences or barbed wire, followed Indian trails between Van Horn and Artesia, Eddy, and communities such as Malaga, close to the state line. Families coming into Van Horn moved into the Guadalupe Mountains in New Mexico, seeking land, better climate, healthier soils, and water. The Cox family is one of the families who moved into the mountains to take advantage of forest allotments and a more vibrant economy.[35]

Modernization in an Arid Environment

Railroads transformed these dispersed communities from isolated outposts to small but bustling towns. They also complemented the irrigation projects and artesian wells because they enabled farmers and ranchers to move their products across the nation. In turn, the push to develop water resources increased the demand for railroads because access to water made the region more attractive, thus railroads fueled immigration to the region.

Yet railroad construction in the region was delayed by the vast distances separating the Guadalupe Mountains Trans-Pecos region from the rest of the United States. Lack of minerals, water, timber, and construction materials stalled the extension of major lines into the area. The Atchison, Topeka, and Santa Fe Railway (ATSF) entered Las Vegas, New Mexico, from Colorado in 1879 and in 1880 it entered Albuquerque and then went south to join the Southern Pacific line in Deming.[36] The Texas and

Pacific reached El Paso in 1881, connecting with western lines through Arizona to California and northward to Colorado through Albuquerque. By 1883 four railroads ran into El Paso: the Southern Pacific; Atchison, Topeka, and Santa Fe; the Texas and Pacific; and the Galveston, Harrisburg, and San Antonio. A year later they were joined by the Mexican Central Railway. The railroads circumvented the Guadalupe region, and individual freighters and cattlemen still had to rely on the old trails between Eddy and El Paso to bring goods back and forth.[37]

As the railroads moved through El Paso and Albuquerque, they bypassed southeastern New Mexico, leaving the region at the periphery of western industrial growth. The first line between the Guadalupe Mountains and the Pecos River was the aptly named Pecos Valley Railway (PVRy), which extended from Pecos, Texas, to Eddy in 1890 and became operational on January 13, 1891. This line entered Roswell in 1894. Financial problems led to bankruptcy of the PVRy in 1896, so James John "J. J." Hagerman approached the ATSF. In 1897 the ATSF bought the PVRy and incorporated it as the Pecos Valley & Northeastern Railway Company (PV&NE), with plans for lines between Roswell and Amarillo. The whole set of companies were known as the "Pecos Valley Lines." But even these lines still did not connect the region with El Paso and the larger Santa Fe line.[38]

One of the most important events in the Guadalupe Mountains Trans-Pecos history was the extension of a railroad between El Paso and eastern New Mexico. The Santa Fe Pacific rail line was built from El Paso northeast into New Mexico, through Roswell, in 1902. The Pecos Valley Railroad brought people from around the world and facilitated the export and import of numerous products. These lines, combined with the frenzy of well drilling and the growth of irrigation projects, helped the population of Roswell nearly triple between 1894 and 1900.[39]

As the region developed ties with the nation, securing a stable source of water remained a central priority.[40] The earlier eras of water development associated with shallow wells dug by Native people in the area, the failed efforts of John Pope, and the expansion of springs at Frijole Ranch and McKittrick Canyon foreshadowed efforts of later generations. The next phase of water use followed two parallel paths: individual artesian wells and irrigation efforts funded by out-of-state investors. Irrigation mirrored many extractive industries at the turn of the century. Individual ditches evolved into large scale endeavors controlled by conglomerates with access to capital, technology, and political power. As these projects failed, the federal government stepped in. Irrigation in the Texas-New Mexico borderlands, though sparse, became a large scale process much faster than in other parts of the West.[41]

As Roswell resident Nathan Jaffa sunk his first well in 1890, irrigation organizations emerged to control water extraction and distribution along the Pecos River.[42] The first major water development company was the Pecos Valley Irrigation and Investment Company (PVIIC), founded by Pat Garret, Charles Greene, and Charles B. Eddy, who was the manager of the Eddy-Bissell Cattle Company. Eddy came to the region in part because of the invitation of Joseph Lea, the founder of modern Roswell. The trio formed the company in 1885, and digging began north of Carlsbad and required a thousand workers and hundreds of mule teams, as well as an enormous ditch digging machine, the likes of which had never been seen in the region. The machine cut out a mile of ditch every week, and the canal itself was eighty-five miles long, six feet deep, and thirty-five feet wide. After numerous delays, the company completed its work in 1890 with a dam on the Hondo River and a system of ditches bringing water to farmers.[43]

They quickly exhausted their financial resources and Eddy sought deeper pockets, such as J. J. Hagerman who made his wealth from western land sales and railroad building. Hagerman lived in Colorado Springs when Eddy met him, and Eddy was hopeful that Hagerman's ties to individuals such as Mark Hanna of Ohio, who made a fortune in mining and railroads, could help him realize his dreams for southeastern New Mexico. Hagerman came out of retirement and agreed to partner with Eddy and bring his enormous personal and political resources to bear upon transforming the region.[44]

After gaining investors and settling on Chicago as the headquarters of the firm, Eddy and Hagerman changed the name to the Pecos Valley Irrigation and Improvement Company, expanded its scope, and built a railroad spur to Pecos, Texas. From this they began six other water development projects: the Hondo Reservoir south of Roswell, the Northern Canal between Roswell and south of Hagerman, the Eddy (Avalon) Dam and Reservoir, the Southwestern and Southeastern Canals from Eddy Dam down the Pecos, the Hagerman Canal on the east of the Pecos, and the Pecos Land and Water Company Canal, which they hoped would irrigate land along the Texas-New Mexico border. The PVIIC was one of the largest privately funded irrigation projects in the world.[45]

Irrigation brought homesteaders from across America and Europe and transformed a small corner of the Southwest borderlands. The settlement of Eddy emerged from Charles B. Eddy's attempt to create a town near his Halagueno Ranch, as Eddy and Hagerman bought land from the Pecos Valley Town Company, a subsidiary of Hagerman's company. This boom attracted international interests seeking irrigation communities for colonization. In 1890 a representative from the Swiss government, Henri Gaullieur, arrived in the United States to determine whether the region was suitable for a colony. He believed it was, but he sent highly educated yet unskilled men from aristocratic families. The newspaper *Eddy Argus* nonetheless opined that they would make great farmers. The town of Vaud was established in 1891 by these immigrants who purchased forty-acre plots from the Pecos Valley Town Company, between Eddy and the town of Black River. Similarly, Italian settlers moved to Malaga, south of Eddy, and the newspaper thought they would be the best gardeners, second only to the Chinese. The Swiss and their colony failed, and Anglos moved into Vaud and changed the name to Florence, and then in 1908 to Loving, in honor of the cattleman. Italians in Malaga fared only a little better.[46]

The initial years of dam building and large scale irrigation yielded promising results. The Eddy (Avalon) Dam was so successful that the company initiated another project known as the McMillan Dam and Reservoir between Eddy and present-day Artesia. Completed in 1893, the dam contributed to the population boom and a frenzied search for water. Just as quickly as the boom had begun, a national depression and local flooding brought it to a halt. Demonitization of silver caused a large-scale banking crisis, but for locals, the failure of the Eddy (Avalon) Dam to hold back heavy rains led to regional flooding.[47]

The disaster caused Hagerman to break ties with Eddy and initiate his own attempt to revitalize the irrigation business. Hagerman reconstituted the irrigation company, changed its name to the Pecos Valley Company, and embarked on another attempt to control the waters of the winding river. He had reason to believe that he could succeed. By the mid-1890s, the area had a railroad line connecting it to the rest of the world, and despite the disaster with the Avalon Dam, other irrigation projects brought water to farmers. People had access to fruit and vegetables, cattle fed from alfalfa, and these local products could reach national markets. National and international products also made their way to this remote corner of the West.[48]

Hagerman moved forward in the wake of the flood, silver crisis, and departure of his partner Eddy, but his fortunes began declining. His eastern backers refused to supply him with loans, immigration to the region slowed, and he had to put his Pecos Valley Railway Company into receivership in 1896. His irrigation company suffered the same fate in 1898. Within five years of the original Avalon disaster, Hagerman realized that he could not transform the West Texas borderlands into an agricultural Eden. It was too far from most major industrial centers, the Pecos River was too difficult to harness, and the bottoms of the dams leaked. Additionally, the walls of the canals crumbled and clogged up the ditches. Excessive irrigation from the canals and the unregulated pumping of artesian wells saturated the land. These realities combined with financial difficulties to cause Hagerman to leave southern New Mexico.[49]

A technical report in 1898 provided a sobering assessment of the situation along the Pecos. It estimated that the PVIIC cultivated 12,500 acres of the 200,000 it promised. The report noted that the canal system suffered from seepage because the canals were built with soil that had a high gypsum content, which did not hold up well under pressure. Seepage caused many of the farms to over-saturate because water went underneath the canals and ditches into the cultivated areas, killing many of the crops with overwatering. The final blow came in 1904, when another flood on the Pecos broke through the Avalon Dam and destroyed the towns in the region. The following year the system was sold to the new U.S. Reclamation Service.[50]

Despite the problems faced by the first generation of irrigation companies, settlers still sank wells in the area. When people saw it was relatively simple to tap into the aquifer, individual efforts yielded a boom of small scale drilling. By 1900 there were more than 1,000 wells, from 240 to 1,000 feet deep, allowing nearly 200,000 acres of crops to be cultivated. By 1903 wells had expanded to ten inches in diameter, and initial exploration revealed that the artesian basin spread out across roughly 660 square miles. In 1907, the New Mexico Territorial Water Code regulated surface water, but not ground water. The alleged size of the aquifer and the lack of regulations, combined with the ubiquity of these small wells, encouraged the belief that the water, and expansion of the region, was endless. The problem with this view was that residents wasted water by failing to cap the wells and allowing them to run freely. People imported exotic flora and planted crops that required large amounts of water, rather than cultivating drought resistant plants.[51]

Locals began to notice that water became more difficult to pump, and in 1908 the Pecos Valley Water Users Association submitted a bill to the territorial legislature to regulate drilling. The legislature rejected the bill and these early conservationists could not counter the claims of boosters and civic leaders that the "vast ocean of underground water" was infinite. Contrary to their pronouncements, and true to the warnings of the conservationists, wells began drying up. The reservoirs built by the El Paso and Southwestern Pacific Railroad stopped the rivers from flowing south, and farms in the Bonito Valley lost their water. Users in the Roswell Artesian Basin filed suits against the project in 1907 on the basis that the railroad destroyed their farms, but a local court dismissed the case.[52] The proclamations of builders and boosters, rather than government reports and the concerns of conservationists, had won the day. The artesian wells and large scale irrigation projects led to massive declines in the aquifer in the 1920s. By 1927, when the state legislature began regulating ground water use, it was nearly too late for a region whose economy had been battered by flood, overwatering, sinkholes, and drought.[53]

As irrigation projects proceeded sporadically, development of extractive industries such as guano mining captured the imaginations of developers. Before Carlsbad Caverns became a national park, locals mined the caves for guano left behind by thousands of years of occupation by birds and bats. During the nineteenth century, guano, especially from Peru, was an important source of fertilizer, and between 1856 and 1903, America claimed a string of atolls, islands, keys, and other formations in the Pacific to mine and harvest guano under the Guano Islands Act of 1856. The U.S. government protected corporations' transferal of workers to these islands where they labored under extreme conditions to mine mountains of guano. Until new synthetics became cheaper, guano was integral to America's economy.[54]

Guano in small quantities was relatively easy to mine in West Texas and southern New Mexico because the limestone caverns in the region provided shelter for bats and birds. Ranchers were on the lookout for holes leading to caves, and it was the good fortune of Abijah Long, a recent emigrant from Goldthwaite, Texas, who in 1903 stumbled upon a cavern while working for the Carlsbad-based Joyce Pruitt freighting company. Long and his partner, Sam Evans, found one cave and began exploring for others. Their curiosity led to the discovery of a fairly large cave entrance that was too intriguing to ignore. They entered the cave and ran headlong into a pungent odor emanating from tons of guano produced by millions of bats. After having a sample certified and a mining claim approved, the partners sparked a Trans-Pecos guano boom.[55]

Long and his associates expanded the scope of their guano project with mechanization and capital from investors across the country. However, the toll of the work and the rising costs of production forced Long to sell his business in 1906 to H. F. Patterson. Later that year, the El Paso Fertilizer Company purchased the property from Patterson and then sold the cave to the General Fertilizer Association of Los Angeles in 1911. Though an offensive source of employment, guano mining provided jobs for hundreds of men between 1903 and 1923, the peak years of the industry. Six main corporations dominated guano mining in Carlsbad, and they left a distinct impact on the region until 1930, when new fertilizers replaced guano, and by World War II, when synthetic chemicals dominated the industry.[56]

As the guano industry declined, a new industry emerged from the caves that yielded so much guano. James Larkin "Jim" White moved to the Carlsbad area in the 1890s, and after working on a ranch as a young man, stumbled onto a cave that was home to numerous bats. He came upon the cave in 1898 and although he was not the first to "discover" it, he is famous for his messianic belief in the geological uniqueness of what locals called the "Bat Cave." White began offering tours to a local audience after the turn of the century. When he died in 1946, he had transformed the caves into the Carlsbad Caverns National Park.[57]

This trajectory from eccentric marketer to "father" of the caverns is an exceptional story. Few people wanted to climb into a deep hole in the desert when it smelled of bat droppings, but White transformed the geologic oddity into a tourist attraction. He created an ingenious system of walkways, lights, railings, and other amenities to make the cave more welcoming to visitors. In 1913 he employed photographer Ray V. Davis to help him advertise the cave. The images and exaggerative language of White, combined with sprinklings of "scientific" explanation, changed the caverns from a source of fertilizer to a wonder of nature. After World War I, White and Davis convinced a group of local dignitaries to descend into the caverns and spread the word about the magnificent features in the darkness below the desert floor. The strategy worked and newspapers across the country advertised the caverns as a natural wonderland, thereby launching the tourist industry in the region and paving the way for the Guadalupe Mountains National Park.[58]

The history of the Guadalupe Mountains from 1880 through 1915 mirrored much of the rural American West, but it differed in important ways. Anglo-American and European immigrants displaced Mexicans, while Mescalero Apaches struggled with removal from their homelands. Many migrants from Texas brought with them racial attitudes that included a virulent anti-Indian and anti-Mexican tendency. They rarely married Mexicans as some of their ancestors had done in El Paso, southern Texas, and northern New Mexico. As they colonized lands recently wrenched from Indians and Mexicans, they tried to recreate their lives in a region marked by a lack of water. This aridity, coupled with the distance from urban centers, made life difficult for the people in this remote outpost of the borderlands.

And yet, several small communities did emerge here. Queen, New Mexico, was one of the most successful, with its network of families, farms, schoolhouse, and post office. Smaller settlements in Pine Springs, the Frijole Ranch, Nickel Creek, and Crow Flats failed to evolve into towns, but families lived there into the late-twentieth century. Radiating outward, other communities took root to become present-day Roswell, Carlsbad, and Artesia. To the south in Texas, a few towns such as Dell City, Van Horn, and Sierra Blanca dotted the landscape despite restrictive land policies and the lack of water.

Before the entrance of the railroads and concomitant development of resources, these nascent towns constituted a dispersed network of settlements tied together by their mutual struggles with aridity and isolation. Despite changes wrought by eventual connection with the national economy and an influx of new immigrants, the Guadalupe Mountain region remained relatively distant from the commercial centers of power.

Many people continued to use horses, as modern inventions such as electricity, municipal plumbing and sanitation, paved roads, and the telephone remained dreams of the future. Nonetheless, the communities that dotted the landscape had proven that families, schools, and public institutions could survive despite aridity, alkaline soils, a mercurial river, and continued isolation.

CHAPTER SEVEN
The Interwar Years, 1919–1941

If the Guadalupe Mountain region of the mid-1800s was a remote yet surprisingly active site of exploration, immigration, and Indian Wars, the interwar years of the twentieth century were a quiet interlude until the campaign to create the national park after World War II. Gone were the Mescalero bands, the Cavalry and Buffalo Soldiers chasing after them, the explorers and topographers such as Pope, the westward migrants seeking fortunes in the gold fields, and the cowboys driving cattle to market. Villages such as Queen and Dog Canyon dotted the region around the present-day park, while a few families, such as the Raders, Smiths, Belchers, and Williams, eked out a living in the mountains. Only slightly larger communities in Carlsbad, Van Horn, Sierra Blanca, and Dell City emerged where livestock outnumbered people ten to one.

To most Americans this remote corner of the Southwest was little more than windswept desert, a dry and brittle void on the national landscape. As late as 1929 there were no paved roads connecting El Paso with Carlsbad. A few dirt roads followed cattle trails, which followed old wagon trails, which followed Indian trails, which were based on the migratory routes of animals inhabiting the region for millennia. And even after considerable sums were spent under the auspices of the New Deal to tie together these two very different cities (El Paso was shaped by Mexico, copper mining, immigration, and a recent revolution, and Carlsbad was a product of Texas expatriates and capitalists dreaming of an irrigated desert empire) very few souls followed that asphalt ribbon through stands of creosote, mesquite, cholla, agave, and Texas Madrone. Indeed, to live around the Guadalupe Mountains required a very specific intent. One had to embrace its expansive sky, its blistering heat, mercurial monsoons, hardscrabble soil, and astonishing distance from other people. And yet, those who lived here left behind traces of their lives in oral history, family memory, and a very scant documentary record.

Although the two wars had minimal direct impact on the area, it did see some growth. Early attempts at oil and gas exploration, struggles with aridity, transportation, the impact of the Great Depression, the decline of the ranching industry, and the birth of tourism all figure into this chapter of the mountain's history. In addition, we meet three of the most important people in the history of the national park: J. C. Hunter, J. C. Hunter Jr., and Wallace Pratt. Although they figure most prominently in the postwar history, their relationship with the mountains starts in the 1920s, decades before Congress preserved El Capitan, Guadalupe Peak, McKittrick Canyon, and this rugged wilderness for the enjoyment of the American public.

Hard Soil, No Water, and a Few People

The Guadalupe Mountain and Trans-Pecos region during the early twentieth century evolved in fits and starts, with the aspirations of empire builders such as James J. Hagerman falling victim to aridity and a mercurial Pecos River. By the beginning of World War I, railroads serviced Van Horn, Carlsbad, and Roswell, and locals could purchase goods from around the world. Rural electrification was still on the horizon, so families used root cellars and small streams to keep their food cold, gas lamps to brighten their homes, and the kindness of neighbors to make phone calls. A few homes boasted indoor plumbing, but most families continued to cook their meals outside. Horses and wagons commonly plied the dirt streets of towns alongside Model Ts.[1]

By the late 1910s one could surely speak of a Guadalupe Mountain community that was comprised of some interesting people. One of the most colorful characters in the area was James Adolphus "Dolph" Williams. Referred to by his family and friends as Uncle Dolph, Williams moved to the west side of the Guadalupe Mountains around 1915. He purchased the ranch house from Henry Belcher, who had taken over the property from his brother, Robert, after he built the house for his wife.[2]

Williams left Louisiana, and after moving to the mountains, he brought several family members to join him during the 1920s.³ The most useful information on Dolph Williams comes from a relative. Tom Williams was a much younger "double first cousin" to Dolph Williams. In 1930 he heard through family connections that Dolph needed assistance with his ranch. Tom left Montgomery, Louisiana, and traveled to the Guadalupes for what he thought would be a summer "respite." Struck by the mountain landscape, Tom ended up staying there for years.⁴

Tom recalled that Dolph was a kind person who seemed equally at ease with the solitude of the Southwest as well as the camaraderie of friends and family. He spent most of his time alone on the ranch until Tom and his cousins arrived in the early 1930s. Dolph had a great sense of humor and frequently played jokes on people. One incident was especially memorable. Tom said that he and Dolph were working with Mexican cowboys loading cattle in Van Horn. They had just purchased several head from ranchers in Mexico, but there was one particularly ornery cow left after loading. Not wanting to antagonize it, the cowboy left it in the corral. Dolph noticed this and decided to play on the cowboy's reluctance. Dolph bet his colleague two quarts of whiskey that he could ride it around the corral without falling off. The cowboy took the bet. Dolph jumped on the cow, was immediately thrown, and ran out of the corral with the angry ungulate chasing him. Although he was short two quarts of whiskey, Dolph had the men laughing all the way back to the ranch.⁵

Tom noticed a lot about the region while visiting the mountains. He recalled an old stagecoach line that ran from New Mexico through El Paso Gap to Bone Springs and then trailed southwest to El Paso. Occasionally a few travelers stopped at Bone Springs for water, and Dolph entertained and fed them. In addition, lawyers and businessmen mainly from El Paso ventured out to Dolph's ranch and used it as a base of operations for hunting expeditions in the Guadalupes. These trips were infrequent, but they provided Dolph with extra income and unexpected socialization.⁶

Like Dolph, the families in the region were usually ranchers struggling to survive in a harsh environment. Labor and sacrifice were central to their lives but so was the education of their children. There were a few small schoolhouses in the region, and the teachers were paid in cash or with produce, while a few families sent their children to Van Horn, El

Paso, or Carlsbad. Sometimes teachers traveled from ranch to ranch to help families that were isolated, living in their homes and assisting with chores. Families came together for holidays, birthdays, and other celebrations. They tried to maintain support networks in times of economic trouble and drought. Families that owned wells allowed neighbors to truck out water, and in return, those families reciprocated with beef, milk, tools, or other items. On more than one occasion Dolph took Tom to Queen, New Mexico, where he knew most of the families. He lived approximately five miles, "as the crow flies," from the Hammacks, and Williams would go to their ranch for his mail. They also occasionally made the difficult trek under El Capitan to the Smiths who lived at the present-day Frijole Ranch House.[7]

Of all Dolph's friends and associates, the most enigmatic was Geronimo Segura. Segura was a regional folk figure whose history is as fascinating as it is obscure.[8] It is difficult to piece together the heritage and early life of Segura. Geronimo Segura's ancestry was probably tied to the captive-taking that characterized the Spanish and U.S.-Mexican borderlands.[9] Segura was allegedly the son or grandson of a captured Mexican boy possibly named Cayetano Segura. Colonel Benjamin Grierson found Cayetano among the Mescalero bands that Grierson attacked in the 1870s. Grierson seems to have left the boy with the Mescaleros on the reservation, many of whom referred to him as "the Mexican Indian."[10] Geronimo Segura could have been a member of several different groups in northern Mexico. He could feasibly have been an Apache living in Chihuahua, but captured by Mexicans, Comanches, or a rival Apache band north of the Rio Grande, as they ventured southward for livestock, horses, or humans. The ancestor could have been traded to the Mescaleros, or they could have captured him from the group that initially captured him. The ancestor could also have been Jumano, Suma, Manso, Piro, or even Ysleta (Tigua). There is the slim chance that they could have been Comanche, but held by one of the aforementioned groups in Mexico.[11] Either way, Geronimo Segura was raised by the Mescaleros and worked closely with Williams for several years.[12]

In addition to the murky details of Geronimo Segura's past, we have little historical evidence to reconstruct the relationship between the two men. Tom recalled that Segura was married to a Mexican woman and that several of Segura's eight daughters worked for a Mrs. Glover at Pine Springs. There is a well-known photograph of Dolph standing in between two women, perhaps Segura's wife and a daughter.[13] After several years of an amicable relationship, the two parted ways sometime in the late 1930s. Dolph and Segura had a falling out when one of Segura's children allegedly stole from Dolph. Whether or not this happened is hard to substantiate. If it had, Segura surely felt ashamed by the actions of his daughter and may have had a hard time facing his friend and employer. On the other hand, if the daughter was innocent, Segura may have been angered by the accusation. Regardless, Segura and Dolph seem to have broken off their ties by the late 1930s.[14] It is not clear what became of Segura, but his descendants make a semiregular pilgrimage to the Guadalupe Mountains to honor his life there.[15]

Tom Williams, the "double half-cousin" of Dolph, remained in the mountains for more than a decade. He appreciated the wide-open spaces and relished the fresh mountain air. He met numerous fascinating people and saw a glimpse of the last vestiges of the "old west." With these memories as the context for his youth, Tom left the region in 1939 when he joined the navy. While in the war he served in the European and Pacific theaters and received a Purple Heart. While Tom was gone, the Great Depression must have taken its toll on Dolph, and he sold his land in 1941 to the expanding Hunter Ranch. Taking what little he had left after decades of ranching, he moved to Black River, New Mexico, to try farming yet again. He had little success and died there in 1942 after the bank foreclosed on his property.[16]

If the ranch established by Belcher and purchased by Dolph Williams barely survived the heat and winds of the western face of the Guadalupes, the more favorably situated Frijole Ranch was a veritable oasis in the desert. The Frijole Ranch is best associated with the John Thomas "J. T." Smith family, which lived there during the early twentieth century, and later with the Guadalupe Mountain Ranch, owned by J. C. Hunter and his son. It is presently an interpretive site oriented toward educating the public about rural culture in the American West.[17]

Smith and his wife Nella lived there for two decades, transforming the farmstead into an incredibly productive oasis. In 1920 they added a guest house to the main building, and a new outhouse was built nearby. They built a school house in 1921 and taught their own children and those of their neighbors.[18] The family irrigated their land from one of the three nearby springs and grazed their cattle on the open range. In the 1920s the Smiths took in boarders who helped with chores around the ranch, and guests that enjoyed the mountain scenery. Even J. C. Hunter Jr. made the trip up from Van Horn and frequently stayed with the Smiths. By the 1930s much of the Frijole Ranch had been developed: Juniper Spring and the surrounding land, which they purchased in 1925, proved to be a valuable addition to the homestead; the spring in the front yard provided water for home use; and the decision to dam Manzanita Spring and create a pond yielded water to fields of corn, peas, and pumpkins.[19] Smith also developed a carbide generator to pump acetylene gas into outlets inside the house for lights, and in the early 1920s, he built a wind-generated battery charger for electricity.[20]

As was the case with the Dolph Williams ranch history, little documentation exists to provide a window into life at the Frijole Ranch. Fortunately there are interviews with family members who remember what it was like to live at the base of the Guadalupes. During a 1992 Smith family reunion, Larry Henderson talked with the children of J. T. and Nella Smith about growing up at Frijole.[21]

Joe T. Smith was the son of J. T. Smith, and went by the name Joe Jr. He was born on July 3, 1912, in East Texas. He grew up at Frijole but moved to Abilene when he turned twenty-one. Joe recalled that they tapped Manzanita Spring to pipe water to the orchard, where they had "about ten acres . . . where we raised corn, peas and first one thing then another." The spring supplied water for the crops, but after they dammed its lower end, the family used it as a swimming hole. Joe Jr. recalled, "that's where I got my swimming lessons. I learned to swim there, oh, we all swam in there." During the long summers the cool water gave a much needed reprieve for the youth in the family. "Yes, our initials are still on that old tree up there, some place on that old middle tree some place," right next to the water. They went fishing in the pond. Joe Jr. said there were "Croppie, Blue Gill, Bass, and [some other] game fish! I remember Uncle Willis one time; he tried to shoot them one time. He tried to shoot them in the water. He climbed up in a tree that's still there, and he tried to shoot them, and the bullet would hit the water and go off to the side." He also remembered that they would grab some of the smaller fish and let them grow larger in a tank they kept outside of the house.[22]

Joe Jr. had an exciting youth at Frijole, but when he left as a young man, he did not return for several years. When he did, he brought his wife Madelyn with him. She recalled coming to the ranch, "I was Madelyn Judson and I married Joe Smith in Abilene in 1933, [and] in October [that year] we came out here." When Joe Jr. returned Judge J. C. Hunter hired him to serve as a cook and guide because he had an intimate knowledge of the mountains. Madelyn remembered getting off the train and gathering up horses to bring with them to Frijole, where she was struck by the profile of the mountains: "The thing I remember, that was most outstanding, and still is, is El Capitan. Looking from a distance, coming from Van Horn, it looked like a Cathedral, that's what I thought of, and that's what I think of today. It's always been beautiful to me for sure."[23]

J. C. Hunter and Wallace C. Pratt: Early Conservationists

As families struggled to survive, one important individual quietly entered into the history of the mountains. Jessie Coleman "J. C." Hunter, an energetic and shrewd businessman, wore many hats. He first moved to Van Horn in 1911 as the superintendent of schools, and then became county treasurer, judge, and the director and vice president of the Van Horn State Bank. He made his money during the oil and gas boom during the 1920s, and out of his offices in Abilene served as president of the Mid-Continent Oil and Gas Commission.[24]

His introduction to the Guadalupe Mountains came in the mid-1910s while living in Van Horn. Like many Texans, Hunter joined the race for oil. He went into partnership with Matt Grisham in the early 1920s. After scouring the Trans-Pecos and digging wells, Hunter became enthralled with the mountains and began purchasing land.[25] Within a few years Hunter had purchased thousands of acres, mostly through the Grisham-Hunter Corporation. This is how he met the second large landholder in the area, Wallace Pratt, the petroleum geologist who amassed land in McKittrick Canyon. Pratt later recalled that he and Hunter were in a race to purchase sections of McKittrick Canyon during the 1920s. Hunter knew more than he, according to Pratt, and Hunter purchased some of the best sections of the Canyon.[26]

Hunter bought numerous ranches during the Great Depression. The records of the Texas General Land Office in Austin are littered with foreclosures in the Guadalupe region and many of these properties ended up in the hands of Hunter. He purchased the Dolph Williams property, and several sections of the Cox family holdings on both sides of the state line.[27] In 1926 the Grisham-Hunter outfit purchased four sections of T&P land near Devil's Den Canyon on the state border, and one section inside McKittrick Canyon. He also purchased two more sections north of Lost Peak near Dog Canyon from a man named J. R. Bonin in 1928. In 1931 Hunter had purchased much of the McCombs property, including a six hundred and eighty-three acre plot between Smith Spring and the state line.[28]

During one of his transactions with the Cox family he met Noel Kincaid, who had married into the family and was managing the Cox properties. Hunter was so impressed with Kincaid that he hired him to oversee his growing Guadalupe Mountain Ranch. Kincaid was born in Dog Canyon near the old post office at El Paso Gap. His parents arrived in 1912 in covered wagon, traveling west from a small town north of Dallas where his father, who was born in Tennessee, met his mother. The Kincaids went to Rio Grande around 1920, and then to an area between Seminole and La Mesa in Texas. The elder Kincaid ran out of money. The family picked cotton until 1931, and they backtracked to New Mexico and remained in Dog Canyon. Kincaid and his seven siblings went to school north of Crow Flats, just above the state line. He visited the Mescalero campgrounds, which attracted tribal members into the early twentieth century. Trails to Lost Creek, Bear Springs, Pine Canyon, and even trails on the eastern side of the mountains down into McKittrick Canyon kept Kincaid busy.[29]

With a stoicism that is common to many from his generation, Kincaid accepted the good times with the bad. The harsh weather, lack of conveniences, and the distance from medical care were balanced out by the beauty of the scenery and the kindness of neighbors. At the schoolhouse and at various homesteads, residents had dances, parties, and celebrations for holidays. Even during the Great Depression Kincaid remembered that people did the best they could. Although he recalls "we just didn't have much to eat," he also added that because they lived on the farm, they had chickens, milk, beef, and numerous vegetables. Like many rural homesteads that escaped the Dust Bowl and survived bank foreclosures, the Kincaid household enjoyed a degree of self-sufficiency that enabled them to endure the Depression. Indeed, Kincaid said that

FIGURE 2. Noel Kincaid and Guadalupe Peak, circa 1960.
—Glenn Biggs Collection, Southwest Special Collection,
Texas Tech University, Lubbock, Texas.

children today have more problems and that he would never have traded his youth back then for a chance to live with modern conveniences.[30]

With this vast experience in the Guadalupes, Kincaid was a perfect choice to oversee Hunter's Guadalupe Mountain Ranch. Kincaid and Hunter struck a good bargain, according to Kincaid, when they began working together. Hunter paid Kincaid a small salary but let him take a percentage of the stock and profits from running the outfit. Kincaid enjoyed near total independence running the ranch. Hunter brought friends and associates to the ranch, and Kincaid took them on hunting trips through the trails he had known since he was a boy. With his deep ties to the region, his personal connections to ranchers, and his love for the rural lifestyle, Kincaid was not only central to Hunter's successful operation, he was a pivotal figure in the history of the Guadalupe Mountains.[31]

As Kincaid ran the ranch, Hunter and his associate, Matt Grisham, decided to make an offer to J. T. Smith for his Frijole property. Smith agreed, and in the early 1940s the Grisham-Hunter operation made the Smith home the headquarters for their ranch. Hunter soon bought out his partner and assumed control of the property. To offset the costs of maintaining the ranch, Hunter diversified his business dealings in three ways. First, he leased sections of the ranch to oil and gas companies. Second, Hunter purchased sheep and goats because they could withstand the heat. Third, he began transforming his ranch into a hunting preserve and imported elk, Merriam Turkey, and trout for recreational purposes.[32]

Although Hunter was a businessman, he was also a nascent conservationist. Some historical studies claim that the genesis for the creation of a park in the Guadalupes originated with Wallace C. Pratt, but as far back as the 1920s Hunter thought they deserved protection. As he purchased land that became the present-day park, he hoped that the state would buy the property and preserve it. Tentative talks with Texas quickly disabused him of that notion, but he continued to hope that the lands could be protected. When J. C. Hunter died in 1945, his son, J. C. Hunter Jr., inherited the ranch. Hunter Jr. followed in his father's footsteps. He continued acquiring sections of land until he owned seventy-two thousand acres in the immediate vicinity of the mountains. And, like his father, Hunter Jr. had an abiding interest in conservation and harbored similar dreams of seeing the mountains protected in perpetuity.

Wallace C. Pratt followed a slightly different path in life compared to J. C. Hunter. Born on March 15, 1885, Pratt grew up in western Kansas. He received a BS in Geology and Mining in 1908, an MA in 1909, and a PhD in Engineering from the University of Kansas. Pratt traveled throughout Mexico, Costa Rica, and the Philippines working for U.S. interests in natural resources held by American colonies and potential territorial acquisitions. In 1917 Pratt became the first professionally trained geologist employed by Humble Oil Corporation, an early player in the oil and natural gas industry. He moved up the ranks to serve as the chief geologist and director of the land, lease, and exploration department for Humble Oil. Under his guidance, Humble leased or purchased twice as many properties for exploration as its competitors. He is credited for the long process of negotiation with the King Ranch that opened it up to oil exploration and production. After working for Humble another twenty years, he accepted a position on the board of directors for Standard Oil Company of New Jersey.[33]

Pratt first came to the Guadalupe Mountains in 1920 during a trip to explore for oil. While exploring sections east of the mountains, he met a

Pecos banker and judge who told him about the Guadalupes. Pratt soon joined the judge on a bone-jarring trek to McKittrick Canyon. Pratt recalled in a 1973 interview, that when he saw McKittrick Canyon after a full day of travel, he believed "It was the most beautiful spot in Texas." Being the geologist that he was, he added that the mountain was a "magnificent cross section of fossil reef of Permain age." Enthralled with the area, Pratt contacted his friends and convinced them to join him later that year to purchase eleven sections in McKittrick Canyon.[34]

Pratt was especially interested in the 7,700-acre McComb Ranch, in the center of McKittrick Canyon. In 1921 Pratt convinced his colleagues to help purchase the old ranch after the owner went bankrupt. In 1925 the group learned that J. C. Hunter was also buying up land in the region, and in particular, sections in McKittrick Canyon. Pratt knew Judge Hunter well, and despite their competition, said he was a good friend. Pratt said Hunter was a "man of some means" due to his success in the "oil producing game." Pratt said that Hunter must have "perked up his ears" after Pratt and his colleagues began purchasing land in the canyon. Pratt said that his "broker friends were in charge of the land purchases, and they were no match for Judge Hunter. He was just smarter than they were." Hunter knew more about the surveys and purchased property that the group had thought it had purchased. In the end, Pratt recalled that Hunter had "simply beat [them] to it."[35]

Pratt bought out his associates and began purchasing new sections. In the early 1930s he commissioned Houston architect John Staub to design a house at the junction of North and South McKittrick Canyons. "Pratt Lodge" was built from local stone by stonemason Adolph May, had four rooms, and a two car garage. This cabin served as Pratt's summer home through 1945.[36] Pratt used the cabin as a base of operations while purchasing lands during the Depression. He increased his holdings in the mountains in 1934, and in 1937 he bought the neighboring seven-thousand-acre ranch owned by Tom Gray. His total holdings in the region, though not all in the area to become the park, reached sixteen thousand acres. He used some of the land for ranching, built windmills and water tanks, but he kept all livestock out of McKittrick Canyon.[37]

But not all was perfect for the Pratts when living in the mountains. The stone cabin that Pratt built became a prison for more than a week when a tremendous rainstorm trapped Pratt and his wife, Suzanne. That harrowing incident, along with the tendency of thick fog to blanket the canyon, convinced Pratt to build a house outside the canyon on an open-air ridge jutting out from the reef. The architect, Newton Bevin, said it would be just like a "ship on the desert" with beautiful vistas embracing the Permian Basin. Pratt began construction of "The Ship" in 1941 and completed it in 1945.[38]

Although he continued to spend summers in the mountains, Pratt moved up the ranks of Standard Oil of New Jersey, eventually serving as the vice president and a member of the Board of Directors. Upon his retirement in 1945, he moved permanently to the Guadalupe Mountains and lived in his "Ship on the Desert" for years. This undoubtedly confirmed a belief that Pratt, and Hunter as well, had harbored for several years: that the Guadalupes were too beautiful for their own private enjoyment. The mountains deserved protection and despite their previous tentative attempts to that end, only the postwar years would bring a full-scale campaign to preserve the Guadalupes in perpetuity.[39]

Development, Oil and Gas Exploration, and Tourism

The hopes of empire builders such as James J. Hagerman to transform the region into the breadbasket of the nation died a hard death as the costs of controlling the Pecos River proved insurmountable. This was not the Colorado River and Grand Canyon, where the high canyon walls lent themselves to the construction of massive dams that could meet the electrical and water needs of millions. The Pecos River and landscape were much more problematic in subtle yet critical ways. After a generation of Herculean efforts, major problems remained with flood control, irrigation, and the system of dams in the Middle Pecos region. What private capital could not solve, the federal government inherited and tried to manage.

Elwood Mead, chairman of the Central Board of Review on the Carlsbad Irrigation Project, noted numerous shortcomings with the irrigation system received from Pecos Valley Irrigation and Improvement. Problems included silting, flooding, and sinkholes at the base of the dams. Continual water shortages, due to flooding and leaking upstream, led to problems for farmers downstream in Texas. By 1914 ten irrigation cooperatives in Texas sought to protect their one hundred and seventy-three thousand irrigable acres from water shortages that allowed them to only irrigate thirty thousand acres. They formed the Texas Pecos River Systems Association in 1914 and hired P. M. Fogg to investigate and make suggestions for system-wide rehabilitation that increased water flow and decreased seepage from reservoirs. Fogg recommended a large reservoir just north of the state line to help Texas systems tied to the Pecos. They then formed the Pecos Valley of Texas Water Users Association in 1916 and petitioned the secretary of the interior for aid from the U.S. Bureau of Reclamation for construction of Red Bluff Dam and Reservoir. New Mexico fought the proposal and forced the issue to court.[40]

As stakeholders struggled in court, the Pecos River Compact Commission in 1923 and 1925 tried devising policies and procedures to move forward. They defined the sectional basins of the river, the division of water, protected present users, outlined future projects, and crafted methods for settling disagreements. Governor Arthur T. Hannett of New Mexico rejected the agreements because the Pecos Water Users Association of Carlsbad said that sedimentation of McMillan Reservoir prohibited them from providing water to Texas as stipulated in the compact. Failure to provide the water could lead to another lawsuit. In 1926 Congress authorized the Department of the Interior to construct a new dam, but again New Mexico refused.[41]

As the reservoir remained in limbo, irrigation from individual wells continued. Regional users drew from two related aquifer systems: a shallow one that was part of the Seven Rivers formation and an artesian aquifer in the upper carbonate-evaporite member of the San Andres formation. Rapid expansion of wells only led to moderate economic growth. The high point of well drilling was between 1906 and 1910, and there were approximately 1,424 wells in the early 1920s. By the onset of the Great Depression, many required gasoline or diesel pumps to offset the loss of head pressure. This, in turn, not only increased the demand for electricity to run pumps located at homes, but it also tied the region to oil and gas exploration. Overuse of individual wells also pushed the New Mexico state legislature to enact a series of laws regulating how much water individuals could pump from artesian wells. The regulations became more stringent and in 1912, 1925, and 1927, the office of the state engineer increasingly cracked down on waste.[42]

Unlike the failed attempts to harness the Pecos River, oil and gas exploration progressed quickly. The history of oil and gas in Texas is legendary and has constituted a central element of the state's identity. Hundreds of corporations rose and fell with the ability to tap into two resources that were synonymous with progress and modernization. One could not imagine Texas, not to mention the country, without the oil boom and ensuing restructuring of the global economy toward fossil fuels.[43]

After the Spindletop well in East Texas kicked off the boom, oil rigs dotted the state. For the Guadalupe Mountains, however, oil and gas played an indirect role because most wells came up dry. Initial problems ranged from locating petroleum deposits by random drilling and surface geology, to delays in drilling, insufficient machinery and poor casings, to water intrusion, and numerous other errors. Nonetheless, W. W. Turney drilled a well in 1900 near Fort Stockton, and a few early exploratory wells in Pecos, Reeves, and Eddy Counties in the 1910s yielded little. Wells north of Van Horn yielded oil in 1901, and caused a great fervor from El Paso to Lubbock and Amarillo. According to Van Horn judge Llew Davis, "oil is being struck all over the Salt Flat Region." Ernest Bridges of El Paso struck oil west of Van Horn. According to Bridges, "All through the Salt Flat Country the evidence that oil exists in paying quantities are very pronounced, and the wildest kind of excitement is likely to break out."[44] The Pecos Refining Company, organized in 1913, processed small amounts of local oils, mainly for lubricants, but little else. With the onset of World War I, the oil and gas industry in West Texas, despite proclamations of a boom, remained in its infancy.[45]

After World War I oil exploration technologies improved rapidly. On May 28, 1923, Santa Rita No. 1 well exploded, spewing oil across the Ollie Parker Ranch, eleven miles from Big Lake, Texas. Oil men flocked to Midland and exploration continued unabated for decades. In return, El Paso became an important refining location, and its extensive railroad connections made it a valuable transport hub. Eastern New Mexico also experienced an oil boom. Wells drilled near Dayton in Eddy County in 1909 failed to produce, but in 1924 oil was struck south of Artesia. The implementation of new technologies near the Twin Lakes site allowed the Picher Oil Company to achieve the first major oil strike in New Mexico. Oil production in the state surpassed one million barrels in 1925 and in 1926, and Picher alone produced two million barrels. The

Texas Production Company discovered massive natural gas fields in 1927 near Jal in Lea County. The smaller towns in southeastern New Mexico became centers for the services that emerged from the oil boom.[46]

Oil and gas exploration and production quickly changed the economy of southeastern New Mexico and western Texas, and by 1930 the region seemed destined to become a major player in the new industries. Independents such as the Maljamar Oil Company had several wells near Artesia and the Midwest Company struck it rich near Hobbs. By 1931 the millions of barrels of oil that were being pumped out of the earth had transformed Hobbs. As oilmen punctured the earth's crust, they encountered natural gas, which they believed to be a useless byproduct of drilling. The El Paso Natural Gas Company, formed in the late 1920s, took advantage of the gas byproduct, and during the 1930s, the company became a major engine for the border economy by supplying natural gas. These developments attracted workers, brought income into the city, and raised the standard of living for many people.[47]

The hopes that oil and gas profits would improve the region's economy seemed to echo the older dream that empire builders could harness the Pecos River. The industries made a few people wealthy, and they altered towns in important ways. By the 1940s and 1950s, much of the Permian Basin in Texas witnessed a boom in oil and gas exploration and production.[48] World War II and the need to find and supply oil and gas for the Allied war effort facilitated the boom. By 1941, West Texas and southeastern New Mexico boasted 12,000 wells. Under wartime restrictions, West Texas was pumping 279,000 barrels per day, while New Mexico was pumping 215,000 barrels per day. The oilfields of twenty-four counties in West Texas contributed to Texas' total oil production, which accounted for 40 percent of global oil production. Over 13,000 people found employment in the West Texas oil industry, and their combined incomes approximated $16,000,000 annually. In several counties, more than 75 percent of their tax revenues came from oil and natural gas and associated industries.[49]

In the early 1960s, the area east of the salt flats, just south of the Guadalupe Mountains, experienced a spike in oil and natural gas exploration, with petrochemical giants such as Mobil sinking wells in the shadow of El Capitan. These exploratory wells sat next to natural gas wells owned by El Paso Natural Gas that were pumping 13,500,000 cubic feet daily.⁵⁰ Individual property owners, wildcat operations, and giant oil companies ran pipelines across the region as the transient population, especially of young men searching for fast money, drastically altered the socioeconomic landscape. But as is the case with most economies based on a boom and bust cycle, the majority of the wealth flowed away from the region. Like the aspirations of those promoting irrigation, the oil and gas industry did not bring stability to Artesia, Roswell, Carlsbad, or Van Horn. With the exception of the landowners that leased property to the corporations, profits went to bankers and investors across Texas, the east coast, and Europe.⁵¹

As oil and gas wealth left the region, industries such as potash attracted the attention of investors. Potash was a fertilizer found in the Salado geological formation between salt deposits containing sylvite and evaporate minerals. World War I forced America to replace potash from Germany with domestic sources. Cast as a national security concern, the federal government subsidized exploration for potash. Building on the 1912 discovery of potash salts outside of Amarillo by John Udden of the University of Texas, deposits were found across the Permian Basin. Postwar prices plummeted, and only the American Potash and Chemical Company survived the downturn. American Potash pursued Udden's prewar plans for expansion and utilized federal funds in 1926 to facilitate exploration in the Permian Basin. With the assistance of the Bureau of Mines, the industry developed newer and less expensive technologies to extract potash from surrounding materials. By 1929, the potash industry had stabilized.⁵²

Potash became an important part of the history of southeastern New Mexico and western Texas. V. H. McNutt, a geologist for the Snowden and McSweeney Corporation, was central to this expansion of the industry, and in 1925 he found potassium in tailings from a local well. Within the next few months they conducted test bores and discovered sylvinite, a combination of potassium chloride and salt, near Carlsbad. They sought leases to fifteen thousand acres of land near Carlsbad and established the United States Potash Company, to deal exclusively with potash.⁵³ The new endeavor faltered, and the Pacific Coast Borax Company (PCBC) purchased half of the stock in an attempt to influence its mining policies. PCBC was a subsidiary of Borax Consolidated Limited of London, which had extensive political connections with the elite of America.

They sought to capitalize on these ties by asking Stephen T. Mather, the director of the National Park Service, to serve as the president of U.S. Potash. This was not an unusual request because Mather made much of his personal wealth by promoting 20 Mule Team Borax (a product of U.S. Potash) and because Mather was close associates with Christian Zabriskie, the chief executive for PCBC. After some reluctance, he left the park service in 1932 to become vice president and general manager of U.S. Potash.[54]

As word spread about the region's potash deposits, new companies began exploration and production. The Potash Company of America (PCA) sank exploratory shafts, and by 1934 it boasted a crushing mill and a twenty-mile railroad between Carlsbad and its drilling operations. In 1936 a third corporation, the Union Potash and Chemical Company, set up shop, pushing the region further into the forefront of domestic potash production. By 1942 the Carlsbad area was responsible for the majority of the nation's 1.2 million tons of potassium salts, in large part due to the massive plant built by U.S. Potash. The industry brought notoriety, employment, and development to southeastern New Mexico, but the overall impact fell short of what the early promoters of potash mining had predicted.[55]

As oil, gas, and potash transformed the Texas-New Mexico borderlands, a budding tourist industry took shape in the shadows of the mountains. The popular image of the American Southwest has roots in the late nineteenth century when reformers followed ethnographers and anthropologists that streamed into the reservations and pueblos hoping to catalogue what they believed were the vestiges of dying cultures. Similarly, entrepreneurs of tourism such as Fred Harvey marketed the image of an "American exotic": an ancient and foreign place within the boundaries of the United States. By World War I, Americans had begun their love affair with a Southwest where time stood still, old civilizations spoke strange languages, echoes of the Indian Wars lingered in the air, and where modernity had yet to take root.[56]

This was the script that the tourist industry offered as it courted the middle class and its expendable income, and the cultural progressives searching for "authenticity" in a world torn by industrialized warfare and material excess. The epicenter of this journey in time was the string of pueblos, reservations, and Hispano villages stretching from Taos to the

Hopi Mesas. Santa Fe, Mesa Verde, Canyon De Chelly, and the Grand Canyon as well, drew scientists, tourists, and urban expatriates, such as Georgia O'Keefe, seeking refuge from the "ills of modernity." While the intellectuals and artists valued the landscape and apparent egalitarianism of the indigenous cultures, their search for primitive simplicity in the communities denied those communities historical agency and adaptation. Fred Harvey and the Santa Fe Railway employed crass marketing techniques that promoted what constituted an ethnographic zoo, with the Indian and Hispano communities as the attraction.[57]

Grafting this scenario onto the Guadalupe Mountains Trans-Pecos region was difficult because there were very few Indians, Hispanos, and their "ancient cultures" to attract outsiders. To most Anglos, the Indians and Hispanos that did live in the towns and on the Mescalero reservation were lazy people suited to manual labor. Essentially, these people did not follow the romantic script of the imagined Southwest because they were wage laborers, who wore "White man's clothes," spoke English, and, in the minds of the dominant society, had lost their culture.

FIGURE 3. Postcard circa 1930s.
—Glenn Biggs Collection, Southwest Special Collections,
Texas Tech University, Lubbock, Texas.

The Interwar Years, 1919-1941   139

Although the Southwest mystique was somewhat incongruous with the Guadalupe region, boosters promoted a modified version of the popular script. Three themes dominated the imagery that locals embraced: the healthful qualities of the desert, the rough and tumble history of the Old West, and the wars against the Comanche and Apache. Promotional material emanated from the local chambers of commerce with stories of salubrious springs, desert air that could cure common illnesses, and an expansive sky that was itself a wonder of God's creation. Sanatoriums cropped up and people flocked to the region, hoping to improve their health. The town of Eddy changed its name to Carlsbad because it wanted to promote its hot springs by associating them with the springs of Karlsbad, Germany. Hotels in Carlsbad and Roswell catered to tourists seeking the twin benefits of the hot springs and the dry desert air. During the 1930s, Van Horn completed construction of the El Capitan Hotel along the Southern Pacific Railway, with the hopes of cashing in on the health craze and the allure of the Guadalupe Mountains.[58]

Parallel to the "therapeutic Southwest," locals altered the common historical narrative of the Old West. Rather than the ancient homes of Taos and the Hopi Mesas, southeastern New Mexico and West Texas were closer to an Old West of the "classic frontier" where outlaws, lawmen, gunfights, and desperados predominated. This narrative connected the northern parts of the region, which were home to the Lincoln County War and thus the famous Pat Garret and Billy the Kid, with El Paso, the border, and its flamboyant characters. Although El Paso tried to situate itself within the Old West narrative, it walked a fine line due to its proximity to Juarez. Promotional material utilized tropes of the lawless frontier even though boosters were ambivalent about how Ciudad Juarez impacted their claims to "American-ness." Pivotal events such as the Salt War of 1877 and the Battle of Juarez during the Mexican Revolution destabilized a classic western identity, so boosters recast them as colorful episodes in the "wild and wooly" history of the borderlands, a history that paralleled the "lawless frontier."[59]

The Old West provided the perfect mix of "true history," nostalgia, and kitsch for tourism in the Trans-Pecos region. It tapped into longings for a lost past of rugged individualism and frontier excitement while extolling the victories of Manifest Destiny and American civilization. The twin accomplishment of rooting the region in the central narrative of American history, westward expansion, and selectively utilizing the "other" histories of the border associated with Indians and Hispanos was a great feat. But even though boosters inserted the region into the Old West narrative they could not attract very many tourists on the scale seen in Santa Fe.[60]

There were, however, enormous caverns that had become a regional curiosity with great potential for tourism. By the late 1920s their growing popularity kept southeastern New Mexico and Carlsbad from sliding into obscurity as agriculture and extractive industries sputtered. The rising attention to the caverns coincided with the expansion of the young National Park Service, which had been established in 1916. During its early years, its two leaders, Stephen T. Mather and Horace M. Albright, strengthened the agency that competed with the U.S. Forest Service and the Bureau of Land Management for oversight of public lands. Local politicians, state representatives, and county commissioners contacted federal officials about the geological qualities of the caverns and their promise to resuscitate the economy. Federal representatives visiting the region because of work on irrigation projects also learned more about the caverns.[61]

Official interest in the caverns by the Department of the Interior began in 1923 and expanded slowly. The Government Land Office dispatched mineral examiner Robert A. Holley to explore the caves for the Department of the Interior. Holley understood that the local population supported protection even though most westerners cringed at an increased government presence in their backyard. He also realized that any future reserve had to include participation by James Larkin "Jim" White, who was eccentric but possessed sharp marketing skills and ties with local leaders. When Holley wrote to his superiors that the caverns evoked in him "deep conflicting emotions, the feelings of fear and awe and the desire or an inspired understanding of the Divine Creator's work," he expressed his enthusiasm to the Department of the Interior and spread word about the caverns.[62]

The relationship between White and Holley expanded into a powerful partnership that led to the creation of the Carlsbad Caverns National Park. An important step in that direction began when W. F. McIlvain, president of the El Paso Chamber of Commerce, organized a trip to the caves. Richard L. Burges, an El Paso attorney, joined them and was astonished by the caves. Burges contacted Willis T. Lee, a geologist with Johns Hopkins University. Lee was impressed with the caves and drew upon his influence in intellectual circles to broaden the base of support for federal protection. Within the year President Calvin Coolidge used the Antiquities Act of 1906 to set aside land above the caverns in the Guadalupe Mountains as a national monument.[63]

The protected designation served as a stepping-stone to the highly prized status of a national park. Monument status also enabled Lee to justify throwing himself into scientific investigation of the caverns, the result of which he published in a 1924 article in *National Geographic* that vaulted the caverns into the international spotlight. The article led to a $16,000 expedition funded by the National Geographic Society to map and photograph the caves. Another article in *National Geographic*, the second within two years, confirmed that Carlsbad Caverns were a natural wonder that people from around the world had to visit. With the scientific value of the Caverns above doubt, locals such as McIlvain took over promotion and marketing when Lee returned to work for the USGS. McIlvain accepted an offer from NPS acting director Arno B. Cammerer to work as "custodian" for the monument as he promoted the site. By 1929 annual visitors jumped to nearly 76,000 people.[64]

The growing popularity of the monument had myriad unexpected consequences. Director Cammerer had become suspicious of White's tourist operation, especially his inability or refusal to maintain the infrastructure and his increasingly expensive tours of the site. Cammerer lacked the funds for upgrades so he contacted a U.S. senator from New Mexico, Andrieus A. Jones, to help draft an appropriation for the monument. Cammerer hoped Carlsbad would create a bipartisan coalition that could rise above the disputes associated with the proposal from Albert B. Fall, the former secretary of the interior, for a park near his ranch, which had been carved out of Mescalero homelands. The NPS increased funding for the monument, appointed White as the chief ranger, built a new road to the cave, and upgraded visitor amenities. In 1928 the Cavern Supply Company offered lunch to visitors seven hundred and fifty feet below the surface.[65]

At roughly the same time, C. L. "Charlie" White, no relation to Jim White, developed a "tourist town" at the junction of the state highway and the road to the park. Charlie White was a colorful character who had a varied life. He and his wife Emma arrived to New Mexico in 1906 hoping that the dry air would improve their health. He taught elementary school in Francis, New Mexico, raised sheep, tried to start a bank, and installed the first gasoline station in Loving, New Mexico. After Charlie accidentally met Jim White in 1926 and learned about the caverns, he filed for a homestead, sight unseen, near the monument. Within a few years, he transformed the entrance to the monument. Although the NPS lacked jurisdiction over "White's City," the gas station, cafe, and other amenities proved attractive to visitors, and by 1940 his strategically situated hotels were booked solid for the summer.[66]

Charlie White's tourist city, along with the efforts of Jim White, local boosters, and Senator Jones pushed the park service to lobby Congress to approve the creation of the national park. It transferred Colonel Thomas Boles, an Arkansas native and a trained engineer, from Hawaii Volcanoes National Park to Carlsbad Caverns in 1927. Boles remained in the position for nineteen years. In addition to Boles and the stable leadership he provided, Stephen Mather brought members of Congress to the park, drawing upon the assistance of the Fred Harvey Company. Mather was especially hopeful that Michigan Congressman Louis Cramton, a great friend of the NPS, would sponsor a bill for park status. Indeed he did, and President Hoover approved the creation of the park in 1931. It was the first national park in New Mexico and brought southeastern New Mexico into the national spotlight. These events, along with growing interest in preserving Big Bend, were crucial to the future park in the Guadalupe Mountains.[67]

The Great Depression and World War II

One of the most intriguing aspects of the creation of the Carlsbad Caverns National Park was that Congress and the president approved it when the national economy was in a free fall. National parks such as Carlsbad were located a great distance from urban centers and required considerable effort to visit them. Such travel cost money and few Americans had spare change in their pockets during the 1930s. And yet the caverns caught the imagination of a country that was gripped by a financial crisis that was unparalleled in history.

The Depression had an ambivalent impact on the Guadalupe Mountain region. On the one hand, the impact was comparable to other rural areas of the Southwest, particularly those struggling with aridity. Many people lost their homes, jobs, and properties, while farms and ranches withered and blew away in Dust Bowl conditions. Into this vacuum came individuals such as J. C. Hunter and Wallace Pratt who purchased land from the banks that foreclosed on ranchers. Thus, as the immediate mountain area saw a net population decline, it also witnessed the rise of the two people that amassed the lands that became the Guadalupe Mountains National Park. If this story of broken dreams, environmental catastrophe, and wealth accumulation marked a bittersweet chapter in American history, another dimension of the 1930s indicated the varied trajectories of the people and land of the Guadalupe Mountains.

The Great Depression forced homesteaders away from the region, but a few individuals nonetheless survived the economic crisis. For many years the Signal Peak Café was a cultural landmark and a monument to the persistence of rural folk in West Texas. In his recollections of life in the mountains, Ben Gilmore said the café was built in the late 1920s but was unclear who first built it. J. T. Smith added on to it. When Gilmore came to Salt Flat in 1937 to work for the Texas Highway Department, Mr. and Mrs. Earl Selman were running the café. Jim and Eva Driggers took over until 1941. Dolph Williams and a prospector named Ben Watson helped occasionally. The Driggers became ill and Fred Cox and his wife took over in early 1940s. After Noel and Lucille Kincaid left Frijole, they helped the Coxes run the café. The Coxes ran it for two or three years. The Sadlers then ran the place for several years until the completion of Interstate 10 diverted a lot of traffic from the region, thus hurting their business. Since then the café has limped along, closing and opening its doors sporadically.[68]

The Signal Peak Café was perhaps the only business in the vicinity not focused on ranching or oil exploration, but it was impacted by the land use policies of the state of Texas. The state held some lands to sell for public school revenue, and it sold a lot of its land to the Texas and Pacific Railway, which in turn sold sections to private individuals. Thus, at the beginning of the Great Depression, nearly all of the Guadalupe Mountains in Texas sat in the hands of private citizens. Due to the extent of private property and the lack of federal land in Texas, New Deal programs were scarce in West Texas. The New Deal programs that did exist were generally in towns and urban areas, rather than rural areas, forests, mountains, and grazing regions lands.

The Guadalupe Mountains in Texas were still impacted by New Deal activity in the Guadalupe District of the Lincoln National Forest and towns in southeastern New Mexico. The most relevant New Deal program was the Civilian Conservation Corps (CCC), which helped build roads, fences, and lay telephone wire in rural regions of the American West. It was an iconic agency dedicated to, among other things, combating the environmental degradation caused by unchecked development such as clear cutting of forests and unregulated grazing of stock animals. The CCC also helped build many of the camping sites throughout the forest. Thus, the New Deal programs indirectly affected the lands that became the national park.[69]

The Lincoln National Forest is located in south-central New Mexico in Lincoln, Otero, Chaves, and Eddy Counties. It is composed of three districts, including the Guadalupe District. The elevation varies from four thousand to just above ten thousand feet. Since it spans a variety of ecosystems, including Chihuahuan desert, piñon-juniper forest, and high altitude conifer-hardwood forests, the activities on the forest and surrounding lands have included logging, ranching, mining, farming, and tourism. To assist the economy and create work for the public, the CCC provided incentives for the forest service to develop projects in the districts. Lower altitude CCC camps on the Lincoln became winter camps for seasonally occupied, higher altitude "Fly Camps" in the colder sections of the Lincoln. The CCC also sent enrollees to New Mexico from as far away as Wyoming during the winter.[70]

Roosevelt and an emergency session of Congress created the CCC in 1933 and deployed men in temporary relief positions across the country. Although the New Deal programs alone failed to end the crisis, the CCC signaled that the government possessed a route toward recovery. By May 1933, the first one hundred and five "CCC boys" and three officers bound for the Sacramento Mountains had been through a basic training program at Fort Bliss and were transported to High Rolls and then the Sacramento CCC camp. This was one of the three original CCC camps in the forest and the very first in operation. Other nearby camps associated with the forest service near Cloudcroft were 16 Springs, High Rolls, Upper La Luz Canyon, Mayhill, and Bear Springs. Additional camps were located in the Smokey Bear Ranger District (Cedar Creek, Baca, Devil's Canyon, Capitan Fly Camp, Jernigan Ranch, and Angel Canyon

Fly Camp) and the Guadalupe Ranger District, in Dark Canyon, west of Carlsbad.[71]

The November 1933 issue of the *Lincoln Forest Notes* covers the Sacramento Camp's first seasons, including completion of telephone lines, forestry work, road and trail construction, tree seed collection, and erosion control. The Sacramento Camp collected one hundred and fifty pounds of Douglas Fir seeds and planted Englemann Spruce and Douglas Fir seeds from Colorado. The CCC boys from High Rolls and Sacramento assisted with road construction, built rock culverts, and whenever a fire was spotted, went into action, sending out crews to stop the flames. CCC-built roads covered the Lincoln National Forest, including Karr Canyon, Haynes Canyon, La Luz Canyon, National Ranch Road, and the Guadalupe Rim Road.[72]

The entrance of America into war led the federal government to wind down its New Deal programs. In 1940 and 1941, the Mayhill CCC Camp shifted its headquarters to the Dark Canyon Camp in the Guadalupe Mountains for the winter months. Other agencies, such as the Soil Conservation Service, also moved personnel into forest service camps, as was done between camps in Tularosa and Mayhill. The La Luz Crew moved to the Bighorn National Forest in 1934 while the Mayhill crew went to Colorado for the summer. These shifts were part of a regional consolidation of conservation efforts.[73]

The CCC employed young men in labor that was fulfilling and that gave them a sense of honor. They were paid $30 a month, of which $25 was sent to their families. Leaders made $45 a month while the assistant leaders made $36. Those that could pass the civil service examination were eligible for $85 a month and a possible agency appointment. In 1937 a majority of the regular enrollees in New Mexico camps were Hispanic. A majority of the assistant leaders were also Hispanic, but leaders and those above them were Anglo. Thus, the programs were open to experimentation that crossed normally rigid ethnic lines.[74]

Of the many CCC enrollees in the region, George Walker recalled spending time in Dark Canyon in the Guadalupe Ranger District. In a 2006 interview, he recalled that life in the camps was pretty slow, with much of the spare time spent giving each other haircuts. He remembered that his parents received $25 of his $30, but his $5 stretched rather far, if "you were smart and didn't gamble it away." Bull Durham tobacco and papers were a nickel, and Prince Albert tobacco was a quarter. Meals and transportation were free. He remembered one hike down past Dog Canyon, when he looked out over "the Bowl" of the Guadalupe Mountains, and was impressed by the view.[75]

The Civilian Conservation Corps and the New Deal programs did not officially penetrate the Guadalupe Mountains in Texas, but as Walker recalls, the workers explored the mountains. The programs introduced them to Carlsbad Caverns, and in turn, they could have learned about the efforts to create a new preserve below the state line. Moreover, the programs made improvements in infrastructure by laying down hundreds of miles of roads, building bridges, shoring up erosion-prone mountainsides, and planting trees. CCC enrollees also strung telephone and electrical wires that brought communities into the modern era. These developments not only reshaped the mountains of New Mexico, but they also impacted the area south of the state line by facilitating development, easing tourist travel, and breathing new life into national concerns about the conservation and preservation of national resources and scenic landscapes.[76]

Like the Great Depression, the impact of World War II on the American West is well known. Military spending grew exponentially as the federal government established new or overhauled old bases across the West. Phoenix, Denver, Los Angeles, Albuquerque, Salt Lake, Tucson, San Francisco, Seattle, and Portland saw an influx of federal dollars in an attempt to increase the production of military weapons, vehicles, plants, and arms. In conjunction with the explosion in the size and scope of military bases such as Fort Bliss and White Sands, contracts to corporations such as Boeing, Motorola, and General Dynamics spurred private-sector production. Industries such as coal, oil, gas, steel, rubber, copper, and aluminum enjoyed astronomical spikes that rippled throughout the West.

As military spending and defense related industries boomed, millions of people poured into Colorado, Washington, Oregon, California, and Arizona in search of employment in wartime industries. In addition to this massive internal migration of workers, the war spurred the movement of soldiers and their families to the West. After the war these families remained in states that had seen little population growth, with the exception of California. It comes as no surprise, then, that this demographic and economic growth was felt in the Trans-Pecos region.[77]

As the hot war died down, the Cold War continued transforming the Southwest. The Manhattan Project, the government program to develop and test an atomic weapon, brought thousands of highly skilled workers to the Los Alamos region of New Mexico. Cold War development continued in White Sands and Fort Bliss as the Department of Defense tested rockets, bombs, fighter jets, and other weaponry. This expanding defense network was closely tied to private oil and gas exploration and uranium mining. Thus, as the United States entered the Cold War, the Trans-Pecos region became enmeshed with the postwar economy of militarization.

When testing at the Trinity Site in New Mexico vaulted the desert Southwest into the atomic era, the Guadalupe Mountains stood at a turning point. During summer 1945 when the first bomb lit up the night sky, one can just imagine the view from the top of El Capitan as the bright flash forever changed human civilization. Locals recalled that they felt something shake them in their beds as they enjoyed what they thought would be a typical night in the desert. If the Hunters or the Pratts, or any of the families in the Guadalupes, did actually feel the shock waves, it would have been significant only in hindsight. They could not have fathomed what their government had unleashed.[78]

With that blast in the summer of 1945, America and the world ended one of the worst wars in history. In closing that chapter, it opened up another one marked by a new kind of uncertainty. Technological and scientific advances that should have ended illness and poverty, and political developments that should have ended tyranny, had ushered in the atomic age. What were the new rules of international relations? How would the United States deal with the Soviet Union? As America became ensconced in the Cold War, political debate was poisoned by accusations of Communism. A new kind of conformity and authoritarianism blanketed the country.

Americans still found some solace in a quarter century of growth and prosperity, despite the uncertainties of the atomic age. The decades of personal sacrifice seemed to bear fruit afterward, as Americans bought homes and cars, attended college, and enjoyed a spike in their standard of living. Families could point to new consumer goods and summer vacations. The Eisenhower Interstate System enabled middle-class Americans to jump into their Fords and Chevrolets and see America. This marriage of new personal wealth and geographic mobility put the middle class on the new roads, and many of those roads led to America's national parks. And it was this development, the postwar boom in leisure travel for the middle class, that made it perfect timing for the creation of Guadalupe Mountains National Park.

CHAPTER EIGHT
The Creation of Guadalupe Mountains National Park

The creation of a national park out of the rugged and isolated Guadalupe Mountains—in the northern Chihuahuan Desert, in far West Texas—was a great achievement. Early efforts before World War II set the foundation for boosters such as Glenn Biggs and property owners such as Wallace Pratt and J. C. Hunter Jr. The long-term interest in establishing a park facilitated the plans of Hunter and Pratt, planted a seed in the institutional culture of the National Park Service, and provided continuity for politicians in Texas. Additionally, the establishment of Guadalupe Mountains National Park symbolized a turning point in the policies of the NPS because Congress used federal monies to purchase private property. Congress and the president primarily created parks out of lands already owned by the federal government, or it encouraged private foundations to purchase and donate the land to the federal government. Alternately, the park was also one of the last established for the traditional purposes of preserving natural scenery for the enjoyment of the American public. El Capitan, McKittrick Canyon, and the Bowl were iconic symbols of the mountains and their importance for decisions about preservation cannot be overstated. This combination of traditional justifications and newer scientific rationales, along with the efforts of boosters and supporters, facilitated a shift in policy represented by the use of federal monies to preserve lands held in private property.

None of this would have been possible without the dedication of a small group of people whose sheer willpower made the park a reality. The principals in this case were Wallace Pratt, a petroleum geologist and vice president for Humble Oil who owned portions of McKittrick Canyon; J. C. Hunter and J. C. Hunter Jr., wealthy oilmen who owned the 72,000-acre Guadalupe Mountain Ranch; Glenn Biggs, the indefatigable real estate broker and promoter of the park; Joe Pool, the congressman-at-large for Texas; and Ralph Yarborough, the legendary U.S. senator. The supporting yet crucial cast included Stewart Udall, the secretary of the interior; William O. Douglas, chief justice of the U.S. Supreme Court, and President Lyndon Baines Johnson. These characters worked not only in conservative Texas, but also in far West Texas where cattle and oil wells outnumbered people. And yet, they moved the proposal forward at lightning speed. President Johnson approved creation of the park in 1966, six years after J. C. Hunter Jr. decided to sell his ranch and three years after the first congressional hearing on the park. More surprisingly, the park supporters succeeded in the midst of one of the most tumultuous eras in U.S. history.[1]

Preservation and Conservation before World War II

Talk of creating a park in the Guadalupe Mountains began decades before Glenn Biggs and J. C. Hunter Jr. decided to sell Hunter Ranch in the early 1960s. The impetus came from boosters, chambers of commerce, and conservationists in El Paso, Carlsbad, and Abilene, as well as some local property owners such as Hunter Jr. and Wallace Pratt. These groups embraced the idea of a park because it might stimulate development through tourism and because many people believed that the geologic and ecological characteristics of the mountains needed protection. The early efforts lacked the coordination and support that surfaced in the 1960s, but they emerged alongside the creation of parks in Texas and throughout the Southwest borderlands.

Early advocates of a park had several problems to resolve. First and foremost was the size and scope of the park. Aside from McKittrick Canyon, "the Bowl," and the El Capitan-Guadalupe Peak complex, what else should be protected? A second question centered on the rationale for a park. NPS policy embraced a set of values known as "monumentalism" and a reverence for natural landscapes defined as sublime or stunning. Although El Capitan was a striking example of a one-thousand-foot sheer rock wall, and McKittrick Canyon possessed beautiful streams and stands of trees, park service administrators did not believe that it equaled the gems of the system: Grand Canyon, Yellowstone, and Yosemite. Third, the mountain region in Texas was private property.[2]

The Guadalupe Mountains attracted the attention of many people long before President Johnson signed legislation in 1966. One of the earliest references to creating a park out of McKittrick Canyon dates to 1925. J. C. Hunter was a prominent judge, oilman, and community leader in Van Horn, Texas, south of the Guadalupes. To stimulate tourism he participated in a 1925 promotional event located in McKittrick Canyon. Along with nearly one hundred people—including the highway commissioners of Texas and New Mexico, Governor Pat Neff of Texas, and members of the recently created Texas State Parks Board—Hunter visited Carlsbad Cave and McKittrick Canyon. The meeting guided Hunter's future advocacy for conservation. Second, the meeting and larger lobbying effort led to construction of Highway 61/180 from El Paso to Carlsbad, which promised to ease access to the caverns, Guadalupe Mountains, and McKittrick Canyon. This development had long-term consequences for tourism and marketability of the mountain region even if the State Parks Board backed off its initial interest in the mountain.[3]

There were several visits to the Guadalupe Mountains and McKittrick Canyon over the decades that sought to raise awareness about the wildlife characteristics of the region, or to promote it as a tourist destination. Willis Lee led a 1925 *National Geographic* expedition to Carlsbad that included a trip to the mountains, and in his article for the magazine, supported a park in the Guadalupes, specifically the beautiful McKittrick Canyon.[4] J. Stokely Ligon did a wildlife study for the U.S. Biological Survey for the state of New Mexico, and he supported public access to the Guadalupes. He also suggested a tourist loop from El Paso to El Capitan, Roswell, and White Sands in an effort to increase awareness of the regional landscape.[5] In 1931 Ben Thompson and George Wright from the University of California conducted a wildlife survey in several national parks, and when they visited Carlsbad they explored the lands included in a proposed extension of Carlsbad. They suggested protection.[6]

These initial expeditions were part of the tentative interest by the National Park Service in the Guadalupe Mountains, which sprung out of investment in Carlsbad Caverns, and perhaps momentum on the creation of Big Bend National Park to the south.⁷ In 1930 Roger Toll, the superintendent of Yellowstone National Park, visited Carlsbad and West Texas, where he spent four days in the proposed extension of Guadalupe into Carlsbad. He suggested transferring fifty-five square miles of high desert grassland and mountain range from the Lincoln National Forest. This addition would include the New Mexico sections of the Guadalupe Mountains down to the state line. The transfer of national forest land would connect Carlsbad with proposals to acquire land in McKittrick Canyon, "the Bowl," and the Guadalupe Peak-El Capitan complex. Toll believed that one large park was more manageable than two separate parks. Park service advisors Harold Brodie of Winnipeg, Manitoba, and Vance Prather, the secretary of the Kentucky State Park Commission, both suggested park status in the region.⁸

Park service employees, scientists, and boosters such as J. C. Hunter kept the idea of a national park alive. After Hunter purchased land in and around McKittrick, he hosted five hundred people at McKittrick Canyon in 1928. Members of the regional chambers of commerce attended as did politicians and newspaper reporters. This event kept the Guadalupe Mountain Park in the public eye. In 1931 the Guadalupe Mountain Park Association (GMPA) emerged as a branch of the El Paso Chamber of Commerce, with E. H. Simons, the manager of the chamber, serving as the secretary for the association. The GMPA and the chamber of commerce approached the chairman of the Texas Highway Commission to support the park.⁹

As boosters worked to convince state legislators and well-connected citizens to support a park, J. C. Hunter continued to purchase land and discuss his plans with park service officials. In 1934 Hunter invited Roger Toll back to the area. Hunter said that he was willing to sell his forty-three thousand acres to the NPS for $237,000. He even offered a one-thousand-acre section of McKittrick to the Texas State Parks Board in the hope that the board would donate that land to the NPS and stimulate acquisition. Lyndon Johnson worked as the state director of the Texas National Youth Administration to build roadside parks across Texas, thus making efforts like Hunter's more attractive. Hunter even worked with E. H. Simmons to convince Herbert Maier of the NPS to join representatives from the Texas State Parks Board for a visit.¹⁰ In 1934 Arno B. Cammerer, who replaced Horace Albright as director of the park service, listened to Toll.

Cammerer proposed to the secretary of the interior Harold Ickes that the Guadalupe Mountains in Texas and land in New Mexico be administered under Carlsbad. In 1938 an expedition comprised of Cammerer, Herbert Maier, and the acting regional director of Region III in Santa Fe traversed the high country of the Guadalupes. The group endorsed a park and sent their findings to the secretary of the interior.[11]

Hunter moved forward even though the NPS remained lukewarm. In 1938 he again offered to sell a one-thousand-acre site in McKittrick Canyon to Texas, but he said that the CCC needed to build a road connecting it to the new highway. Texas Highway Commission officials visited McKittrick and agreed that an access road would be necessary, but the state legislature balked at the cost. Hunter pressed ahead with E. H. Simons to convince the State Parks Board to visit. Simons brought the *El Paso Times* to cover the event, and it published a full-page story with photos. D. D. Obert, the assistant landscape architect for the NPS, prepared a report for the board, recommending purchase of Hunter's land.[12] These efforts tried to capitalize on the decision of President Franklin D. Roosevelt to add 39,488 acres to Carlsbad Caverns, bringing the boundaries of that park relatively close to the Guadalupe Mountains.[13]

The expansion of Carlsbad, Hunter's offer to the state, and the advertising campaigns of boosters sustained the park idea. Wendell Little, the planning coordinator for the NPS, wrote to Director Newton Drury about his trip to the Guadalupes in 1940. Little recognized the scenic value of Guadalupe but pointed to NPS policy against purchasing land from private entities. He agreed with an idea floating around to use funds from the visitor center of the relatively new Carlsbad Caverns National Park to purchase land in the Guadalupes, but that option gained little traction.[14] To make matters worse, expansion of the NPS slowed during the 1940s due to the war and the leadership style of Director Drury.[15]

Environmental Politics and the National Park Service at Mid-Century

Extensive societal changes contributed to a shift in park service policy after the war, which in turn improved the chances for the creation of Guadalupe Mountains National Park. After surviving the Great Depression and fighting World War II, many Americans hoped to enjoy the prosperity that they believed they had won after decades of sacrifice. The G.I. Bill opened higher education and FHA loans made homes a reality for many families. Economic growth and rising wages increased Americans' hopes that their standard of living would steadily improve. Booming highway construction and a desire for leisure led Americans to jump into their cars and drive to the national parks. At the same time, a growing concern about pollution and development pressured the NPS and Congress to reevaluate policy toward land acquisition, which opened the door for the creation of Guadalupe Mountains National Park.[16]

The creation of a park in the Guadalupe Mountains revealed a system in transition. Many of the reasons behind Guadalupe reflected traditional rationales for preserving natural places. From the establishment of Yellowstone National Park in Wyoming during the 1870s through the creation of the park service itself in 1916, the approval of parks emphasized "monumental" and sublime characteristics, as well as their protection of wildness for the spiritual sustenance of an industrializing nation. These objectives reflected Victorian Romanticism and Progressive Era concerns about nature and the need for respite from the ills of modernity. Occasionally the park service promoted, and Congress approved, parks for their cultural and historical value. Nonetheless, NPS policy remained ensconced in the philosophy of monumentalism and America's national identity, something that resembled a "nationalism of nature."[17]

During the 1930s these values undergirded a handful of landscapes in the Southwest, but support for a Guadalupe park remained elusive. Grand Canyon, Mesa Verde, Big Bend, Carlsbad, and sites in New Mexico formed a ring around the Guadalupes, and served as models for advocates of the West Texas park. In particular, Big Bend seemed to offer a particularly appropriate example of state purchase of private land and the eventual transfer of that land to the federal government.[18] Supporters argued that Carlsbad and the Guadalupes could contribute to a regional loop of monuments and parks throughout the region.[19] And finally, the 1930s and 1940s saw the park service wanting for the "visionary" leadership of Horace Albright and Stephen Mather, as more bureaucratic directors such as Arno B. Cammerer "doggedly followed existing policies without the innate flexibility and responsiveness of their predecessors."[20] Supporters appealed to traditionalism, but entrenched policy hampered efforts to use federal dollars to purchase private land.

Despite the desire among middle-class Americans to visit the national parks, divisions within the NPS mitigated against a park in the Guadalupe Mountains. Thomas Boles, the superintendent of Carlsbad Canyon, complained about the 1935 decision to divide the park system into regional districts because it forced superintendents to deal with regional directors instead of the central office in Washington, D.C. This added layer of bureaucracy made it more difficult to convince Congress to consider protected status for the Guadalupes. It arguably placed the decision in the hands of the regional director, who might have been more amenable to increasing the numbers of parks within his jurisdiction, but he could just as easily have been beholden to local property owners and the needs of preexisting sites. The park service also inherited a greater number of responsibilities during the 1930s that increased the workloads and demands upon superintendents.[21]

During the 1940s the National Park Service stood at a crossroads. The Victorian and Progressive Era pillars of romanticism and nationalist conservation dominated policy, but new scientific rationales for protecting natural areas emerged. The pressures of rampant growth alarmed a cadre of professionals espousing ideas about ecology and ecosystems. Many of these scientists embraced policies to protect natural places for their biological characteristics, as well as for the wellbeing of the planet. Scientists and scientifically oriented individuals entered the park service and began influencing policy. Newton Drury, though restrained by budgets and ideology, was the "first true preservationist to take the reins of the agency and the first from a professional conservation background." In 1941 the park service had already incorporated public education into its mission, so it could use the sciences and the young field of ecology to preserve natural areas. For instance, the creation of Everglades National Park in 1947 marked the first park based on ecological uniqueness, and thus opened the door for the Guadalupe Mountains and their geological importance.[22]

As the NPS moved through this era of transition, the professionalization of staff left an important legacy. It hired more employees holding degrees in science related fields, rather than landscape architecture. It also began limiting an individual superintendent's tenure at a park to three years. This policy sought to reduce entrenched interests and subsume personalities to park service regulations. In light of this shift, the NPS transferred Carlsbad Caverns superintendent, Thomas Boles, to Hot Springs National Park in Arkansas, after twenty years at the caverns. In that transfer the caverns lost their most enthusiastic, if unorthodox and temperamental, advocate, who took with him the institutional memory associated with the creation the park.[23]

Professionalization evolved in tandem with competition for control over Western landscapes as the U.S. Forest Service, the Bureau of Reclamation, and the Department of Defense grew. Congress supported the new goals of the NPS, symbolized by MISSION-66, a decade-long program to expand the park system between 1956 and 1966. This effort reflected the consensus on public recreation as a national good, the link between park visitation and "patriotic feeling and participation," and the booming economy. In addition, scientists that once stood on the fringes of the bureaucracy were now gaining employment within an evolving park service that increasingly embraced its role as protector of wildlife, natural scenery, ecological marvels, and American cultural history.[24] MISSION-66 also sought to increase visitor attendance in time for the fiftieth anniversary of the creation of the park service. The NPS modernized its facilities, improved its educational component, and revised its interpretation purposes. The traditional characteristics of parks—natural beauty, wildlife preservation, and national pride, though on a smaller scale—helped the advocates of a Guadalupe park. The growing influence of science also benefited Guadalupe because El Capitan was an unrivaled example of a Permian Basin geological feature, and because "the Bowl" was a nearly pristine wildlife habitat. With MISSION-66 in the background, each of these shifts helped set the stage for the creation of a national park in the Guadalupe Mountains.[25]

Creating Guadalupe Mountains National Park

The creation of Guadalupe Mountains National Park benefited from shifts in policy and the convergence of regional, state, and national interests. Importantly, it was one of the first, if not the first, park created by outright purchase of private property. This was in contrast to its neighboring parks: Carlsbad was underneath the Lincoln National Forest, which the federal government already managed, and Big Bend, which the state of Texas transferred to the federal government. The park is also important because of the cast of characters involved with its creation (a petroleum geologist, a wealthy rancher, a real estate broker, a U.S. senator, a U.S. congressman from Texas, and a chief justice of the U.S. Supreme Court); the speed in which it was created (six years); and its location within Texas, a state skeptical of the federal government.

Wallace Pratt, J. C. Hunter, and J. C. Hunter Jr. contributed the largest amount of land to the park. Before a heart attack killed Hunter in 1945, he had amassed forty thousand acres to which his son added over thirty thousand. Indeed, Hunter influenced Pratt to transfer McKittrick Canyon to the park service, which Pratt eventually did after the Pratts made McKittrick their home. Between 1958 and 1961, Pratt donated 5,632 acres to the park service.[26] Hunter Jr. followed the lead of his father, but after Pratt donated his land, Pratt helped Hunter Jr. decide the fate of the 72,000-acre Guadalupe Mountain Ranch. Hunter Jr. could not donate his land like Pratt, and he operated the ranch as a hunting and recreational site with a few sheep, goats, and cattle. Hunter Jr. kept the land healthy through the careful management of elk, turkey, trout, and other animals that his father had introduced. But as he grew older, he worried that he would leave his family with a large piece of property and large taxes, so he entertained ways to sell the ranch.

Hunter Jr. hired Glenn Biggs, an employee of the Abilene based real estate firm of Millerman and Millerman, to help sell the Guadalupe Mountain Ranch. This was one of the single most important decisions in the struggle to create the park. Biggs was born in 1933 in Eola, Texas, and attended Baylor University. A Southern Baptist with a big personality and restless energy, Biggs graduated in 1956, and after a brief stint in law school, he landed a job with the Abilene Chamber of Commerce. Biggs stayed with the chamber until 1959 when he joined Millerman and Millerman. Here he honed his innate people skills with professional experience and gained contacts through the firm and his membership in the First Baptist Church. He met Hunter Jr. through the church, and they became good friends.[27]

When Hunter and Biggs began working together in late 1960, they agreed on three main options: sell the ranch as a private operation, trade it for mineral investments of equal value, or sell it to a philanthropy that would donate it to the NPS. Although the idea to sell the ranch directly to the government had entered their minds, it had not fully formed because of the NPS policy against purchasing private property.[28] Biggs jumped into the project with vigor. They advertised the ranch for $1.5 million due to the scenic value.[29]

After six months trying to sell the ranch, Biggs's feelings shifted. He embraced Hunter Jr.'s view of the scenic and ecological importance of the mountains and agreed to preserve them in their present state.[30] Several concurrent events influenced Hunter Jr.'s decision to instruct Biggs to explore selling the ranch to the government. Pratt endorsed the creation of a park through letters to newspapers, businesspeople, congressional leaders, and colleagues in the oil and gas industry. In addition, NPS officials conducted investigations in 1961 to assess the biological and geological resources of the ranch. Finally, regional chambers of commerce supported a park. In the light of these developments, Biggs ramped up his promotion of the ranch and the idea of creating a national park.[31]

FIGURE 4. Glenn Biggs sitting atop the Guadalupe Mountains, circa 1963.
—Glenn Biggs Collection, Southwest Special Collections,
Texas Tech University, Lubbock, Texas.

At the behest of Biggs and Hunter, in 1961 the NPS surveyed the ranch and mountains. The NPS became more interested when it realized it might lose lands that were in great condition. In March 1962, after receiving the NPS report on the ranch, the secretary of the interior Stewart Udall indicated that the property merited consideration, but he reminded advocates of the difficulties involved with transferring the land to the federal government. The open interest of the secretary and the NPS in the ranch, as well as a concern about sale to a private corporation, redirected the political winds toward transferring the lands to the government.[32]

Biggs maintained communication with the NPS and the Department of the Interior, hoping to bring representatives to the ranch. Writing to the regional director Thomas J. Allen, Biggs expressed his hope of bringing Secretary Udall to the mountains, "if we could ever get him on the Ranch so that he might see this beautiful part of the country, we would have an excellent chance to push this through."[33] Hunter also knew that Udall was crucial to approval of the park. In one of several letters to Udall, Hunter wrote, "This letter is to invite you to make a personal visit to the Guadalupe Mountains of Texas to view the area that has been proposed by the Park Service as a desirable addition to the McKittrick Canyon property now held by the Park Service. If you are able to accept this invitation, all arrangements will be made strictly in accord with your wishes. It is my belief that you will enjoy an outing in the Guadalupe Mountains." Udall replied he was interested in learning more.[34]

Wallace Pratt was an important ally to Biggs and Hunter Jr. In one of his early letters to Pratt, Biggs informed him of their efforts to sell the ranch and obtain federal support. Biggs confided in Pratt that he thought Hunter Jr. had a fifty-fifty chance to convince Udall to visit the ranch, and if Udall did so, Biggs believed their chances increased considerably to preserve the land. He also knew the value of Pratt's endorsement, so Biggs invited Pratt to join a group of people to visit the ranch. In his characteristic earnestness, Biggs wrote, "Although I have not yet met you I feel I know you, for I have met many individuals who know you personally and who have expressed to me the vast source of knowledge which you hold regarding the fabulous Guadalupe Mountains."[35] Pratt agreed with Hunter Jr. and Biggs, and in one of his several letters he wrote, "I think you are aware that I should like very much to see all the

Guadalupe Mountain area go into a public recreation park and wildlife refuge."[36]

By 1963 Biggs, Hunter Jr., and Pratt had created a network of boosters, lobbyists, politicians, newspapers, and naturalists supporting a park. The tactic of bringing people to the ranch was especially ingenious. This was part of his goal to get people to have a sense of personal ownership in the idea of making the ranch into a park. This, in turn, formed the core of Biggs's broader strategy: advertise the historical, environmental, geological, and scenic attributes of the ranch to newspapers, chambers of commerce, and philanthropic organizations; contact and educate politicians; and work closely with the NPS and secretary of the interior. In the process he hoped to work the Texas connection via people such as Senator Ralph Yarborough to gain the attention of President Johnson and Congress more broadly.[37]

This strategy bore fruit as local groups and politicians joined in the cause. Importantly, U.S. congressman at large for Texas, Joe Pool, picked up the idea of a park and ran with it across the state. In January 1963 Pool introduced House Bill 3100 to the U.S. House of Representatives. Pool was motivated as much by politics as conservation, and he saw it as an avenue to increase his own profile.[38] Pool's action surprised Hunter Jr. and Biggs, but they supported the effort. Biggs wrote to Pool, "Inadequacy of words prohibit me from truly expressing to you my appreciation for your interest in the Guadalupe Mountain ranch. It is a tremendous undertaking and I am firmly convinced that a successful effort can be achieved."[39] With an endorsement from Joe Pool, the attention of Udall and the park service, and the momentum of local boosters, in 1963 Biggs confirmed local support for the proposal. The chambers of commerce endorsed a park, as did the El Paso Women's Club, the local chapter of the Sierra Club, the El Paso Democratic Party, and the El Paso mayor. El Paso County judge Glenn Woodward wrote to Biggs, "The country is certainly some of the most beautiful I have ever seen and I agree wholeheartedly that it should be part of a National Park."[40]

As Biggs and Hunter Jr. organized trips and wrote letters to newspapers across New Mexico and Texas, they crafted a historical narrative of the mountains to create an enticing sense of place time. Biggs wrote to Olin Ashley, editor of the *Odessa American*, providing him with this emerging narrative about the mountains and Hunter Jr.'s ranch. Its unique geological and biological features attracted Native Americans, and as the Spanish entered the region, they noted its monumental stature. Migrants going west used it as a geographical marker and the Butterfield Overland Mail established a refilling stop at the Pinery. The mountains were a site for conflicts between Indians and the military, and eventually they were settled by rugged settlers and plucky homesteaders. In the twentieth century, farmers and ranchers tried to make the region productive but aridity stunted their efforts. Only the Frijole Ranch flourished. In the 1920s, J. C. Hunter Sr. and Wallace Pratt began purchasing the land to create a national park. The Guadalupe Mountains were a symbol of the open spaces and grand vistas of the American West, and although Texans had their suspicions about federal activity, this park would bring the state national recognition.[41]

The cadre of proponents solidified the narrative of the mountains through invitations to nature and sports writers and newspaper editors to visit the ranch and pen their own stories extolling the region's beauty. A trip in May 1963, organized for more than fifty writers, was especially crucial for advertising the park.[42] An impressive six page article in the May 14, 1963, Sunday edition of the *Carlsbad Current-Argus* included photographs of the "breathtaking wilderness scenery" of the Guadalupe Mountains.[43] In an article in the *Dallas Morning News*, the popular nature writer Frank Tolbert talked about his trip to the mountains, where he learned about stories of hidden gold, Native Americans and the military, the geological qualities of the region, and how Hunter Jr. had preserved the mountains in a "pristine state."[44]

With a chorus of advocates from Santa Fe to Dallas, Biggs widened the campaign. Biggs wrote to O. C. Fisher in the U.S. House of Representatives, urging him to use federal funds to purchase the ranch: "Mr. Hunter, under personal financial sacrifice, has preserved the Ranch just as it was in the days of the Apaches. Very little grazing has taken place on a great part of the Ranch." Biggs added that Hunter Jr. "preserved it as well as if the National Park System had been operating it for 30 years. The very interesting part of this great piece of land relates to the fact that it is located in a semi-arid section and out of this dry section is this oasis. In my mind it should clearly be preserved for it is an unusual piece of property and as you very well know, none of it has been today."[45] Fisher replied that he had enjoyed the visit to the ranch last December: "I certainly share your views about the Guadalupe Mountain Ranch. I think it would be wonderful . . . for the public."[46]

As Pool pressed a national park bill in Washington, D.C., and Texas, and as Hunter Jr. and Biggs firmed up regional support of the park, word spread of the beauty of the ranch. The principals organized another trip to the mountains in July 1963 for luminaries in El Paso and far West Texas. Talking with the *Carlsbad Current-Argus*, Pool claimed that the ranch was "the only place in our state where you can find such a wide variety of wild life. This is exactly the type of natural beauty that we need to preserve." The growing knowledge about the park eased communication with higher-level political leaders and civic organizations. Biggs gained the ear of Senator Ralph Yarborough, who shepherded the Padre Island National Seashore legislation through Congress, and they began correspondence.[47] Yarborough wrote to Biggs, "Your aggressive efforts on behalf of the preservation of this beautiful site have been instrumental in pushing this worthy proposal to this stage. Be assured that I shall certainly do everything possible to obtain early and favorable action on this bill."[48] Even Texas governor Connally was reportedly planning a trip to the ranch.[49]

In fall 1963 political momentum swung toward creation of a national park. Due in large part to Biggs's efforts, on October 31, the National Parks Advisory Board inspected the ranch and McKittrick Canyon, and the Advisory Board of the Big Bend National Park supported the idea. The Carlsbad Caverns superintendent told Hunter Jr. that the NPS Advisory Board visit to the ranch went very well. "I know the board was tremendously impressed with the potential of the entire area proposed as a National Park." The secretary of the interior Stewart Udall announced the positive results of the NPS survey of the ranch requested by Pool's House Bill 3100.[50] Following this momentum, on November 7, 1963, Senator Yarborough introduced Senate Bill 2296 calling for the creation of Guadalupe Mountains National Park. On December 2, 1963, Pool introduced a new House Bill 9312 for the park, based on the suggested changes of Biggs to Pool, and on December 4 Yarborough adjusted his bill in accordance with Pool's.[51]

Biggs, Hunter Jr., Pratt, and Pool continued promoting the park, and especially Biggs and Pool kept up their efforts across the state and nation. By winter 1964 Biggs had support in New Mexico from Carlsbad, the congressional delegation, the governor's office, and the NPS in Santa Fe. Ralph Yarborough was fully engaged with the process and confirmed that the Department of the Interior and NPS would "formally recommend that the Guadalupe Peak area in far West Texas be made a national park."[52] And Governor Connally visited the ranch.[53]

The proponents of the park struggled to maintain the visibility of the ranch in light of the tumultuous events of the era. In January 1964 Biggs and Tom Diamond, the leader of the El Paso Democratic Committee, planned a trip for the El Paso Ladies Chamber of Commerce to visit the ranch.[54] Talking with the *San Angelo Standard Times*, Hunter Jr. said he was "very pleased as to the progress that has been made in connection with introduction of the bill made by Sen. Yarborough and are quite hopeful that culmination of all efforts will be the creation of the Guadalupe National Park." In his typical humility, Hunter Jr. thanked the "people over West Texas and US who have been very interested in

FIGURE 5. Secretary of the Interior Stewart Udall (with field glasses), J. C. Hunter Jr. (plaid coat), and Glenn Biggs (far right) at the Guadalupe Mountains. —Glenn Biggs Collection, Southwest Special Collections, Texas Tech University, Lubbock, Texas.

passage is best demonstrated by the hundreds of letters, resolutions, and other evidence of support given."[55]

Attention from federal leaders catapulted the proposal forward. Due to pressure from Biggs, on December 13, 1964, Secretary Udall visited McKittrick Canyon on his way to El Paso. Udall endorsed the project and estimated that the park would be approved in two years.[56] The approval from Udall and Connally helped legitimize the Guadalupe park but the support from one unlikely individual, William O. Douglas, Chief Justice of the United States Supreme Court, accelerated the process. Douglas had ties to the region, and he was an avid outdoorsman and naturalist. He was also writing a book in which the Guadalupes would receive their own chapter.[57] Douglas's December 1964 visit was not promoted as widely as those of Udall and Connally, but Douglas was a respected jurist whose support could only help the cause.[58]

In 1965 there was more of the same strategy, as endorsements and

FIGURE 6. Glenn Biggs (left), U.S. Supreme Court Justice William O. Douglas (center), and unidentified individual (right, possible a member of the Rockefeller family).
—Glenn Biggs Collection, Southwest Special Collection, Texas Tech University, Lubbock, Texas.

support continued to stream in. In January, Randal F. Dickey Jr., chairman of the Sierra Club Conservation Committee, informed Henry H. During, the superintendent of Carlsbad Caverns National Park, that the Sierra Club Board of Directors endorsed the park.[59] Tom Diamond informed Senator Yarborough that El Pasoans supported the park, while Sierra Club members in Houston sent a letter of support to Senator Alan Bible of the National Parks Subcommittee within the Senate Interior and Insular Affairs Committee. They told Bible about a trip by Club members to the ranch and referred to a documentary they were using to promote the mountains, which they referred to as a "West-Texas Shangri-La." They even volunteered to testify in Congress.[60]

The group was elated by congressional hearings called for by none other than President Lyndon B. Johnson, and his proposal to use money from the 1964 Land and Water Conservation Fund Act to purchase the land. This fund would help pay for land for parks from new and existing revenues from preexisting parks.[61] Hypothetically this would appease conservatives who opposed use of taxpayer dollars for purchasing private lands for public parks. Johnson's interest in Guadalupe was related to a larger effort, "Parks for America Decade," in recognition of the concerns about pollution and the interest in environmentalism and recreation. The Guadalupes were in this plan to create a dozen new parks across the country.[62]

House hearings were scheduled for July 20, 1965, with the Senate to hold hearings in two weeks. Representative Joe Pool reintroduced House Bill 9312 and Representative Richard White introduced the revised bill, House Bill 698, since the park was in White's district. Yarborough introduced Senate Bill 295.[63] As Pool, White, and Yarborough tinkered with the bills, Biggs organized witnesses to testify in Congress and to write statements for the Congressional Record. Although the hearings before the House National Parks Committee were brief, transcripts were effusive.[64] Wallace Pratt discussed his relationship with the mountain and McKittrick Canyon: "I speak as a geologist at the end of a very long career in the profession of geology, and I speak also as one who has lived and made his home for 15 years at the mouth of McKittrick Canyon." He added, "At the end of the war in 1945 when I retired from active life, Mrs. Pratt and I built ourselves a home on the lower slopes of the Mountains. I know of the interest this territory has for the general public." He complimented J. C. Hunter and his son for their conservation of the mountains. "I want to commend the remarkable wisdom of my neighbor, Mr. J. C. Hunter Jr., and his father before him, whose persistent efforts have brought under one ownership by far the larger part of the area that will constitute Guadalupe Mountains National Park."65

Comments from Senator Yarborough were especially important. Yarborough affirmed that "there is no opposition to this. Never in the history of any bill that I have worked with have I found more enthusiasm and stronger and more unanimous approval of my home state than I have found on the Guadalupe Mountain National Park proposal." He mentioned the role of Hunter Jr., who had "resisted all offers to sell it for uses which would clutter up the area and not be in keeping with a national park area. He has managed his ranch so as to preserve the environmental and wildlife value, in hopes that someday the beautiful area could belong to the public." That endorsement from a popular senator contributed immeasurably to the cause.66

Final hearings in the Senate nonetheless experienced a year's delay. During the interim Biggs and Hunter Jr. organized a trip for U.S. senator Alan Bible and others in April 1966. Bible told reporters that he was "very encouraged the Guadalupe Mountain National Park project will go through this session." He also commented that he "was very impressed with the area—even more so than I'd expected, because of the great variety of plant life and the uniqueness of coming right out of the desert floor into this valley of rich vegetation."67 The June 1 Congressional Record included a report from the Committee on Interior and Insular Affairs acknowledging the creation of Guadalupe Mountains National Park. It authorized the expenditure of $12,162,000 for infrastructure development and the acquisition of 77,582 acres of land: 60,574 in Culberson County and 16,944 in Hudspeth County.68 When the Senate took up the issue of the park in August 1966, Senator Yarborough again made his support clear. He reiterated last year's testimony in the House and added that his personal ties with the mountains made him invested in the park and gave him an insider's view as to the importance of the region. "I lived for three and a half years in El Paso, Texas, and first saw El Capitan, the southernmost bluff of this mountain in 1927." Since that initial view of the highest point in Texas nearly a half-century ago, Yarborough had understood the value of the mountain for the state and nation.69

A late summer recess allowed the Senate to make progress on its version of the bill. On October 6 Senator Alan Bible submitted a report from the Senate Committee on Interior and Insular Affairs favoring the national park. It acknowledged that the NPS would need additional private land beyond the tracts from Pratt and Hunter Jr. It reiterated the geological, biological, wildlife, and scenic attributes that made the park attractive and it quoted Wallace A. Pratt and J. C. Hunter Jr. as the central figures of the campaign for park status. Assistant Secretary of the Interior Stanley E. Cain in his addendum to the report echoed the sentiments of Pratt and Hunter that this site was an important addition. He added that the subsurface oil, gas, and mineral rights within the boundaries of the park were negligible despite the claims of the state of Texas.

After amendments relative to mineral rights and land-acquisition funding limits, President Johnson signed legislation creating Guadalupe Mountains National Park on October 15, 1966.[70] This was the official birth of the park, which after an additional several years of wrangling would encompass over eighty-two thousand acres of desert grassland, salt flats, the highest point in Texas, massive barrier reef geological formations, and more than forty thousand acres of wilderness. Passage of the legislation required the herculean efforts of a small group of individuals who hoped to see this unique ecosystem preserved in perpetuity. It was a bold step for the park service because it signaled a potential shift in policy toward purchase of private property for public benefit. It also epitomized how citizens could cooperate to pull national park policy out of its doldrums and into a more dynamic arena that reflected the new and changing realities of the modern era.

Before Biggs agreed to help Hunter Jr. market his sprawling Guadalupe Mountain Ranch, there seemed to be little chance that Hunter's seventy-two thousand acres would benefit anyone other than a very wealthy individual. Lack of financial wherewithal, disinterest on the part of the state of Texas, insufficient publicity, and NPS policies stymied boosters and preservationists. In particular, the fact that the lands were private property created the biggest obstacle to setting aside the mountains as a park. Regardless of the geological and scenic value of El Capitan, Guadalupe Peak, and the mixed conifer forest of "the Bowl," legislators at the state and national level could not fathom purchasing property and changing its status to a public park. It would take a small revolution in thinking to consider such a measure.

That great leap occurred after World War II when Hunter Jr., Pratt, Biggs, and a dedicated cadre of individuals decided to preserve the Guadalupe Mountains in perpetuity for the benefit of the entire nation. Thus, after decades of frustration, Biggs and Hunter Jr. vaulted forward in the 1960s to wage a nonstop advertising campaign to educate the public about the scenic beauty and the geological value of the mountains and the highest point in Texas. Building upon local and national allies, such as Joe Pool, Ralph Yarborough, William O. Douglass, and others, the group persevered through the Cuban Missile Crisis, the Bay of Pigs, the assassinations of President Kennedy and Martin Luther King Jr., and important civil rights legislation. After less than a decade, a short time in the history of establishing national parks, the efforts of Biggs and Hunter Jr. came to fruition. Though complex issues such as surface and mineral rights had to pass through the state of Texas, by 1972 the park was established and officially open for business. Since then, it has been a small but sparkling gem in the system of public lands across the United States.

CHAPTER NINE
A National Park for the Twenty-First Century

As a new addition to the National Park System within the conservative state of Texas, the Guadalupe Mountains National Park followed only some of the common paths traversed by larger and more iconic units of the park system. This "desert island," in an isolated corner of the Southwest borderlands, suffered from a paucity of federal funding. It sat in the shadow of the Grand Canyon, Yellowstone, and Yosemite, and it lacked the allure of Big Bend with its precipitous canyon walls and winding Rio Grande. Even Carlsbad Caverns attracted a tenfold greater number of visitors with its foreboding depths and its whimsical rock formations. The park nonetheless sparked the imaginations of Texans as the highest point in the state, and it enjoyed a period of stardom as it was supported by political luminaries such as Ralph Yarborough and President Johnson himself. But federal funds to build a visitor center, establish trails and campgrounds, and hire permanent staff were hard to squeeze from an increasingly embattled Congress. The boundaries of the park were fraught with contested land titles, and oil and gas companies continued to claim that they could find oil underneath the mountain and salt flats. In short, after the fanfare associated with the establishment of the park died down, the difficult business of opening the park to visitors began.

Guadalupe Mountains National Park lurched forward during the late 1960s and early 1970s, as the country faced one of its most tumultuous eras. During the first decade of its existence, park staff coped with rudimentary conditions on the ground: lack of water, electricity, and infrastructure; organizational challenges that included oversight by the Superintendent at Carlsbad; and unanswered questions about land titles and property boundaries. Employees worked with the regional headquarters in Santa Fe to draft a management plan, stabilize historic structures, conduct wildlife surveys, and tackle questions of access to "the Bowl" at the top of the mountain. Moreover, the staff held public meetings to discuss the designation of a large percentage of the park as wilderness, or, alternately, to construct a road or tramway in the park.

The end of the twentieth century brought great changes in the American economy and political system, both of which directly impacted the national park. The election of Ronald Reagan and his appointment of James Watt as the secretary of the interior ushered in an era of reduced spending for public projects, which translated into austerity in the park system. Local resistance to the perceived heavy hand of the federal government reflected opposition to centralized control of public lands and resources. Alternately, the elections of George H. W. Bush, and to a greater degree Bill Clinton, caused the pendulum to swing back to policies favoring national parks. The Guadalupe Mountains saw the construction of the headquarters and visitor center, elaboration of the trails, and acquisition of new properties. Thus, the national politics of environmentalism loomed large over this Southwestern park.

The new millennium was also characterized by shifts in management of wildlife and natural resources, low visitor attendance, expansion of educational interpretation, and swings in federal appropriations. The terrorist attacks on September 11, 2001, transformed national priorities and diverted funds to the new Department of Homeland Security and agencies associated with national defense. Parks such as Guadalupe had to survive on shoestring budgets that barely met the basic needs of payroll, utilities, and infrastructure maintenance. Alternately, a greater awareness of fire management techniques helped managers shift away from practices that allowed fuels to build up and cause megafires, to new regimes of selective burning and natural fire burning cycles. Lastly, the Guadalupe Mountains made strides reaching out to the general public, attracting visitors, and building bridges with the Mescalero Apache. In sum, the Guadalupe Mountains National Park has met its mandate to make accessible the wonders of the natural world and the beauty of wilderness in the American Southwest.

Environmentalism and the Changing United States

The National Park Service rapidly expanded during the 1960s and 1970s, one of the most tumultuous eras in U.S. history. While the service added parks and grew the bureaucracy, the nation as a whole returned to a familiar series of debates about the reasons for creating parks and how they represented the nation's heritage. Traditionalists embraced monumentalism and the epic narratives associated with American history, while newer voices promoted ecological rationales alongside the preservation of culture and history. Robert Sterling Yard's pre-WWII beliefs in the sanctity of parks as places to worship God through nature now complimented the scientific and cultural advocates who were less concerned about Yard's purism than the creation of the parks to protect species habitats in the wake of environmental pollution. These rationales sometimes conflicted as they were rooted in different though not incompatible paradigms.[1]

In fact, the romantics and the scientists found common ground in the protection of natural places from the excesses of the modern world. Monumentalism and the nascent field of ecology, along with growing concerns about suburban sprawl and industrial pollution, spoke to the cultural, economic, and political shifts bracketing the years surrounding the approval of the park and its official opening in 1972. The Land and Water Conservation Fund Act, passed by Congress in 1965, provided a mechanism to fund new parks and reflected a congressional sea change in views about nature. Approved before America became embroiled in Vietnam, when President Johnson rode a wave of support for the Great Society programs that promised to end poverty and provide "guns and butter" for a booming nation, the fund reflected optimism about the country's ability to protect its natural resources. Specifically, the fund used revenues from offshore oil and natural gas production for expansion and improvement of parks and national recreation areas. It also stipulated cooperation with state and local agencies.[2]

As the American GDP increased, the federal government passed legislation advancing environmental protection and natural preservation. The 1964 Wilderness Act established the National Wilderness Preservation System, which consisted of areas within a park that were in a "pristine" state and that warranted additional protection from development. As the trend toward preservation grew, it also included elements of national heritage and culture, as seen in the 1966 National Historic Preservation Act, which mandated assessing, preserving, and managing those resources. In 1970 the Nixon Administration passed the National Environmental Protection Act, which was the foundation for the Environmental Protection Agency.[3] All of these policies created a fertile ground for strengthening the National Park System in the 1970s.

Opening the Park's Doors and Welcoming Visitors

These national debates structured the realities facing local residents, park employees, and regional supporters during the early years of advocacy in favor of establishing Guadalupe Mountains National Park. The signature of President Johnson in 1966 enabling the establishment of the park, for instance, did not immediately lead to a new and functional unit, as there were numerous details to address that escaped policy makers in Washington, D.C. One of the most nettlesome issues was the clarification of boundaries and the purchase or transfer of additional lands into the new park. The enabling legislation that gave birth to the park provided that land would be accessible per the map drafted by the Department of the Interior and that the sections owned by families such as the Hammack's would be purchased or traded. Contracts for purchase of new lands would be available upon appropriation, but the staff at the regional office in Santa Fe foresaw difficulties. Funds for the administration of McKittrick Canyon, the most dynamic and highly visited section, would be shifted to Guadalupe Mountains National Park immediately. Additionally, Congress envisioned appropriating $1,800,000 for land and $10,400,000 for development of trails, roads, facilities, and infrastructure within the next few years to make the park accessible to visitors.[4]

With the Texas legislature, the issue of mineral rights and oil and natural gas leases remained a subject of great debate. Senator Joe Christie of El Paso and Representative Gene Hendryx of Alpine introduced bills for the conveyance of mineral rights tied to forty-five thousand acres of Hunter's land to the federal government even as Texas land commissioner Jerry Sadler believed the state should retain them. Sadler argued that the state was better suited than the federal government to run a park funded by the very mineral leases tied to the land, although he seemed to have forgotten that Texas historically refused to support a park in the Guadalupes. The West Texas Geological Society, which was difficult to portray as a liberal environmental group, opposed Sadler and asserted that the value of the park as a tourist destination outweighed the dollars generated from mineral rights or oil and natural gas leases. Sadler did not pursue the issue because the political winds seemed to be working against him.

After a last-ditch effort by Texaco requesting the state to postpone a decision on the legislation, Texas governor John Connally signed a bill on March 6, conveying mineral rights to the federal government. Texaco relented and donated its remaining mineral rights, hoping to exploit the gesture and improve its profile in the court of public opinion. Congressman Richard White facilitated the donation and praised the company as a "good citizen of West Texas." Proponents of the park accepted the "gift" and moved forward to find the $1.8 million for land purchases and $10.4 million for infrastructure development.[5]

The hoped for momentum did not emerge, and Senator Yarborough decided to exert some of his political muscle in Congress, which had become stingy with its funds as the costs of the Vietnam War grew. According to the *El Paso Herald-Post*, "with the snout of war devouring federal funds in a lather, and the rising clamor in the cities for more spending on urban problems, Guadalupe Mountains National Park has no real crack at getting $1 million out of Congress this year."[6] Surprisingly Congress agreed to $354,000 for the park, particularly for a down payment on 58,878 acres of Hunter Ranch. When it looked less likely that Congress would release the full $1,800,000, the Department of the Interior used some of that amount to purchase various small tracts of land. Funds for the purchase of the Hunter Ranch were harder to coax from Congress as political infighting pushed the Guadalupe park to the bottom of the priority list. The greatest resistance came from Representative Julia Butler Hansen from Washington, who chaired the House Appropriations Subcommittee. When George J. Hartzog, director of the park service, appeared before the committee, Hansen was recalcitrant. Dismissing his request, she said "if you think I am going to throw away money to make someone a millionaire, you are wrong."[7]

Frustrated with the process, Yarborough in 1968 persuaded the Senate Appropriations Committee to earmark $200,000 for land acquisition, which he thought would be enough to serve as a down payment on Hunter's land. He then convinced Secretary Udall to approve a $1.2 million expenditure from the Land and Water Conservation Fund to purchase the remaining tracts of land from J. C. Hunter Jr. With Yarborough pushing it through the committees, and with Udall's support, Johnson endorsed the measure in late 1968. When Congress approved the final funding in September 1969, the money was now in place to conclude the purchase of more than seventy-three thousand acres of land. This was one of the most important measures paving the way for the official opening of the park on October 6, 1972.[8]

Writing the existence of the park in the National Register of Historic Places and "opening its doors" for business did not resolve all of the questions posed by the creation of a new unit in the American West. For instance, debate over how to apply the Wilderness Act of 1964 in the Guadalupe Mountains immediately elicited a range of responses. The act stipulated that the secretary of the interior assess roadless areas of more than five thousand acres within a park and suggest whether they be included in the National Wilderness Preservation System. The genesis for protecting wilderness across the nation dated back at least to Aldo Leopold in the early twentieth century. By the 1930s the U.S. Forest Service created mechanisms to protect primitive sections of land, and The Wilderness Society helped raise awareness of the issue. The idea languished during World War II, until the posthumous publication of Leopold's *Sand County Almanac* revived it through a poetic defense of what he termed a "land ethic." Leopold's philosophy contributed to the postwar growth of environmentalism and ecology and framed the growing interest in protecting wild spaces. This shift in Congress was also a reaction to public outcry about the declining state of the parks themselves: the boom in visitation and tourism strained the resources of the NPS and threatened to ruin the very qualities of nature and solitude that made these places unique. Thus, pressure grew from myriad sectors of society to create a distinct and protected status of land within the parks wherein no motor vehicles, additional roads, or structures could be built.[9]

There were contending philosophies within the park service, ranging from preservation of natural landscapes to the view that "use" and access were central objectives of park managers and superintendents. The objective of access dated back to the creation of the NPS itself articulated by Horace Albright and Stephen Mather, which stated that parks should be open and accessible to the public. This view echoed the claims of modern chambers of commerce, which viewed parks as potential engines of tourism and development. On the other end of the spectrum was the more recent emphasis on preservation based on science, reflected in the Leopold Report of 1963, which stated that parks protected "vignettes of primitive America." These philosophies made it difficult to agree upon objectives internal to the NPS, and they complicated efforts to handle the reactions to local political groups and myriad state pressures.[10]

As knowledge of the Wilderness Act grew, so did concerns about its impact across the park service. In theory it protected some of the most "pristine" lands within preexisting parks, and this was a boon for proponents. For those who hoped to develop some of the most remote sections of a park, the act provoked criticism. And these concerns dominated conversations during public scoping meetings across the nation, as park staff tried to develop long-term plans that balanced the institutional prerogatives of the NPS with the opinions of local communities. As the master plan was being drafted in 1970, the concept of wilderness provoked controversy at multiple levels. The issue seemed simple for some people invested in the Guadalupe Mountains National Park: the Hunter family had protected the land for decades, they made minimal "improvements" on their property, and accessing the top of the mountain was incredibly difficult. These facts resulted in a fairly healthy forest that sustained a vibrant array of flora and fauna, and categorizing most of the park as wilderness did not drastically deviate from its present condition. Moreover, most visitors remained close to amenities such as restrooms, paved roads, "modern" campgrounds, water and electrical utilities, and visitor centers. Very few ventured out into the wilderness areas that lacked such luxuries, so the new designation would not significantly change their experience with the parks. Guadalupe Mountains National Park fit the profile that to reach the potential wilderness, one had to hike up a slope of three thousand feet in less than three miles of trail. Only the most physically fit, highly determined, and well-equipped hikers were prepared for such a trek.[11]

A range of perspectives emerged during public meetings and in newspaper editorials. Much of this discussion reflected volatile emotions, entrenched interests, political ideologies, and half-truths. First, park staff had to clarify the misunderstanding that the entire park would be a wilderness, rather than roughly forty-six thousand acres at the top of the mountain. The Sierra Club of El Paso supported the wilderness designation. Joseph Leach, the regional chairman, hoped it would protect the near-pristine Chihuahuan Desert and high country.[12] They believed that parks best served the nation as defenders of primitive nature accessible to people who left their cars behind and trekked into the backcountry to embrace nature on its own terms. Others opposed the designation on ideological, policy, or financial grounds. Ideologues critiqued the designation because they believed that it was a federal land grab that locked up acres from public use. Others believed that the designation reduced access to the park even though its very topography already limited visitor access to the Bowl, where most of the wilderness sections were proposed.

The discussions about wilderness sparked debate about two old and interrelated issues. The first was a tramway to the Bowl, and the second was the construction of a road, dubbed "Skyline Drive," from Carlsbad Caverns through the Lincoln National Forest to Dog Canyon at the state line and then throughout the forest at the top of the park. The proposed tramway consisted of a high wire tramway that brought people, like a ski lift, from the base of the mountain to the Bowl, where the wilderness designation was. Proponents argued that the tramway would itself attract visitors due to its inherent novelty, the epic views of the desert it provided, and of course the greater access to the Bowl that it afforded. Even factions within the park service supported the tramway because the compliance report required by section 106 of the National Historic Preservation Act of 1966 indicated that the tramway would not significantly damage cultural, natural, or historic resources. "Skyline Drive" was an especially popular proposal during the 1950s, and the tramway gained traction during MISSION-66 as a great way to bring more tourists into the heart of a wilderness area and open up the park to more visitors. Even Congressman Richard White pressured the park superintendent, Donald Dayton (1972–1981), to support the road from Carlsbad, New Mexico, through the Lincoln National Forest and across the state line to the national park.[13]

The tramway and road sparked debate for park service officials, public representatives, and various interest groups. Superintendent Dayton was hesitant about both projects but agreed to follow the will of the people if they supported either one. White told Dayton that he did not support a wilderness designation if the NPS opposed the tramway, which White believed would increase tourism and jobs. In contrast, the National Parks and Conservation Association mounted a vocal campaign against both projects. President Joseph Leach and the Sierra Club surprisingly saw no harm in the tramway because he believed it would leave a relatively small footprint on the land. Newspapers came alive with opinions for and against. A small survey administered at the park had a major impact when it revealed that most visitors opposed the tramway, a few supported the road, and a majority supported traditional hiking and horse trails instead. Moreover, when high cost estimates for the projects soured supporters, the ideologues remained the sole voices in favor of the tramway and road.[14]

Debate about a wilderness designation continued throughout the region. Frank F. Kowski, the director of the NPS Southwest region, said public scoping meetings were supposed to inform the public about the park master plan and the wilderness proposals.[15] Regional heavyweights offered opinions, from promises that wilderness protected nature and provided year-round access to the public, to worst-case scenarios wherein the government "locked up" land through prohibitions on all development. The Carlsbad Chamber of Commerce opposed any master plan that included a majority of the park as wilderness and that lacked roads for easy access to scenic vistas. Representatives from the U.S. Geological Service wanted open access, while the Sierra Club supported a near ban on roads into the park. Surprisingly, by fall 1971, newspapers, such as the *Carlsbad Current-Argus*, shifted from skepticism to support for the wilderness designation, while the tramway fell victim to doubts about the cost of construction. Even the chamber of commerce switched in favor of the wilderness area as proposal in the draft management plan. In October 1972, President Nixon recommended to Congress the wilderness proposal for the park, which included 46,850 acres out of 77,500 acres as wilderness. This seeming consensus in favor of wilderness—and in opposition to the tramway and road, as well as oil and gas exploration—provided considerable protection for the Guadalupe Mountains. Unfortunately, the wilderness designation did not become official until passage of the 1978 National Parks and Recreation Act.[16]

After quieting the debates about mineral rights and the tramway, and the tabling of discussions about wilderness designations, the park officially opened during the fall of 1972. At the official park dedication, Julie Nixon Eisenhower, the daughter of President Nixon helped dedicate the new national park. At a well-attended gathering at the Frijole Information Station, she reminded the public that her father supported the designation of 46,850 acres the park to serve as a wilderness area. She said, "We hope that many of the acres here at Guadalupe Mountains will be named a wilderness area and for these mountains what will remain is the natural beauty of the region. What will remain for us is the opportunity to visit again and again." Donald Dayton, the superintendent for Carlsbad Caverns and Guadalupe Mountains National Park, oversaw the event. In attendance were Senator Ralph Yarborough, William Collins of the Texas Parks and Wildlife Commission, Stanley Hulett, the assistant director of the National Park Service, and dozens of local leaders and members of the community.[17] It was an important milestone in the history of the park.

After the fanfare died down and the political luminaries moved on, the daily operations of the new park loomed large for the staff at Carlsbad. Key to the opening of the new park were the dedicated souls working out of Carlsbad Caverns and locals such as Noel Kincaid who lived on location and oversaw daily operations. Dayton managed the park for several years until a separate superintendent was appointed by the regional office and funds were allocated for a headquarters and staff housing. Roger Reisch, working under Dayton, shepherded the park from approval by Congress through the opening of its doors in 1973. Reisch, headquartered at the Frijole Ranch House, oversaw rangers based at Frijole, McKittrick, and Dog Canyon. He began expanding park staffing immediately but continued to serve a dual function as chief ranger and superintendent. The staff oversaw natural resources, managed daily operations, visitor services, interpretation, and offered hikes and tours through the rudimentary trail system.[18] In addition, staff faced the daunting tasks of stabilizing historic structures, cataloguing and protecting cultural patrimony, addressing the health of wildlife, and tackling budgetary shortfalls. Additional issues occupied employees: property owners adjacent to the park feared that the government wanted to purchase their lands or obtain them through eminent domain, local ranchers demanded protection of cattle from increased road traffic, and there were episodic assertions of untapped reserves of oil and natural gas underneath the park.

As staff focused on the important duties associated with getting a new park up and running, they contemplated a "story" of the park that both justified its existence and attracted visitors. Although national parks protect the animals, plants, and landscapes that strike us as "beautify, sublime, or monumental," they also preserve and narrate our shared heritage. No physical place or landscape in North America is void of human activities, and thus they contain myriad stories about the activities of cultures and peoples. Thus, the national parks showcase those histories through visitor centers, educational endeavors, museums, printed materials, and the protection of cultural artifacts and physical structures. In effect, they encapsulate large and small stories through a particular identity.

In the case of the Guadalupes, that history included a combination of Native, Spanish borderlands, western, and U.S. histories. As noted previously, the Guadalupe Mountains and surrounding regions were part of larger historical processes unfolding in the American West, even though at times their inclusion in those events seemed peripheral. Incorporating thousands of years of history into the regional narrative presented by park officials presented myriad challenges, but some events and eras stood out because of the documentation left behind. The Pinery, which was associated with the Butterfield Overland Mail route across the U.S. West, was the most easily protected, and it was added to the National Register of Historic Places in 1975. The Frijole Ranch House was also on the National Register, while simultaneously housing Roger Reisch as he served as park ranger. The other prominent structures, the Pratt Stone Cabin in McKittrick Canyon, Williams Ranch on the west side of the mountain, and the Ship on the Desert, were too remote for visitors to access in the 1970s, but they served as reminders of the regional history. They too, however, were eventually added to the National Register.[19]

Like debates about cultural resources and historic properties, tensions between the NPS, tourists, and ranchers served as a central theme in the history of the park service in the West, and the Guadalupe Mountains were no different. Several large ranches surrounded the park in Texas, and ranchers leased land in the Lincoln National Forest in New

Mexico from the forest service. Soon after the opening of the park, tensions flared when A. L. Parker, who leased ranchlands from the Lincoln National Forest at the eastern base of the Guadalupe Mountains, complained that tourists vandalized his fences and hit cattle with their cars. He also claimed that some individuals hunted out of season. Parker said, "If I could take fifty per cent of the public and drop them in the ocean, I could leave my gates open." Like many residents in the region, he crossed the state line to work in multiple jobs and oversee a private ranch in Texas and run cattle on federal land in New Mexico. He lived here most of his life, raised a family in the mountains, and served as a Van Horn County commissioner. As a rancher and long-time resident, he resented the change to his lifestyle, which he considered to be "Western" solitary.[20]

Parker's hope for a quiet life screeched to a halt as the park opened for operations. The particular issue that rankled him was access to the upper elevations of McKittrick Canyon, one of the most scenic spots in the park. Tourists had to cross land leased by Parker to enter McKittrick Canyon because the land deeded to the government by Wallace Pratt included an extremely rough road that engineers deemed unsafe for public use. Parker and Suzanne Pratt, the widow of Wallace Pratt, agreed to allow tourists access via their land, but Parker did not expect the numbers. The federal government proposed trading some park land for the private leased land to improve access the canyon, but the deal required congressional approval. Superintendent Dayton said that he lacked the staff to properly protect the area from poachers and vandals. He said that the park received more attention from tourists than expected, and it had been difficult to obtain funds to provide services and infrastructure. Dayton noted, "We're having to provide a park without the facilities and staff needed." Parker, Dayton, and Ranger John Chapman devised a solution where they kept the entrance gate locked but provided keys to a few visitors. Parker remained suspicious that this would solve their problems. He also feared that when Congress approved the land swap and more tourists had access to the canyon, the NPS would be unable to protect the fragile ecosystem.[21]

The lack of public access to McKittrick Canyon became an urgent matter because of the growing numbers of tourists hoping to see one of the most scenic areas of the park. It was increasingly difficult to expand public interest in the Guadalupes if visitors had to use a privately owned road and borrow a key to open a gate. Considering this, in 1975 Congressman Richard White introduced a bill as an amendment to section 2 of the 1966 legislation creating the park, providing for an exchange of land to build an access road on federal land. The Senate proposed an identical bill and the Congress enacted Public Law 94–174 on December 23, 1975, approving the transfer and appropriation of funds to construct a public road from Highway 180 directly to McKittrick Canyon. Until the new road was completed, employees shuttled hikers from the visitor center to McKittrick via a seven-mile gravel road.[22]

Although the tourists wanted to see the remote sections of the park, the status of those sections was undergoing important transformation that would soon facilitate greater access. After the initial passage of the Wilderness Act of 1964, several developments stalled designation within Guadalupe. Local concerns, divisions within the NPS, and explosive national events diverted the country's attention. The issue reemerged with a wilderness designation supported by Nixon, which included the Bowl as well as additional acreage. This designation did not become actual law until 1978 under President Carter.[23] The wilderness designation for the Guadalupe Mountains was part of the National Parks and Recreation Act (an omnibus bill) of 1978, which reflected a watershed moment in history of national parks. Championed by Philip Burton of California, the chairman of the House Subcommittee on National Parks and Insular Affairs, the bill contained a major expansion of the system. According to Alfred Runte, the omnibus bill "included increased appropriations and acquisition ceilings for existing parks, boundary changes, wilderness designations, and final authorization for new parks, historic sites, and wild and scenic rivers." Overall, it designated 1,854,424 acres of wilderness in parks including Guadalupe Mountains.[24]

The staff at the park worked tirelessly to expand its system of trails and campsites into the area designated as wilderness. Between 1973 and 1978, of the total $10,362,000 approved by Congress for the Guadalupes, very little went toward building visitor facilities, the headquarters for employees, housing, roads, and trails, and $7,462,000 went toward planning, building temporary employee facilities, exploring for water, and stabilizing the historic structures and crumbling buildings. The Department of the Interior sought an increase to their funds and in 1978, Congress raised that ceiling to $24,715,000 in the National Parks and Recreation Act. Unlike other requests for parks, which were based on needs assessments through the early 1980s, this boost in funds was supposed to cover all requests indefinitely.[25]

Park Stabilization and Political Conservatism

The initial years of the park yielded several problems for the staff, but employees remained resolute despite worries about visitor access, land disputes, and limited budgets. Nonetheless, they made important gains due to additional funds in the omnibus bill of 1978. These encouraging developments came to a halt in 1980 with the election of Ronald Reagan as president. Reagan promised to reduce government size and shift money and control of programs and resources to the states. Reagan attacked the regulatory powers of the Environmental Protection Agency and advocated for leasing lands and increasing the number of exploratory permits for drilling on properties overseen by the Bureau of Land Management. These and other policies resounded in the West where tension with the federal government was common.[26]

President Reagan ushered in a new era in the park service with the appointment of James Watt as secretary of the interior. Born in Wyoming to a conservative evangelical family, Watt enjoyed a long career in politics and government service, ironic considering his antigovernment rhetoric. He was an aide to Republican senator Millard Simpson of Wyoming, held the position of deputy assistant secretary of water and power development at the Department of the Interior, and served as vice chairman of the Federal Power Commission in 1975. Before Reagan chose him as secretary of the interior, Watt was head legal officer and president of the Mountain States Legal Defense Fund, which staunchly defends and promotes individual liberties, private property, and limited government.[27]

Often known as the most conservative secretary to hold the position, historians likened him to the Albert B. Fall, who in 1922 was indicted for fraud in the Teapot Dome scandal. True to form, Secretary Watt implemented Reagan's conservative vision. Watt blocked creation of new parks, promoted "efficiency" across the system, and focused on improvements of facilities and access to the public, with an eye toward recreational development. He also loosened regulations governing coal leases on land managed by the Department of the Interior. Several inappropriate comments about disabled Americans and minorities, not his conservative politics, forced Watt to resign in 1983. His successor, William Clark, pursued a similar agenda and implemented deeper budget cuts.[28]

The rise and popularity of Reagan and Watt were part and parcel of the "Sagebrush Rebellion," a loose array of individuals, organizations, lobbyists, and special interest groups concerned about government management of lands in the West. As part of the conservative backlash against the perceived excesses of the 1960s and 1970, the "Rebellion" lacked cohesion, but it did shift the political culture in the West as it stressed a variation of states' rights and the "return" of federal lands to the states. As Hal Rothman notes in *The Greening of America*, notions of custom and tradition guided the politics of states' rights, even when states such as Nevada, ground zero for the rebellion, forfeited much of their control over land when they gained statehood. Lands under the Bureau of Land Management were typically considered "wastelands" until ranchers seeking cheap grazing land, and companies exploring for coal, oil, and natural gas sought leases to drill and mine. But even then, these interest groups paid minimal amounts in leases compared to the costs of owning the land outright. Thus, in practical and legal terms, the Sagebrush rebels stood on shaky ground.[29]

The real weight of the rebellion can be seen in the threat it posed to environmentalism. Closely tied to the antigovernment rhetoric was the desire to "open up" and privatize federal lands and make them available for individual and corporate development. Watt and his allies created a false dichotomy between macrolevel federal stewardship of public lands and the narrowly vested interests of locals who had allegedly been marginalized from the land. This "us versus them" narrative of David (westerners supporting local control) against Goliath (the federal government) appealed to many Westerners as they believed various groups of outsiders—environmentalists and bureaucrats from Washington, D.C.—gained control over their communities.[30]

These epic battles played out all across the West in the late twentieth century. As if it was orchestrated by James Watt himself, during the early 1980s the Guadalupe Mountains experienced a classic battle over oil and natural gas drilling on public lands. Questions about drilling in and around the Guadalupes dated back to the West Texas oil boom of the 1920s that brought Wallace Pratt to the region. Since then, the belief that the Guadalupes contained oil and gas reserves sparked debate: during the 1940s war effort; during the 1950s explosion of automobiles and the construction of the interstate highway system; during the 1960s when the state of Texas feared it would lose oil, gas, and mineral rights; and into the 1970s oil and gas crisis associated with OPEC (Organization of Petroleum Exporting Countries). The 1980s manifestation of this perennial question revealed the modern contest over development vs. nature as well as intergovernmental rivalries between the Lincoln National Forest, which promoted a multiuse agenda, and the National Park Service that emphasized preservation.

The debate focused on oil and natural gas drilling in the Lincoln National Forest next to the national park, as well as in Texas along the eastern face of the Guadalupes. Drilling in McKittrick Canyon, which extended into New Mexico, was proposed. This raised alarm bells as the canyon and the surrounding region was home to Peregrine Falcons, and the McKittrick Pennyroyal was being considered for the endangered species list. With these traditional battle lines drawn, the groups took aim at each other. Environmental groups such as the Sierra Club worried that drilling would ruin the habitat of the falcons and Pennyroyal, while C. Wesley Leonard, chairman of the Guadalupe Wilderness Committee and member of the Sierra Club, called the canyon one of the "finest cave regions in the Southwest."[31]

The prodrilling side lined up to state their opposition to wilderness and their support for access to subsurface resources. Peter Hanagan, of the New Mexico Oil and Gas Association, said that "operators feel that the area has a very, very real potential for oil and gas." However, the uppermost reaches of the canyon were declared part of the wilderness area established in 1978. Oil and gas exploration in the New Mexico sections of the Guadalupe escarpment, which sat within the boundaries of the Guadalupe section of the Lincoln National Forest, had been approved by Senators Pete Dominici and Harrison H. Schmitt, through a bill that reduced acreage from the area proposed by Carter as wilderness. New Mexico governor Bruce King and the state delegation also supported drilling.[32]

The situation was complicated, however, by discussions about categorizing a 22,800-acre section of the Lincoln National Forest as wilderness under President Carter's proposed National Heritage Trust in 1978. The Lincoln National Forest in southern New Mexico stood out from other national forests, where timber cutting was a prominent activity. The Guadalupe section was especially unattractive to logging interests, but it was popular for cattle grazing and potential oil and natural gas drilling. Additionally, due to its relative remoteness from large urban areas, the national forest remained fairly healthy and attracted outdoorsmen and campers seeking solitude. For these reasons the national forest and the Guadalupe and Carlsbad Caverns parks explored the possibility of a larger wilderness area that linked the two parks.[33]

With this history of oil and gas exploration, the age-old question of "development vs. preservation," and the nuanced relationship between the national park and national forest serving as the context for the recent debate, the future seemed uncertain. The stalemate shifted as the oil and natural gas lobby gained prominence and the forest service embraced the New Mexico delegation's proposal to explore along the escarpment. The groups thus dug into camps that reflected the classic dilemmas facing communities in the American West. Conservationists decried the destruction of natural habitat by "big oil," and developers protested the "obstacles" placed in front of them by "big government."[34]

And yet this most recent iteration of a classic battle yielded surprising perspectives from influential players in the region. The *Carlsbad Current-Argus*, which typically supported development, questioned the logic of oil and gas exploration and even promoted conservation and alternative sources of energy. To be sure, they wanted energy independence and feared the threat to national security posed by OPEC, both of which were fresh in the minds of many, but the editors revealed a surprisingly philosophical stance on the issue. Although the newspaper could not have been solely responsible for the shift away from drilling, it played a key role. Testing in the mid-1980s failed to discover oil deposits on the escarpment, and as oil prices dropped, the impetus for exploration waned.[35]

Echoing the debate over "wilderness vs. development," questions about large game and predatory animals again brought the park into the spotlight. Mountain lions were considered a scourge by ranchers who feared they would kill livestock, and the big cats had been exterminated or brought to the brink of elimination across the West. More recently the animals, along with wolves and coyotes, had become new icons of the environmental movement. Debates over their numbers, impact on cattle and domestic animals, and their function as symbols of wild nature or as barometers of ecological health revealed deep divisions between communities across the American West. Like other regions, southern New Mexico and far West Texas had their share of mountain lions as well as highly charged debates about their population, health, and future.[36]

New Mexico had a policy of mountain lion control during the 1980s that alarmed environmental and animal rights groups. In response to a vocal campaign protecting the big cats, the state promised to hold public hearings in pursuit of a new policy. The policy adopted by the New Mexico Game and Wildlife Commission in 1987 would have allowed for expanded hunting of lions into the Guadalupe and Sacramento districts of the Lincoln National Forest. A lawsuit filed by environmentalists blocked implementation of the policy because of alleged violations by the commission of the open meetings act. The lawsuit alleged that the members took a rancher-sponsored trip into the Guadalupe Mountains to inspect areas where the lions lived and preyed on nearby flocks of sheep and cattle, on the New Mexico side of the state line. Thus, the national park, which sat in Texas, was pulled into a debate in New Mexico because the mountain lions allegedly sought refuge in the Bowl. The NPS was also interested in the hunting policies because the lions killed deer and other animals living in the park.[37]

New Mexico state game director Harold Olson told the commission that the old hunting policy was still in place while the lawsuit played out. During one meeting, environmentalists said that the hunting of lions contradicted popular will. Claude Bentley from Sangre de Cristo Animal Protection said the problem of lions killing cattle was minimal and limited to southern New Mexico. He said lions attacked cattle because of the decimation of the deer population due to hunting, grazing of cattle on their land, and incursions into their home territory by housing. Olson disagreed with Bentley's claim that lions were killing cattle because of the decline in the deer population, stating that the deer population was the healthiest in the state. Rather, he said that the cattle deaths by lions had increased and that the state policy supporting targeted hunting of lions would protect the cattle and enable the deer populations to grow. Although the commission rescinded support for killing mountain lions, the issue reemerged several years later and the big cats did not fare as well.[38]

As debates over resource exploitation and mountain lion control played out during the 1980s, Guadalupe Mountains National Park became ensconced in the region's identity as a permanent monument to the Chihuahuan Desert: the millennia-old rock wall known as El Capitan, and the surprisingly lush landscape of the Bowl. Environmentalists proclaimed the presence of a national park in West Texas, and longtime residents, many of whom remained skeptical of big government, even embraced the mission to preserve and protect the land. As the park shaped and was shaped by the culture of far West Texas, it grew as an engine of economic development. In short, those who expressed reservations about "locking up resources" saw the park as a magnet for tourism. For instance, during the early 1980s the park and Carlsbad Caverns had generated $45 million in tourist expenditures and related construction projects and taxes amounted to $2,250,000 for Eddy, Culberson, and Hudspeth Counties. These numbers approximated if not exceeded revenues projected by oil and natural gas drilling, and they definitely came at a lower cost to the environment.[39]

By the end of the decade, the two parks had attracted the attention of communities across the nation and of visitors around the world. Newspapers in Australia, England, Germany, and Canada ran stories about the mountains and caverns punctuating the expansive Chihuahuan Desert. Reporters and authors for outdoors and hunting magazines extolled the nearly pristine high desert and woodlands with eighty miles of hiking trails. Journalists visited, took photographs, and hiked throughout the park. Their glowing words and flattering photographs helped craft an image of the Guadalupes as a mountain island in a desert sea where the closest town of consequence was an hour away.[40]

In the shadow of the epic battles over public lands, privatization, and natural resources, two important events offered inspiration during an era of conflict and acrimony. In September 1982 a group of six men in wheelchairs, all paraplegics, climbed El Capitan. They called themselves Paraplegics on Independent Nature Trips (POINT), and they were based out of Dallas, Texas. The three who made it to the top, Dave Kiley of

Claremont, California; Donnie Rodgers of Dallas; and Joe Moss of Lancaster, Texas, had to abandon their wheelchairs a few hundred yards before the top of the mountain. Due to terrain that was impossible on wheelchair, the three dragged themselves by their arms over rocks and rugged trail. The entire group consisted of six men who set out upon the trek five days before Kiley, Rodgers, and Moss scrambled to the peak, the highest in the state of Texas. While attending a celebration provided by hundreds of people in Carlsbad, New Mexico, Rodgers said that after he reached the summit, he felt as though he could do anything. He added, "If everybody could work together like this, the world would be a better place." Upon reaching the summit, the three celebrated with a bottle of champagne that one of them had carted up on his back. After a few moments enjoying the view, they were flown back down in military helicopters from Fort Bliss.[41]

The climb has become an inextricable chapter of park history, but in the early 1980s, it was considered nearly impossible for wheelchair bound individuals to accomplish such a feat. In addition to the difficulties navigating a world before the Americans with Disabilities Act (ADA), the group chose to climb a horse trail in this little known national park. When Shorty Powers, the leader of the expedition convinced Dave Kiley to join POINT on this adventure, he admitted that he "had never heard of anyone with disabilities even attempting anything like this." Nearly ten years before the ADA, the group had a mixture of motivations, ranging from an interest in sports, love of the outdoors, attraction to a good challenge, and a desire to "demonstrate the ability and power of the human spirit." Their success was doubly inspiring considering the superintendent nearly cancelled the climb due to inclement weather. The group forged despite injuries, blisters, and the frustration associated with watching able-bodied hikers cruise past them. And yet, decades later, the three who reached the top still consider it one of their greatest achievements.[42]

On a more mundane level, during the 1980s the park service expanded trails, built campgrounds, and upgraded visitor facilities. Superintendent Bill Dunmire said they constructed one campground for visitors interested in laying down their tents near their cars and enjoying access to water and rudimentary privies. Within a year, Dunmire noticed that park usage increased as the majority of campers parked their cars at the new campground and took day hikes to the top of the mountain. He noted in 1982, "The month we opened the campground, we doubled our usage. As soon as we had a spot for them, they started coming here." In 1981 they erected a temporary ranger station and visitor center along the highway. The visitor center, which was essentially a trailer, was all that the park service could afford. In 1987 Texas congressman Ron Coleman, the successor to Richard White, proposed an addendum to the omnibus bill for the National Park Service for $3,650,000 for construction of a new visitor center and headquarters. Those funds remained tied up in Congress for years. Coleman also suggested the addition of 10,000 acres of land comprised mainly of sand dunes on the western side of the mountain. Despite some debate and resistance, Congress approved the proposals, and the construction of the new headquarters and visitor center began in the early 1990s.[43]

The Park at the Turn of the Millennia

As the park approached the twenty-first century, it encountered new opportunities while it continued managing old dilemmas. On the national level, the sentiments articulated in the "Vail Agenda" framed the trajectory of the NPS and its embrace of science and ecology, yet it articulated a number of other important concerns. In 1991 the NPS commemorated its seventy-fifth anniversary with a conference organized jointly with policy-makers, scientists, nonprofit organizations, universities, and myriad affiliate interests to, according to Richard West Sellars, "review the status of national park management and deliberate on future projects."[44] Among the central themes of the conference was a renewed dedication to leadership associated with management of environmental, ecological and cultural resources within park properties that was based on partnerships with relevant institutions (such as universities) as well as long-term research projects that generated scientific data about resources and their management. Although the Vail conference was significant in other ways, these goals were salient for the Guadalupe Mountains as the specter of budget cuts prompted discussions about raising user fees to help maintain park amenities, and as politicians floated a short lived idea to privatize some parks.

A central claim of the Vail Agenda was that the NPS lacked knowledge of the environmental characteristics of the parks themselves and the biological, ecological, geological, and even climactic challenges they faced. According to some, upper administration failed to cultivate a culture of leadership based on scientific data to best manage those resources over time. During the 1990s the park service proposed increases to its research budget, although they made little headway in comparison to amounts dedicated to management. Moreover, internal debates and inertia associated with the bureaucracy of the park service itself stalled change. The example of neighboring Carlsbad Caverns is illustrative of these conflicts. In the late 1980s, the newly discovered Lechugilla Caves, which sat beneath the caverns, prompted extensive exploration that revealed new geological, paleontological, and biological resources. However, when staff proposed designating Lechuguilla a "wilderness cave," their efforts failed as skeptics claimed the designation would duplicate and thus undermine the designation of lands on the surface as a wilderness area. This little-known debate illustrated the challenges associated with resource designation, exploration and scientific research, and resource management at the end of the twentieth century.[45]

Minor tensions such as this multiplied one hundred-fold constituted the challenges facing a park system adapting to an ever-changing political, economic, and cultural landscape that had direct implications for policies guiding superintendents and staff across the nation. Tensions over wilderness designations, cultural resource management, visitor numbers, marketing and advertising, educational programming, compliance, upkeep of infrastructure, and other responsibilities consumed time and effort. Cultural and philosophical differences within the park service bureaucracy also complicated the shifting political terrain of the 1990s, as seen in battles over access to parks, adherence to the National Environmental Protection Act, science-based resource management, historical representations of communities associated with parks, and debates about privatization of public lands.

The presidency of Bill Clinton, particularly his self-representation as a "New Democrat" and the Newt Gingrich–led Republican Revolution, signaled a shift for park service policy and funding and opened the door for renewed debates about fiscal conservatism and "local control." In an extensive reorganization of the park service initiated by the secretary of the interior Bruce Babbitt in 1995, the regional offices, which played a vital role in overseeing and administering individual parks, were either eliminated or greatly reduced in staffing and influence. In addition, the budget and personnel in the national office in Washington, D.C., were similarly slashed.[46] Although the NPS has traditionally struggled to draw funds from Congress, this downsizing hamstrung superintendents and employees across the country. Projects that needed attention fell by the wayside or they piled up at an alarming rate. Soon, and most assuredly by 2015, the National Park Service was looking at a backlog of work to the tune of $11 billion. Considering present political conditions, that number will undoubtedly increase.[47]

Despite the impressive array of challenges facing the Guadalupe Mountains National Park staff, park service employees served a growing number of visitors. Employees built new trails and campgrounds, opened up a ranger station at Dog Canyon, and built employee housing. The park service purchased properties around the original boundary of the park, stabilized historic structures, conducted biological studies, completed another master plan, and moved out from under the jurisdiction of Carlsbad Caverns to become an independent unit of the park service. Debates over oil and natural gas drilling, as well as the economic benefits of tourism, the impacts of pollution, and questions about access continued for more than a decade, but the fundamental infrastructure of the park was sound. A symposium in 1998, designed to commemorate the twenty-fifth anniversary of the establishment of the park, demonstrated the great achievements associated with the first quarter century at the Guadalupe Mountains National Park.

National environmental and cultural trends also impacted the Guadalupes. Drought across the West posed emergency conditions on public lands and strained the ability of local, state, and federal governments to fight increasingly massive super fires. Images of mountains and valleys set ablaze by lightning or the careless tourist alerted Americans to the shortsightedness of a century-long policy of total fire suppression. New policies in the wake of these massive fires resulted in greater acceptance for controlled burns on public lands. Additionally, the NPS had to contend with a new generation of Americans that enjoyed greater access to video games and the internet, both of which reduced visitation to smaller parks such as the Guadalupe Mountains. For instance, in 1994 Carlsbad Caverns ranger Richard McCamant said that roughly

250,000 people visited Guadalupe Mountains compared with 750,000 to Carlsbad Caverns.[48] The park service thus had to repackage itself as a bureaucracy that educated the public, protected cultural history as well as natural resources, and that offered an important function as a site for community building. Like the retooling of public libraries as community centers, the park service had to work harder to get people out of their homes, away from their computers, into their campgrounds, and onto their wilderness trails.

At the turn of the century the park reached important benchmarks and turning points in the area of preserving culturally and historically significant structures and sites. The Frijole Ranch House, one of the most noteworthy properties of the park, was home to the Smith family during the early 1900s. Later it was used by J. C. Hunter as the headquarters for his sprawling cattle ranch. After Hunter Jr. sold his properties to the NPS, the structure was used by park employees, especially superintendents, as a home and base of operations. As park staff moved into new housing and when Congress appropriated funds for a new headquarters and visitor center, it seemed like an opportune time to investigate the cultural significance of the building and landscape to determine procedures whereby it could serve a greater role in narrating the region's history.

Noting in the 1988 Statement for Management, the mission of Guadalupe Mountains National Park included the preservation of natural and cultural resources that reflected the significance of the mountains for the Southwest borderlands. The Frijole Ranch, also known as the Smith Ranch, served as an example of the interaction between Anglo American settlers and the West Texas environment. The cultural landscape of managed grasslands, drainage and watering systems, innovative farming techniques, and ingenious architecture provide historians and visitors with an important window into early twentieth-century rural life. The significance of the site was recognized with a designation in 1978 of the ranch on the National Register of Historic Places, but a robust and professional assessment of the site was not completed until 1994 by Peggy Froeschauer, a landscape architect out of Santa Fe. This study explained the human occupation of the landscape; traced land ownership; followed the construction of physical structures such as the home, barn, and schoolhouse; and highlighted the management of natural resources by the Smith and Kincaid families, as well as J. C. Hunter. Most importantly, the study recommended steps to preserve this cultural resource as an educational site for visitors.[49]

After a considerable investment of time and money, the Frijole Ranch House serves as one of the key sites of historical representation in the park. The surrounding landscape has been recreated to demonstrate the ingenuity of the Smith family and their advances with gardening and farming, their creative use of natural springs to cool their food supplies and irrigate their crops, while interpretive materials inside the building teach visitors about rural life in the early twentieth century. For those living in the twenty-first century, the thought of cooking outside or receiving an education from a one-room schoolhouse that used to be a storage shed, the Frijole Ranch House is a memorable glimpse into a past that has all but escaped us.

Cultural properties such as the Ship on the Desert, Pratt's first house in McKittrick Canyon, and the Frijole Ranch House all speak to the rich heritage of the park, but they say little about the long history of Native occupancy of the mountains. Anglo settlers noted the ongoing presence of Apaches who occasionally lived in the upper reaches of the Bowl, and archaeological investigations provided irrefutable evidence documenting indigenous occupancy. In the twenty-first century, however, Guadalupe Mountains National Park has had minimal interaction with the Natives in the surrounding region. The most conspicuous group with ties to the park is the Mescalero, who lived within the area for centuries and considered the Guadalupes to be sacred. Spanish archival information, U.S. military reports, records from the Bureau of Indian Affairs, newspaper stories, and the reflections of Mescaleros and Anglos support these claims. However, when the NPS and Congress approved the mission of Guadalupe, it ignored the cultural history of the Mescalero and various groups, such as the Jumano, Tigua, Comanches, and others with ties to the mountain.

After the passage of the Native American Graves Protection and Repatriation Act in 1990, the park began a process of outreach with the Mescalero that generally improved relations with the tribe, but fell short of the hopes of the Mescalero themselves. A series of efforts initiated to recognize the historic presence of Native people in the mountain area, such as portions of a conference in 1998, evidenced growing willingness to incorporate a more robust acknowledgment of cultural resources and historical legacies. And yet, when the conference committee published the proceedings in *The Guadalupe Mountains Symposium*, they segregated the histories of Native people, particularly the Apache, into a section on "Cultural Resources" rather than the section on "History," which contained chapters on the Butterfield Stage Coach—which existed for less than two years—and individuals such as Felix McKittrick and Wallace Pratt. Relevant chapters covered archaeological resources, Apache war sites, and cultural landscapes, but the lack of contributions from Apaches and explanations of the mountains' relevance in Apache culture seemed strikingly out of touch with trends during the era that emphasized multicultural perspectives and diverse interpretations of the past.[50]

Additional events in the twenty-first century punctuated the historical ties between the Mescalero and Lipan Apache with the Guadalupe Mountains. In 2004 Howard University partnered with the National Park Service, representatives and high school students from the Mescalero Reservation, and faculty at Arizona State University and the University of Texas at El Paso in an investigation of the shared histories of Buffalo Soldiers and Apaches in the West. The endeavor included a multiyear summer archaeological dig and a series of exchange programs, conferences, and partnerships collectively identified as the "Warriors Project." The broad goals of these efforts included highlighting the shared and sometimes difficult histories of Buffalo Soldiers and Apaches within the framework of diversifying the stories examined in National Park System units. Incorporating the histories of Apaches and African Americans into the narratives, educational materials, and exhibits helps to inform visitors about the diverse, contested, and intriguing stories that constitute our nation's past.[51]

Most recently park staff tried to host an annual Mescal Roast that highlighted the importance of the plant for the cultural identity of the Mescalero people. Although the history of the creation of this national park revealed the difficulties of the park service to recognize Native occupancy and history, the future relations between the park and the tribe seem optimistic. And if the park can build bridges with the Mescalero and other Native people, particularly the Tiguas due to their use of the salt beds in the park, it would serve as an important act of friendship and understanding in the long and complicated history of the Guadalupe Mountains.

◀▶

Although the centennial of the park service—and the fiftieth anniversary of Guadalupe Mountains National Park—in 2016 was marked with great fanfare, the park still faces major battles and obstacles. Restraints associated with limited funding, climate change and its impact on wildlife, and moderate attendance numbers require constant attention and monitoring. Occasional moments of cooperation with the Mescalero and Carlsbad as seen in the Mescal Roasts signal an optimistic future for the park's relationship with surrounding communities. Indeed, the simultaneous celebration of the park's fiftieth anniversary and the centennial of the entire National Park System, heightened public awareness about the importance of protecting natural spaces and maintaining the parks themselves. As the nation struggles with political controversy, heightened ubiquity of technology, and accelerated cultural change, national parks such as the park in the Guadalupes continue to offer a respite for everyone seeking access to nature, wilderness, open skies, and narratives of our shared past.

Conclusion
A National Park in the Southwest Borderlands

The Guadalupe Mountains captured the imaginations of generations that marveled at their sheer rock wall and enjoyed the unlikely forest that sits above the arid Chihuahuan Desert. Slow geological processes spanning millions of years brought forth from a vast ocean an awe-inspiring Permian reef that has attracted indigenous peoples, Spaniards, scientists and explorers, soldiers, cattle rustlers, overland migrants, tourists, and entrepreneurs. Native peoples such as the Mescalero incorporated the mountains into their spiritual and cultural landscape, and the Piro, Manso, Tiwa, and Tigua placed a high value on the salt beds, deer, and rabbits associated with the mountains. Spaniards and overland migrants used El Capitan as a navigational tool while crossing the open spaces of the Trans-Pecos. Individuals fleeing urban America found the solitude of the mountains to be an antidote to the complexities of modernity. Lastly, for J. C. Hunter and Wallace Pratt, as well as myriad conservationists, boosters, and park service employees, the mountains deserved protection so that everyone could enjoy the unique geological, biological, and ecological qualities of this "island in the desert."

Although the Guadalupe Mountains found a home in the imaginations of many, the park came into being at a moment of national transition. The civil rights movement, Vietnam War, suburbanization, and a nascent environmental movement contextualized a National Park Service that was experiencing great change. The park was established at the end of MISSION-66, which sought to modernize national parks and monuments to make them more accessible and attractive to the public. George Hartzog, the NPS director who oversaw the creation of Guadalupe Mountains National Park and the successor program to MISSION-66, Parkscape USA, helped open the doors of these institutions to a wider audience. The changes that characterized the park service mirrored the changes taking place across the country as the nation collectively grappled with the meaning of wilderness, our valuation of nature, and our larger relationship with the environments in which we live.[1]

Similarly, the reasons and rationales behind the creation of parks echoed the tensions in the United States over "modern" and "traditional" values. Whereas many Americans fretted over the new gender, social, and racial relationships that challenged the norms of pre–World War II public culture, advocates of these changes believed that a new era of equity and progress stood before them. Likewise, the park service had begun to rethink the processes, goals, and objectives associated with the sites they protected. Culture, history, and ecological diversity factored into the creation of parks, along with the older rationales of monumentalism, nationalism, and landscape aesthetics. Guadalupe Mountains National Park was one of the last parks created for traditional "monumental" characteristics, but it was also significant because of its scientific qualities. The looming rock wall of El Capitan as it rises above the desert floor speaks to the sublime dimensions of the natural wonders that the park system sought to preserve. Although parks contained mountains, forests, waterfalls, and animal populations that dwarfed Guadalupe, this spot in Southwest borderlands was visually striking within the context of the arid Trans-Pecos region. And this point reflected its "modern" justification: the geological, biological, and ambient characteristics attracted scientists from around the world who believed that the mountains could help them understand the history of the earth itself.[2]

Despite the unique qualities of the park, its establishment was hard fought and complicated. It required an array of forces and larger-than-life personalities to come into alignment. The purchases of Wallace Pratt and the Hunter family represented an exceptional accumulation of property, without which the government purchase would have been wildly more complicated. The personal and political ties of Wallace Pratt were helpful, as was the relationship between Pratt and Hunter Jr. The reverence that they held for the land was crucial because they understood that they owned a piece of the West that all Americans would enjoy.

The supporters that visited the site created a pool of good will and personal investment in the park. Hundreds of people came to the mountains and hunted, hiked, and marveled at the vastness of the Trans-Pecos region. This network of supporters was cultivated by Glenn Biggs, the real estate agent and marketing wizard who campaigned to preserve the Guadalupes. Biggs worked with Noel Kincaid, the foreman of Hunter Ranch, state representatives Joe Pool and Richard White, and U.S. senator Ralph Yarborough. Yarborough was particularly key because he had spent several years as a young man in West Texas, and he had actually visited the mountains during the 1920s. This personal charm and political acumen enabled Biggs to cultivate relationships and nurture friendships in such disparate groups as the West Texas Chamber of Commerce, Carlsbad mayors, the Sierra Club, the National Park Service, and the state legislature. He even convinced Secretary of the Interior Stewart Udall and Supreme Court Justice William O. Douglas to visit the mountains and support the national park.

Although the interest groups associated with the park were important, no amount of support could have preserved the site if the timing had been different. People in West Texas and southern New Mexico talked about creating a park for decades before President Johnson approved it in 1966. These previous efforts fell apart because of the distance of the mountains from major highways, the lack of automobiles and expendable income for the middle class, stagnant policies in the NPS, antiquated financial mechanisms for the purchase of private land, and landscape philosophies that valued Victorian Era notions of monumentalism and the sublime. Park service policies shifted after World War II, the science of ecology gained credence in American culture, and U.S. society itself embraced outdoor recreation. More Americans began to worry about the environmental impact of pollution and urban sprawl. By the time the America entered the 1960s, when J. C. Hunter Jr. decided to pursue the creation of a national park, the nation was in the middle of an economic boom that placed it at the apex of its power. Johnson promised Americans they could live in a "great society" where private wealth, government support, and public good will would improve the quality of life for all citizens, and the Guadalupe Mountains National Park comported with that philosophy.

This relative abundance trickled into the coffers of the park service and contributed to a shift in its policies. With the passage of the 1964 Land and Water Conservation Fund, Johnson created a mechanism to shift revenue toward the purchase of private lands, without raiding general appropriation funds. This was a novel solution to the key obstacle behind the creation of the park. Hunter Jr. could not afford to donate his ranch and philanthropies, and conservation organizations refused to purchase the land and transfer it to the public domain. The conservation fund was a step in the right direction, and it surely did not hurt to have a Texan in the White House while proposing a national park in his home state.

And yet, with all of these stars aligned, obstacles remained. Subsurface oil and mineral rights remained a nettlesome topic. Several private landholders in the area refused to sell. Civil rights legislation, the escalating war in Vietnam, and the cultural turmoil of "the sixties" stalled legislation introduced to Congress in 1964. Political debate kept Guadalupe bills from leaving committee and reaching the floor. When bills did see discussion, they were buried under amendments and in more complicated and unrelated bills. After several attempts, myriad hearings, and testimony from people associated with the park, President Johnson signed the bill creating the national park in the Guadalupe Mountains. Although the formal efforts to create the park dated only to conversations between Hunter Jr., Pratt, and Biggs in the early 1960s, in reality, the dreams of preserving the mountains had entertained the thoughts of many for decades.

The Guadalupe Mountains are an engaging and enigmatic place within the Greater Southwest borderlands. Sitting at the nexus of the southern plains and the Chihuahuan Desert, and bisecting two states that have had conflicting histories, the mountains saw their share of colorful characters and important events. The striking geological characteristics and the surprising forest seem incongruent with the surrounding creosote, cholla, salt beds, and sand dunes. It is a landscape characterized by a massive barrier reef jutting out over what was once a vast ocean floor. To those who had lived here—Native, Anglo, Mexican, and immigrant—it was a hard but beautiful land. What it lacked in water and rich soils, it gave back in open skies and intangible charm. And to those that are associated with the mountains and the park today, whether for personal, spiritual, or professional reasons, the national park is a fitting tribute to the fascinating histories and cultures that have graced this small corner of the Southwest borderlands.

Notes

Introduction

1. Fred Philips, G. Emlen Hall, and Mary E. Black, *Reining in the Rio Grande: People, Land, and Water* (Albuquerque: University of New Mexico Press, 2011); Casey Walsh, *Building the Borderlands: A Transnational History of Irrigated Cotton along the Mexico-Texas Border* (College Station: Texas A&M Press, 2008); Evan R. Ward, *Border Oasis: Water and the Political Ecology of the Colorado River Delta, 1940–1975* (Tucson: University of Arizona Press, 2003); Samuel Truett, *Fugitive Landscapes: The Forgotten History of the U.S.-Mexico Borderlands* (New Haven: Yale University Press, 2008); Frederick Gelhbach, *Mountain Islands and Desert Seas: A Natural History of the U.S.-Mexican Borderlands* (College Station: Texas A&M University Press, 1993).
2. William deBuys, *Enchantment and Exploitation: The Life and Hard Times of a New Mexico Mountain Range* (Albuquerque: University of New Mexico Press, 1985), 6.
3. David J. Weber, *The Spanish Frontier in North America* (New Haven: Yale University Press, 1992), 2.
4. Stephen H. Lekson, ed., *A History of the Ancient Southwest* (Santa Fe: School for Advanced Research Press, 2011), 18.
5. Joseph P. Sánchez, Robert L. Spude, and Art Gómez, *New Mexico: A History* (Norman: University of Oklahoma Press, 2013), 101.
6. Carole Larson, introduction to *Forgotten Frontier: The Story of Southeastern New Mexico* (Albuquerque: University of New Mexico Press, 1993); Howard Roberts Lamar, *The Far Southwest, 1846–1912: A Territorial History* (New York: W.W. Norton, 1970), 15.
7. Richard White, *"It's Your Misfortune and None of My Own": A New History of the American West* (Norman: University of Oklahoma Press, 1991), 270.
8. G. Emlen Hall, *High and Dry: The Texas-New Mexico Struggle for the Pecos River* (Albuquerque: University of New Mexico Press, 2003), 28; Patrick Dearen, *Bitter Watters: The Struggles of the Pecos River* (Norman: University of Oklahoma Press, 2016), 5.
9. Hal K. Rothman, *Promises Beheld and the Limits of Place: A Historic Resource Study of Carlsbad Caverns and Guadalupe Mountains National Parks and Surrounding Areas*, National Park Service, Southwest Regional Office, Santa Fe (1998), 4.
10. Neel Baumgardner, "Bordering North America: Constructing Wilderness Along the Periphery of Canada, Mexico, and the United States" (PhD diss., University of Texas at Austin, 2013); Ryan H. Edgington, *Range Wars: The Environmental Contest for White Sands Missile Range* (Lincoln: University of Nebraska Press, 2014), 3.

Chapter One: Geology and Environment

1. Susan Marjorie Applegarth, "Prehistoric Utilization of Environment of the Eastern Slopes of the Guadalupe Mountains, Southeastern New Mexico" (PhD diss., University of Wisconsin–Madison, 1976), 21.

2. Donny L. Hamilton, *Prehistory of the Rustler Hills: Granado Cave* (Austin: University of Texas Press, 2001), 4.
3. Hal K. Rothman, *Promises Beheld and the Limits of Place: A Historic Resource Study of Carlsbad Caverns and Guadalupe Mountains National Parks and Surrounding Areas*, National Park Service, Southwest Regional Office, Santa Fe (1998), 1.
4. Lynne Sebastian and Signa Larralde, *Living on the Land: 11,000 Years of Human Adaptation in Southeastern New Mexico* Cultural Resources Series No. 6 (Roswell, NM: Bureau of Land Management, 1989), 7; Hamilton, *Prehistory*, 5.
5. David H. Jagnow and Rebecca Rowher Jagnow, *Stories from Stones: The Geology of the Guadalupe Mountains* (Carlsbad: Carlsbad-Guadalupe Mountains Association, 1992), 8.
6. Rothman, *Promises Beheld*, 2.
7. Alan Tennant, *The Guadalupe Mountains of Texas* (Austin: University of Texas Press, 1980), 17; Hamilton, *Prehistory*, 14.
8. Sebastian and Larralde, *Living on the Land*, 15.
9. Sebastian and Larralde, 17; Hamilton, *Prehistory*, 13.
10. Tennant, *Guadalupe Mountains*, 20.
11. Tennant, 21.
12. Tennant, 19.
13. Sebastian and Larralde, *Living on the Land*, 9.
14. Tennant, *Guadalupe Mountains*, 48; Robert James Mallouf, "A Synthesis of Eastern Trans-Pecos Prehistory" (master's thesis, University of Texas at Austin, 1985), 16.
15. Rothman, *Promises Beheld*, 5; Mallouf, "Synthesis," 17.
16. Susana R. Katz and Paul Katz, *The Prehistory of the Carlsbad Basin, Southeastern New Mexico*, prepared for the Bureau of Reclamation, Southwest Regional Office, 1985.
17. Ron C. Tyler, *The Big Bend: A History of the Last Texas Frontier* (Washington, D.C.: Department of the Interior, National Park Service, 1975), 105.
18. Frederick Albion Ober, *Travels in Mexico and Life Among the Mexicans* (Boston: Estes and Lauriat, 1884), 592; Mallouf, "Synthesis," 8.
19. Applegarth, "Prehistoric Utilization of Environment," 22.
20. Tennant, *Guadalupe Mountains*, 50.
21. Applegarth, "Prehistoric Utilization of Environment," 26.
22. Applegarth, 29.
23. Applegarth, 31.
24. Sebastian and Larralde, *Living on the Land*, 4.
25. Mallouf, "Synthesis," 9.
26. Mallouf, 15.
27. Michael Baldree, "Diversity of Life in Guadalupe Mountains National Park," in David Love et al., eds., *Carlsbad Region, New Mexico and Texas, New Mexico Geological Society Forty-Fourth Annual Field Conference*, October 6–9, 1993 (in cooperation with the West Texas Geological Society), 55–63.
28. Baldree, "Diversity of Life," 56.
29. Baldree, 56.

Chapter Two: Pre-Columbian Indigenous Worlds

1. Alan Tennant, *The Guadalupe Mountains of Texas* (Austin: University of Texas Press, 1980), 47; Hal K. Rothman, *Promises Beheld and the Limits of Place: A Historic Resource Study of Carlsbad Caverns and Guadalupe Mountains National Parks and Surrounding Areas*, National Park Service, Southwest Regional Office, Santa Fe (1998), 9.
2. Lynne Sebastian and Signa Larralde, *Living on the Land: 11,000 Years of Human Adaptation in Southeastern New Mexico* Cultural Resources Series No. 6 (Roswell, NM: Bureau of Land Management, 1989), 41; David Carmichael, personal communication.

3. Don Clifton, "An Archeological Survey of 26 Miles of the Boundary of the Guadalupe Mountains National Park, Culberson and Hudspeth Counties, Texas," prepared for Guadalupe Mountains National Park, 1992, 9.
4. Susana R. Katz, "Late Prehistoric Period Environment and Economy of the Southern Guadalupe Mountains, Texas" (PhD diss., University of Kansas, 1978); Hal K. Rothman, *Promises Beheld and the Limits of Place: A Historic Resource Study of Carlsbad Caverns and Guadalupe Mountains National Parks and Surrounding Areas*, National Park Service, Southwest Regional Office, Santa Fe (1998), 5.
5. Susana R. Katz and Paul Katz, *The Prehistory of the Carlsbad Basin, Southeastern New Mexico*, prepared for the Bureau of Reclamation, Southwest Regional Office, 1985, 35–61.
6. Katz and Katz, 41–42.
7. Susan Marjorie Applegarth, "Prehistoric Utilization of Environment of the Eastern Slopes of the Guadalupe Mountains, Southeastern New Mexico" (PhD diss., University of Wisconsin–Madison, 1976), 12.
8. Applegarth, 14
9. Applegarth, 15.
10. Applegarth, 16.
11. Applegarth, 37.
12. Applegarth, 53.
13. Applegarth, 57.
14. Applegarth, 65.
15. Applegarth, 78.
16. Applegarth, 81.
17. Applegarth, 87.
18. Applegarth, 90.
19. Applegarth, 105.
20. Applegarth, 122.
21. Applegarth, 125.
22. Applegarth, 148.
23. Katz and Katz, *Prehistory of the Carlsbad Basin*, 90, 393.
24. Katz and Katz, 403.
25. Katz and Katz, 410.
26. R. L. Hunter-Anderson, *Prehistoric Adaptation in the American Southwest* (New York: Cambridge University Press, 1986), 43; Paul S. Martin, "Prehistory: Mogollon," *Handbook of North American Indians, Southwest,* ed. Alfonso Ortiz, vol. 9 (Washington, D.C.: Smithsonian, 1979), 71–74.
27. Martin, 46.
28. Alan H. Simmons et al., *Human Adaptation and Cultural Change in the Greater Southwest: An Overview of Archeological Resources in the Basin and Range Province* (University of Nevada, Desert Research Institute, 1989), 69.
29. Rothman, *Promises Beheld*, 24.
30. Nancy P. Hickerson, "Jumano: The Missing Link in South Plains History," *Journal of the West* 29, no. 4 (October 1990): 5–12.
31. Donny L. Hamilton, *Prehistory, of the Rustler Hills: Granado Cave* (Austin: University of Texas Press, 2001), 7.
32. Applegarth, "Prehistoric Utilization of Environment," 183.
33. Hamilton, *Prehistory*, 268.
34. Hickerson, "Jumano," 7.
35. Applegarth, "Prehistoric Utilization of Environment," 180.
36. Nancy Parrott Hickerson, *The Jumanos: Hunters and Traders of the Southern Plains* (Austin: University of Texas Press, 1994), 23.
37. Hickerson, 25.

38. Elizabeth A. H. John, *Storms Brewed in Other Men's Worlds: The Confrontation of Indians, Spanish, and French in the Southwest, 1540–1795*, 2nd ed. (Norman: University of Oklahoma Press, 1996), 104.
39. John, 267; Morris Edward Opler and Catherine H. Opler, "Mescalero Apache History in the Southwest" *New Mexico Historical Review* 25, no. 1 (January 1950): 1.
40. Applegarth, "Prehistoric Utilization of Environment," 200; Opler and Opler, 3.
41. Tennant, *Guadalupe Mountains*, 50.
42. Tennant, 52; Morris E. Opler, "Mescalero Apache," in *Handbook of North American Indians: Volume 10 Southwest* (Washington D.C.: Smithsonian Institution, 1983), 421.
43. Bill Lockhart, "Protohistoric Confusion: A Cultural Comparison of the Manso, Suma, and Jumano Indians of the Paso Del Norte Region," *Journal of the Southwest* 39, no. 1 (Spring 1997): 129; Edward H. Spicer, *Cycles of Conquest: The Impact of Spain, Mexico, and the United States on the Indians of the Southwest, 1533–1960* (Tucson: University of Arizona Press, 1962), 109; Donald E. Worcester, *The Apaches: Eagles of the Southwest* (Norman: University of Oklahoma Press, 1979), 7.
44. Gary Clayton Anderson, *The Indian Southwest: Ethnogenesis and Reinvention, 1580–1830* (Norman: University of Oklahoma Press, 1999), 12.
45. Jack Forbes, "Unknown Athapaskans: The Identification of the Jano, Jocome, Jumano, Manso, Suma, and other Indian Tribes of the Southwest" *Ethnohistory* 6, no. 2 (Spring 1959): 107–11.
46. Forbes, 116.
47. William B. Griffen, "Southern Periphery: East" in *Handbook of North American Indians: Southwest 10* (Washington D.C. Smithsonian Institution, 1983), 329–42.
48. Griffen, 333.

Chapter Three: Indigenous Peoples, Spain, and Mexico

1. David J. Weber, *The Spanish Frontier in North America* (New Haven: Yale University Press, 1992), 16; Edward H. Spicer, *Cycles of Conquest: The Impact of Spain, Mexico, and the United States on the Indians of the Southwest, 1533–1960* (Tucson: University of Arizona Press, 1962), 5.
2. Weber, 30. See also Andrés Reséndez, *A Land So Strange: The Epic Journey of Cabeza de Vaca* (New York: Basic Books, 2009), 129.
3. Thomas E. Sheridan, *The Bitter River: A Brief Historical Survey of the Middle Pecos River Basin* (Roswell District Office, Roswell, NM: Bureau of Land Management, 1975), 7; Donald E. Chipman, "In Search of Cabeza de Vaca's Route across Texas: An Historiographical Survey," *Southwestern Historical Quarterly* 91, no. 2 (October 1987): 127–48; Nancy Parrott Hickerson, *The Jumanos: Hunters and Traders of the Southern Plains* (Austin: University of Texas Press, 1994), 15.
4. Weber, *Spanish Frontier*, 40; Diego Pérez de Luxán, *Expedition into New Mexico Made by Antonio de Espejo, 1582–1583, As Revealed in the Journal of Diego Pérez de Luxán, A Member of the Party*, trans. George Peter Hammond and Agapito Rey (Los Angeles: Quivira Society, 1929), 1940.
5. Thomas Sheridan, *The Bitter River*, 8; Weber, *Spanish Frontier*, 56; Susana Katz and Paul Katz, *The History of the Carlsbad Basin, Southeastern New Mexico*, preparation for Bureau of Reclamation, Southwest Regional Office, 1985, 17.
6. Hickerson, *Jumanos*, 27.
7. J. Charles Kelley "The Rio Conchos Drainage: History, Archeology, Significance," Bruce Glasrud and Robert Malouf, eds., *Big Bend History: Selections from the Journal for Big Bend Studies* (College Station: Texas A&M University Press, 2015), 109.
8. Reeve, quoted from H. E. Bolton, ed., "Declaration of Bustamante," *Spanish Exploration in the Southwest, 1542–1706* (New York, 1916), 148.

9. Reeve, 148; J. Lloyd Mecham, "Antonio de Espejo and His Journey to New Mexico" *The Southwestern Historical Quarterly* 30, no. 2 (October 1926): 135.
10. Pérez de Luxán, *Expedition into New Mexico*, 121.
11. Pérez de Luxán, 122.
12. Pérez de Luxán, 123.
13. Pérez de Luxán, 126.
14. Hickerson, *Jumanos*, 43. This site should not be confused with a previous one: La Cienega Salada.
15. Pérez de Luxán, *Expedition into New Mexico*, 124.
16. Sheridan, *Bitter River*, 10.
17. Pérez de Luxán, *Expedition into New Mexico*, 125.
18. Pérez de Luxán, 126.
19. Pérez de Luxán, 128.
20. J. Lloyd Mecham, "Antonio de Espejo and His Journey to New Mexico," *The Southwestern Historical Quarterly* 30, no. 2 (October 1926): 136.
21. Hickerson, *Jumanos*, 15.
22. Katz and Katz, *History of the Carlsbad Basin*, 20.
23. Carole Larson, *Forgotten Frontier: The Story of Southeastern New Mexico* (Albuquerque: University of New Mexico Press, 1993), 56.
24. Larson, 20; Gaspar Castano de Sosa, *A Colony on the Move: Gaspar Castano de Sosa's Journal, 1590–1591*, trans. Albert H. Schroeder and Dan S. Matson (Santa Fe: School of American Research, 1965), 54–78.
25. Larson, 62–66.
26. Sheridan, *Bitter River*, 12; Elizabeth A. H. John, *Storms Brewed in Other Men's Worlds: The Confrontation of Indians, Spanish, and French in the Southwest, 1540–1795*, 2nd ed. (Norman: University of Oklahoma Press, 1996), 36.
27. Hickerson, *Jumanos*, 60.
28. Boyd C. Pratt and Dan Scurlock, "Llano, River and Mountains: The Southeast New Mexico Regional Overview, Volume 1, Historic Overview," Historic Preservation Division, Office of Cultural Affairs, Santa Fe, 1989, 55; Sheridan, *Bitter River*, 14.
29. Hickerson, *Jumanos*, 89–91; John, *Storms Brewed*, 79.
30. Hickerson, 95–97.
31. Hickerson; John, *Storms Brewed*, 79.
32. Lockhart, "Protohistoric Confusion," 136.
33. Weber, *Spanish Frontier*, 137.
34. Weber, 138; Spicer, *Cycles of Conquest*, 167.
35. Pekka Hämäläinen, *The Comanche Empire* (New Haven: Yale University Press, 2008), 2.
36. Daniel J. Gelo, "'Comanche Land and Ever Has Been': A Native Geography of the Nineteenth-Century Comancheria," *Southwestern Historical Quarterly* 103, no. 3 (January 2000): 272–301.
37. Gelo, 281.
38. Hickerson, *Jumanos*, 11; Gary Clayton Anderson, *The Indian Southwest: Ethnogenesis and Reinvention, 1580–1830* (Norman: University of Oklahoma Press, 1999), 110.
39. Reeve, "Declaration of Bustamante," 199.
40. Jack D. Forbes, *Apache, Navajo, and Spaniard*, 2nd ed. (Norman: University of Oklahoma Press, 1994), xviii.
41. Forbes, 34.
42. Juliana Barr, *Peace Came in the Form of a Woman: Indians and Spaniards in the Texas Borderlands* (Chapel Hill: University of North Carolina Press, 2007), 2–3; Ned Blackhawk, *Violence over the Land: Indians and Empires in the Early American West* (Cambridge: Harvard University Press, 2007), 5; Hämäläinen, *Comanche Empire*, 4.

43. Dan L. Thrapp, *The Conquest of Apacheria* (Norman: University of Oklahoma Press, 1967), x; Donald E. Worcester, *The Apaches: Eagles of the Southwest* (Norman: University of Oklahoma Press, 1979), 5.
44. Reeve, "Declaration of Bustamante," 200; Weber, *Spanish Borderlands*, 206.
45. John, *Storms Brewed*, 267; C. L. Sonnichsen, *The Mescalero Apaches* (Norman: University of Oklahoma Press, 1965), 52.
46. Gary Clayton Anderson, *The Conquest of Texas: Ethnic Cleansing in the Promised Land, 1820–1875* (Norman: University of Oklahoma Press, 2005), 22; Anderson, *Indian Southwest*, 125; Hämäläinen, *Comanche Empire*, 59–60.
47. W. H. Timmons, *El Paso: A Borderlands History* (El Paso: Texas Western Press, 1990), 31.
48. Pedro Jose' de la Fuente, "Diary of Pedro Jose' de la Fuente, Captain of the Presidio of El Paso del Norte, August–December 1765 trans. and ed. James M. Daniel, *Southwestern Historical Quarterly* 83, no. 3 (January 1980): 259–78; Timmons, *El Paso*, 58.
49. Gelo, "Comanche Land," 270.
50. Reeve, "Declaration of Bustamante," 201; Weber, *Spanish Frontier*, 205.
51. Weber, 217.
52. Weber, 221.
53. Frank D. Reeve, "Apache Indians in Texas," *Southwest Historical Quarterly* 50, no. 2 (October 1946), 257.
54. Sheridan, *Bitter River*, 9; Colin G. Calloway, *One Vast Winter Count: The Native American West before Lewis and Clark* (Lincoln: University of Nebraska Press, 2005), 280–82; Weber, *Spanish Frontier*, 206.
55. Mathew Babcock, *Apaches Adaptation to Hispanic Rule* (Cambridge: Cambridge University Press, 2017), 6.
56. William B. Griffen, *Apaches at War and Peace: The Janos Presidio, 1750–1858* (Norman: University of Oklahoma Press, 1998), 127.
57. Calloway, *One Vast Winter Count*, 384; Weber, *Spanish Frontier*, 234; Hämäläinen, *Comanche Empire*, 265.
58. Reeve, "Apache Indians in Texas," 201; Pratt and Scurlock, "Llano, River and Mountains" referencing Forbes, *Apache, Navajo, and Spaniard*; Max Moorhead, *The Presidio: Bastion of the Spanish Borderlands* (Norman: University of Oklahoma Press, 1975), 37–39; Thomas, *Bitter River*, 11–14; Charles L. Kenner, *The Comanchero Frontier: A History of New Mexican-Plains Indian Relations* (Norman: University of Oklahoma Press, 1995), 60–61.
59. Schroeder and Mason, *Colony on the Move*, 522–23 and Thomas, 27, in Pratt and Scurlock, "Llano, River and Mountains," 56; James F. Brooks, introduction to *Captives and Cousins: Slavery, Kinship, and Community in the Southwest Borderlands* (Chapel Hill: University of North Carolina, 2004).
60. David J. Weber, *The Mexican Frontier: The American Southwest Under Mexico, 1821–1846* (Albuquerque: University of New Mexico Press, 1981), xx, 30–35; Griffen, *Apaches at War and Peace*, 119.
61. Weber, 97.
62. Andres Resendez, *Changing National Identities at the Frontier: Texas and New Mexico* (Cambridge: Cambridge University Press, 2005), 173; Lynne Sebastian and Signa Larralde, *Living on the Land: 11,000 Years of Human Adaptation in Southeastern New Mexico* Cultural Resources Series No. 6, 1989; Overview of Cultural Resources in the Roswell District, New Mexico Bureau of Land Management, submitted by Richard C. Chapman, P.I. January 1989, 93, citing Arthur J. Jelinek "1967: A Prehistoric Sequence in the Middle Pecos Valley, New Mexico" (University of Michigan, Museum of Anthropology, Anthropological Papers No. 31, Ann Arbor); Pratt and Scurlock, "Llano, River and Mountains," 67.
63. Jose Joaquin Calvo, Cuartel General en Chihuahua, Agosto 30 de 1832, Comandancia

General e Inspeccion del Estado de Chihuahua y territorio del Nuevo Mejico, Orden General Circular, eoncosing Bases pincipales para conceder la paz, a los Apaches sublevado en el estado de Chihuahua, Encinillas Julio 28 de 1832, in Alfred B. Thomas, "The Mescalero Apache, 1653–1874," *Apache Indians XI: American Indian Ethnohistory, Indians of the Southwest* (New York: Garland Publishing, 1974), 15.
64. William B. Griffen, *Utmost Good Faith: Patterns of Apache-Mexican Hostilities in Northern Chihuahua Border Warfare, 1821–1848* (Albuquerque: University of New Mexico Press, 1986), 70.
65. Griffen, 72.
66. Griffen, 88.
67. Griffen, 91.
68. Griffen, 97.
69. Griffen, 103.

Chapter Four: War, Exploration, and Conquest, 1836-1865

1. Carole Larson, *Forgotten Frontier: The Story of Southeastern New Mexico* (Albuquerque: University of New Mexico Press, 1993), 27; Gary Clayton Anderson, *The Conquest of Texas: Ethnic Cleansing in the Promised Land, 1825–1875* (Norman: University of Oklahoma Press, 2005), 195–96.
2. Anderson, 211; David J. Weber, *The Mexican Frontier: The American Southwest Under Mexico* (Albuquerque: University of New Mexico Press, 1982), 274; Ernesto Chávez, *The U.S. War with Mexico: A Brief History with Documents* (New York: St. Martin's, 2007), 12.
3. Chávez, 13; Andrés Reséndez, *Changing National Identities at the Frontier: Texas and New Mexico, 1800–1850* (Cambridge: Cambridge University Press, 2005), 24.
4. Anderson, *Conquest of Texas*, 212; Brian DeLay, *War of a Thousand Deserts: Indian Raids and the U.S.-Mexican War* (New Haven: Yale University Press, 2008), 213.
5. DeLay, xviii; Robert V. Hine and John Mack Faragher, *The American West: An Interpretive History* (New Haven: Yale University Press, 2000), 200.
6. Marc Simmons, *New Mexico: An Interpretive History* (Albuquerque: University of New Mexico Press, 1977), 79.
7. Anthony Mora, *Border Dilemmas: Racial and National Uncertainties in New Mexico, 1848–1912* (Raleigh: Duke University Press, 2011), 23.
8. Mora, 24.
9. W. H. Timmons, *El Paso: A Borderlands History* (El Paso: Texas Western Press, 1990), 96–98.
10. Joseph P. Sánchez, Robert L. Spude, and Art Gómez, *New Mexico: A History* (Albuquerque: University of Oklahoma Press, 2013), 108; Mora, *Border Dilemmas*, 43; Simmons, *New Mexico*, 126–131.
11. Simmons, 133–37; Reséndez, *Changing National Identities*, 241.
12. Paula Rebert, *La Gran Línea: Mapping the United States—Mexico Border, 1849–1857* (Austin: University of Texas Press, 2001), 14; David Lavender, *The Southwest* (Albuquerque: University of New Mexico Press, 1984), 148.
13. Howard Roberts Lamar, *The Far Southwest, 1846–1912: A Territorial History* (New York: W. W. Norton and Company, 1965), 72.
14. Chávez, *The U.S. War with Mexico*, 21.
15. Hine and Faragher, *American West*, 236; Gary Clayton Anderson and Kathleen P. Chamberlain, *Power and Promise: The Changing American West* (New York: Pearson, 2008), 99.
16. Kenneth Franklin Neighbors, *Robert Simpson Neighbors and the Texas Frontier, 1836–1859* (Waco: Texian Press, 1975), 70.

17. Neighbors, 76; John S. Ford, "Report upon the practicability of a Route from Austin to El Paso del Norte," *Texas Democrat*, June 18, 1849; Anderson and Chamberlain, *Power and Promise*, 99; W. C. Jameson, *The Guadalupe Mountains: Island in the Desert* (El Paso: Texas Western Press, 1994), 12.
18. Neighbors, 80; Ford, 79.
19. Ford, 81.
20. Jameson, *Guadalupe Mountains*, 15.
21. Lavender, *Southwest*, 145.
22. W. Eugene Hollon, *Beyond the Cross Timbers: The Travels of Randolph B. Marcy, 1812–1887* (Norman: University of Oklahoma Press, 1955), 77; Jameson, *Guadalupe Mountains*, 18; William H. Goetzman, *Exploration and Empire: The Explorer and the Scientist in the Winning of the American West* (Austin: Texas State Historical Association), 271–72.
23. Averam B. Bender "Opening Routes across West Texas, 1848–1850," *Southwestern Historical Quarterly* 37, no. 2 (October 1933): 119; William H. Goetzmann, *Exploration and Empire: The Explorer and the Scientist in the Winning of the American West* (Austin: Texas State Historical Association, 1993), 273.
24. C. C. Cox, "From Texas to California in 1849: Diary of C. C. Cox," *Southwest Historical Quarterly* 29, no. 1 (July 1925): 47.
25. Cox, 48.
26. Murchison to Richardson, Camp near Paso del Norte, June 23, 1849, 213; C. C. Cox, "From Texas to California in 1849,"and appendix, "Letters by Cornelius Cox's Contemporaries," *Southwestern Historical Quarterly* 29, no. 3 (January 1926), 212–22.
27. Cox, 212–22.
28. "Wagon Trains and Cattle Herds on the Trail in the 1850s," *West Texas Historical Association Annual Yearbook* 30 (October 1954): 149.
29. Cox, "From Texas to California in 1849," 181.
30. Brevet Brigadier John Garland to Lieutenant Colonel L. Thomas, June 30, 1854, in F. T. Cheetham, "El Camino Militar," *New Mexico Historical Review* 15, no. 1 (January 1940), 5; Frank D. Reeve, "The Apache Indians in Texas," *Southwestern Historical Quarterly* L, no. 2 (October 1946), 203; see W. C. Holden, "Frontier Defense, 1846–1860" *West Texas Historical Association Year Book* 6 (June 1930), 47.
31. "Fight with the Apaches," Telegraph and Texas Register, January 3, 1850, 2, reprinted in *Southwestern Historical Quarterly* 48, no. 2 (October 1944).
32. J. J. Bowden, "The Captivity and Suffering of Mrs. Jane Wilson" *Password* 17, no. 2 (Summer 1972): 51–72.
33. DeLay, *War of a Thousand Deserts*, xiii.
34. Paula Rebert, *La Gran Línea: Mapping the U.S.–Mexico Boundary, 1849–1857* (Austin, University of Texas Press, 2001), 23.
35. Lavender, *Southwest*, 149; L. David Norris, James C. Milligan, and Odie B. Faulk, *William H. Emory: Soldier-Scientist* (Tucson: University of Arizona Press, 1998), 1967.
36. Jameson, *Guadalupe Mountains*, 20; Robert V. Hine, *Bartlett's West: Drawing the Mexican Boundary* (New Haven: Yale University Press, 1968), 33.
37. Joseph Richard Werne, *The Imaginary Line: A History of the United States and Mexican Boundary Survey, 1848–1857* (Fort Worth: Texas Christian University Press, 2007), 98; Hine, 33.
38. Lavender, *Southwest*, 152; Rachel St. John, *Line in the Sand: A History of the Western U.S.-Mexico Border* (Princeton: Princeton University Press, 2012), 46.
39. Lee Myers, "Pope's Wells," *New Mexico Historical Review* 38, no. 4 (October 1963): 273–99.
40. Myers, 279.
41. Myers, 288; John Miller Morris, *El Llano Estacado: Exploration and Imagination on the High Plains of Texas and New Mexico, 1536–1860* (Austin: Texas State Historical Association, 1997), 313.

42. A. B. Gray, "Survey of a Route for the Southern Pacific Railroad on the Thirty-Second Parallel, for the Texas Western Railroad Company" (Cincinnati: Wrightson, 1856), 24; Morris, 313.
43. Hine and Faragher, *American West*, 278.
44. Waterman L. Ormsby, *The Butterfield Overland Mail: Only Through Passenger on the First Westbound Stage*, Lyle H. Wright and Josephine M. Bynum, eds. (San Marino: Huntington Library, 1942); Hal K. Rothman, *Promises Beheld and the Limits of Place: A Historic Resource Study of Carlsbad Caverns and Guadalupe Mountains National Parks and Surrounding Area* (National Park Service, Southwest Regional Office, 1998), 93.
45. Roscoe P. Conkling and Margaret B. Conkling, *The Butterfield Overland Mail, 1857–1869* (Glendale: The Arthur C. Clarke Company, 1947).
46. Joseph Leach, "Stagecoach Through the Pass—The Butterfield Overland Mail Comes to El Paso," *Password: The El Paso Historical Society* 3, no. 4 (1958): 135.
47. Robert N. Mullin, *Stagecoach Pioneers of the Southwest* (El Paso: Texas Western Press, 1983), 67.
48. C. L. Sonnichsen, *The Mescalero Apaches* (Norman: University of Oklahoma Press, 1986), 67; Alfred B. Thomas, "The Mescalero Apache, 1653–1874" in *Apache Indians XI: American Indian Ethnohistory, Indians of the Southwest* (New York: Garland, 1974), 33.
49. Lieutenant W. H. C. Whiting, as cited in Sonnichsen, 68.
50. Kelly R. Hays, "General Garland's War: The Mescalero Campaign, 1854–1855," *New Mexico Historical Review* 67, no. 3 (July 1992): 251–68; Sonnichsen, 69.
51. Thomas, "Mescalero Apache," 34. Sonnichsen, 71.
52. John A. Rogers, Special Indian Agent and Commissioner, San Antonio, Texas, November 25, 1851, to Governor P. H. Bell, in Indian Papers MS., Texas State Archives, Austin, TX.
53. The 1852 Treaty with the Apache; Hays, "General Garland's War," 254.
54. Hays, 256.
55. Hays, 258.
56. Sonnichsen, *Mescalero Apaches*, 88.
57. Hays, "General Garland's War," 262.
58. Morris E. Opler, "Mescalero Apache History in the Southwest," *New Mexico Historical Review* 25, no. 1 (January 1950), 8; NMSA; Microfilm, NMSU Special Collections; Myers, "Pope's Wells," 100.
59. Thomas, "Mescalero Apache," Hays, "General Garland's War," 270.
60. Agent Michael Steck (Apache Agency, NM, June 16, 1856) to Governor Meriwether (governor and superintendent of Indian Affairs), Microfilm, NMSU Special Collections; Lt. Col. D. J. Miles (Fort Fillmore, New Mexico, September 9, 1855) to Dr. Michael Steck (U.S. Indian Agent, Fort Thorn, New Mexico), Steck Papers, University of New Mexico.
61. Morris Edward Opler and Catherine H. Opler, "Mescalero Apache History in the Southwest" *New Mexico Historical Review* 25, no. 1 (January 1950): 10; correspondence between Steck and Meriwether, 1856, Steck Papers, NMSU.
62. Bender, "Opening Routes," 141; Frank D. Reeve, "The Apache Indians in Texas," *Southwestern Historical Quarterly* L, no. 2 (October 1946): 202.
63. Robert M. Utley, *The Indian Frontier of the American West, 1846–1890* (Albuquerque: University of New Mexico Press, 1984), 67.
64. Howard Roberts Lamar, *The Far Southwest 1846–1912: A Territorial History* (New York: W.W. Norton & Company, 1966), 125; Larson, *Forgotten Frontier*, 44.
65. Opler and Opler, "Mescalero Apache History," 12; Marc Simmons, *New Mexico: An Interpretive History* (Albuquerque: University of New Mexico Press, 1977), 143.
66. Sonnichsen, *Mescalero Apaches*, 112.
67. Larson, *Forgotten Frontier*, 49; Sonnichsen, 31.
68. Sonnichsen, 135.

Chapter Five: Conflict and Early Community Formation, 1865-1881

1. Carole Larson, *Forgotten Frontier: The Story of Southeastern New Mexico* (Albuquerque: University of New Mexico Press, 1993), 6; Howard Roberts Lamar, *The Far Southwest, 1846–1912: A Territorial History* (New York: W.W. Norton and Company, 1970), 136.
2. Richard White, *"It's Your Misfortune and None of My Own": A New History of the American West* (Norman: University of Oklahoma Press), 277.
3. Robert V. Hine and John Mack Faragher, *The American West: A New Interpretive History* (New Haven: Yale University Press, 2000), 432.
4. William Deverell, "Fighting Words: The Significance of the American West in the History of the United States," *Western Historical Quarterly* 25, no. 2 (Summer 1994): 187.
5. Thomas Lloyd Miller, *The Public Lands of Texas, 1519–1972* (Norman: University of Oklahoma Press, 1970).
6. Tom E. Sheridan, *The Bitter River: A Brief Historical Survey of the Middle Pecos River Basin* (Roswell District Office, Roswell, NM: Bureau of Land Management, 1975), 56; Lynne Sebastian and Signe Larralde, *Living on the Land: 11,000 Years of Human Habitation in Southeastern New Mexico*, Cultural Resources Series No. 6 (Roswell, NM: Bureau of Land Management, 1989); Larson, *Forgotten Frontier*, 55; Miller, *Public Lands of Texas*, xii.
7. Roxanne Dunbar-Ortiz, *Roots of Resistance: A History of Land Tenure in New Mexico* (Norman: University of Oklahoma Press, 2007), 5; Larson, *Forgotten Frontier*, 35; Yvonne R. Oakes, *The Ontiberos Site: A Hispanic Homestead near Roswell, New Mexico*, Laboratory of Anthropology Notes 311 (Santa Fe: Office of Archaeological Studies, Museum of New Mexico, 1983).
8. Oakes, 26.
9. Benjamin Levy, *Draft Historic Resource Study, Guadalupe Mountains National Park* (Washington, D.C.: National Park Service, 1971); G. Emlen Hall, *High and Dry: The Texas-New Mexico Struggle for the Pecos River* (Albuquerque: University of New Mexico Press, 2002), ix.
10. Lamar, *Far Southwest*, 139.
11. Lewis Atherton, *The Cattle Kings* (Lincoln: University of Nebraska Press, 1961), 2; Boyd C. Pratt and Dan Scurlock, "Llano, River, and Mountains: The Southeast New Mexico Regional Overview, Volume 1" (Santa Fe: Historic Preservation Division, Office of Cultural Affairs of the State of New Mexico, 1989): 93.
12. Atherton, *The Cattle Kings*, 14.
13. Sheridan, *Bitter River*, 40.
14. Pratt and Scurlock, "Llano, River and Mountains," 94; C. L. Sonnichsen, *The Mescalero Apaches* (Norman: University of Oklahoma Press, 1958), 174.
15. Recollections of Ben Gillmore, typescript in the vertical files of the Guadalupe Mountains National Park headquarters, Pine Springs, Texas.
16. Peggy S. Froeschauer, *Cultural Landscape Report for Frijole Ranch, Guadalupe Mountains National Park* (Santa Fe: National Park Service, 1995), 14–19.
17. Levy, *Draft Historic Resource Study*, 124–28.
18. Pratt and Scurlock, "Llano, River and Mountains," 94.
19. Pratt and Scurlock, 98; Sheridan, *Bitter River*, 55.
20. Pratt and Scurlock, 99.
21. Anthony Mora, *Border Dilemmas: Racial and National Uncertainties in New Mexico, 1848–1912* (Durham: Duke University Press, 2011), 9–10.
22. Larson, *Forgotten Frontier*, 43; Marc Simmons *New Mexico: An Interpretive History* (Albuquerque: University of New Mexico Press, 1988), 141.
23. Oakes, *Ontiberos Site*, 123; Pratt and Scurlock, "Llano, River and Mountains," 60.

24. Hal K. Rothman, *Promises Beheld and the Limits of Place: A Historic Resource Study of Carlsbad Caverns and Guadalupe Mountains National Parks and Surrounding Areas* (National Park Service, Southwest Regional Office, 1998), 97.
25. Pratt and Scurlock, "Llano, River and Mountains," 65.
26. Pratt and Scurlock, 137; Rothman, *Promises Beheld*, 98.
27. Sheridan, *Bitter River*, 35.
28. Pratt and Scurlock, "Llano, River and Mountains," 61.
29. Oakes, *Ontiberos Site*, 32–38; Larson, *Forgotten Frontier*, 45.
30. Pratt and Scurlock, "Llano, River and Mountains," 62; Oakes, 47–48.
31. Oakes, 38.
32. Sheridan, *Bitter River*, 40–41.
33. Ben Gilmore, typescript of personal memories in the vertical files of the Guadalupe Mountains National Park Headquarters, Pine Springs, Texas.
34. Oakes, *Ontiberos Site*, 38. The Texas State Government Land Office confirms that few land claims for northeastern El Paso County came into the office during the 1860s and 1870s. Additionally, research in the Culberson County Records Office shed little light on the colonization of land in the Guadalupes.
35. Miller, *Public Lands of Texas*, xii.
36. Miller, 19; Map of Culberson County, March 22, 1943, in General Land Office, Austin, Texas.
37. Map of Culberson County.
38. Hine and Faragher, *American West*, 290; W. H. Timmons, *El Paso: A Borderlands History* (El Paso: Texas Western Press, 1990).
39. Robert M. Utley, *Fort Davis National Historic Site, Texas* (Washington: U.S. Department of the Interior, National Park Service, 1965).
40. Larson, *Forgotten Frontier*, 81; Christopher D. Adams, Diane E. White, and David M. Johnson, *Last Chance Canyon 1869 Apache/Cavalry Battle Site*, prepared by Lincoln National Forest Heritage Program, Alamogordo, New Mexico, 2000.
41. Averam B. Bender, "A Study of Mescalero Apache Indians, 1846–1880," in David Agee Hoor, ed., *American Indian Ethnohistory: Indians of the Southwest* (New York: Garland, 1974); Lawrence L. Mehren, ed., "Scouting for Mescaleros: The Campaign of 1873," *Arizona and the West* 10, no. 2 (September 1968): 171–90.
42. Frank D. Reeve, "The Apache Indians in Texas," *Southwestern Historical Quarterly* L, no. 2 (October 1946): 210.
43. Sonnichsen, *Mescalero Apaches*, 137.
44. Utley, *Fort Davis*, 41.
45. Thomas Dunlay, *Wolves for the Blue Soldiers: Indian Scouts and Auxiliaries with the United States Army, 1860–90* (Lincoln: University of Nebraska Press, 1987).
46. R. David Edmunds, *The People: A History of Native America* (Wadsworth, 2006).
47. "African Americans in the Frontier Army," Fort Davis National Historic Site, U.S. National Park Service, accessed May 23, 2007, http://www.nps.gov/foda.
48. William H. Leckie, *The Buffalo Soldiers: A Narrative of the Negro Cavalry in the West* (Norman: University of Oklahoma Press, 1967), 84.
49. Leckie, 87.
50. Utley, *Fort Davis*, 42.
51. Leckie, *Buffalo Soldiers*, 90.
52. Bruce J. Dinges, "The Victorio Campaign of 1880: Cooperation and Conflict on the United States-Mexico Border," *New Mexico Historical Review* 62, no. 1 (January 1987): 83, 81–94.
53. Dinges, 88.
54. "African Americans in the Frontier Army."

55. Frank D. Reeve, "The Apache Indians in Texas," *Southwestern Historical Quarterly* L, no. 2 (October 1946): 211; Bruce B. MacLachlan, "The Mescalero Apache Quest for Law and Order" *Journal of the West* 3, no. 4 (October 1964): 441–58.
56. J. J. Bowden, "The Magoffin Salt War," *Password* 7, no. 3, (Summer 1962): 95–121; Paul Cool, *Salt Warriors: Insurgency on the Rio Grande* (College Station: Texas A&M University Press, 2008), 5; *El Paso Troubles in Texas*, Department of War, 1877.
57. Bowden, "Magoffin Salt War," 108.
58. Cool, *Salt Warriors*, 126.
59. Bowden, "Magoffin Salt War," 111; Cool, 13.
60. White, *"It's Your Misfortune,"* 431; Timmons, *El Paso*, 259.

Chapter Six: The Nature of Economic Development in the Texas-New Mexico Borderlands, 1880–1915

1. Richard White, *"It's Your Misfortune and None of My Own": A New History of the American West* (Norman: The University of Oklahoma Press, 1991), 432.
2. Hal K. Rothman, *Promises Beheld and the Limits of Place: A Historic Resource Study of Carlsbad Caverns and Guadalupe Mountains National Parks and Surrounding Areas* (National Park Service, Southwest Regional Office, 1998), 139.
3. Rothman, *Promises Beheld*, 105.
4. Boyd C. Pratt and Dan Scurlock, "Llano, River, and Mountains: The Southeast New Mexico Regional Overview, Volume 1" (Santa Fe: Historic Preservation Division, Office of Cultural Affairs of the State of New Mexico, 1989): 102.
5. Rothman, *Promises Beheld*, 106.
6. Patricia Patterson, *Queen, New Mexico: A Historical Perspective on the Settlement in the Guadalupe Mountains, 1865–1975* (Roswell: Hall Poorbaugh Press, 1985), 14; Carole Larson, *Forgotten Frontier: The Story of Southeastern New Mexico* (Albuquerque: University of New Mexico Press, 1993), 282.
7. Pratt and Scurlock, "Llano, River and Mountains," 103.
8. Patterson, *Queen, New Mexico*, 28–32.
9. Jerry R. Cox, *Ghosts of the Guadalupes: A Factual History of Agriculture, Families and Violence Between 1905 and 1955 in Southern New Mexico* (Lubbock: Action, 2005), 214.
10. Patterson, *Queen, New Mexico*, 28–32; Cox, 244.
11. Dolph Shattuck, not to be confused with James Adolphus "Dolph" Williams, who settled to the southwestern side of the Guadalupe Mountains.
12. Patterson, *Queen, New Mexico*, 45, 72.
13. Patterson, 60–61.
14. Patterson, 67–70.
15. Patterson, 79–88.
16. Patterson, 121, 123.
17. Patterson, 129, 131.
18. Cox, *Ghosts of the Guadalupes*, 3.
19. Interview with T. Holmsley, August 16, 1973, interviewed by Paul Patterson, Sierra Blanca, Texas, Texas Tech University Special/Southwest Collection, Lubbock, Texas.
20. Holmsley.
21. Holmsley.
22. Cox, *Ghosts of the Guadalupes*, 271.
23. Delmar Hayter, "The Early Economic Development of the Pecos River Valley of New Mexico and Texas, 1880–1900" *West Texas Historical Association Year Book* 62 (1986): 69–85.
24. W. C. Jameson, *The Guadalupe Mountains: Island in the Desert* (El Paso: Texas Western Press, 1994), 47.

25. John F. Chapman, "Visit to nephew of Dolph Williams, August 31, 1972," Guadalupe Mountains H2215, Guadalupe Mountains National Park Library, Pine Springs, Texas; and Tom Williams interview, Guadalupe Mountains National Park Library, Pine Springs, Texas.
26. Jameson, *Guadalupe Mountains*, 47.
27. She was looking at the 1881 document, "Assessment Roll of Property in El Paso County; Owned by Non-Residents," Peggy Froeschauer, *Cultural Landscape Report for Frijole Ranch* (Santa Fe: National Park Service, 1995), 16.
28. Froeschauer, *Cultural Landscape Report*, 14.
29. Rothman, *Promises Beheld*, 139; Ben Gilmore, "History of Guadalupe Mountains National Park," unpublished typescript, vertical file, Guadalupe Mountains National Park Library, 4–8.
30. Vivian Grubb, "John Thomas Smith: A Van Horn Pioneer," *Van Horn Advocate* May 5, 1990.
31. Rothman, *Promises Beheld*, 139; Gilmore, "History of Guadalupe," 4–8.
32. General Land Office for the State of Texas, Austin, Texas.
33. Rosa Lee Wylie, *History of Van Horn and Culberson County, Texas* (Hereford, TX: Pioneer, 1973); Hayter, "Early Economic Development," 71.
34. These salt flats refer to the flats of the 1877 Salt War.
35. Wylie, *History of Van Horn*, 25; Delmar Hayter, "The Crookedest River in the World: Social and Economic Development of the Pecos River Valley" (PhD diss., Texas Tech University, 1998), 28.
36. Larson, *Forgotten Frontier*, 28.
37. Rothman, *Promises Beheld*, 104.
38. Pratt and Scurlock, "Llano, River and Mountains," 142.
39. Larson, *Forgotten Frontier*, 29; Rothman, *Promises Beheld*, 105.
40. Donald Worster, *Rivers of Empire: Water, Aridity, and the Growth of the American West* (Oxford: Oxford University Press, 1992).
41. Rothman, *Promises Beheld*, 107.
42. Hayter, "The Crookedest River," 7.
43. Tom Sheridan, *The Bitter River: A Brief Historical Survey of the Middle Pecos River Basin* (Bureau of Land Roswell: Management, Roswell District Office, 1975), 56; Lynne Sebastian and Signa Larralde, *Living on the Land: 11,000 Years of Human Adaptation in Southeastern New Mexico*, Cultural Resources Series No. 6. (Roswell, NM: Bureau of Land Management, 1989), 121. See also Patrick Dearen, *Bitter Watters: The Struggles of the Pecos River* (Norman: University of Oklahoma Press, 2016).
44. Elvis E. Fleming, "J. J. Hagerman and the Pecos River Railroad," *Permian Historical Annual* 33 (December 1973): 21–35.
45. Sheridan, *Bitter River*, 57; Sebastian and Larralde, *Living on the Land*, 122.
46. Sheridan, 62.
47. Sebastian and Larralde, *Living on the Land*, 123.
48. Sheridan, *Bitter River*, 59.
49. Sheridan, 65.
50. Sheridan, 67–68.
51. Sheridan, 68.
52. Pratt and Scurlock, "Llano, River and Mountains," 181.
53. Sheridan, *Bitter River*, 68.
54. Jimmy M. Skaggs, *The Great Guano Rush: Entrepreneurs and American Overseas Expansion* (New York: St. Martin's, 1994), 129–49; Gregory T. Cushman, *Guano and the Opening of the Pacific World: A Global Ecological History* (New York: Cambridge University Press, 2013), 21.
55. Rothman, *Promises Beheld*, 143.
56. Rothman, 145.

57. Rothman, 146.
58. Rothman, 147.

Chapter Seven: The Interwar Years, 1919-1941

1. Carole Larson, *Forgotten Frontier: The Story of Southeastern New Mexico* (Albuquerque: University of New Mexico Press, 1993).
2. Abstract number 6125, file number 100892, title date May 15, 1907, section 46, block 66, TSP 1, Texas General Land Office, Austin, Texas. According to the files of the General Land Office, Williams purchased 653 acres from Henry Belcher in 1917.
3. John F. Chapman, "Visit to nephew of Dolph Williams, August 31, 1972," Guadalupe Mountains H2215, Guadalupe Mountains National Park Library, Pine Springs, Texas; and Tom Williams interview, Guadalupe Mountains National Park Library, Pine Springs, Texas.
4. Chapman, "Visit to nephew of Dolph Williams"; Williams interview.
5. Chapman; Williams interview.
6. Chapman; Williams interview.
7. Chapman; Williams interview.
8. Chapman; Williams interview.
9. See James F. Brooks, *Captives and Cousins: Slavery, Kinship, and Community in the Southwest Borderlands* (Chapel Hill: University of North Carolina Press, 2002); Pekka Hämäläinen, *The Comanche Empire* (New Haven: Yale University Press, 2007).
10. William H. Leckie, *The Buffalo Soldiers: A Narrative of the Negro Cavalry in the West* (Norman: University of Oklahoma Press, 1967), 217.
11. See William B. Griffen, *Apaches at War and Peace: The Janos Presidio, 1750–1858* (Norman: University of Oklahoma Press, 1998), 54.
12. Chapman, "Visit to nephew of Dolph Williams"; Williams interview. Also see interview on file in Guadalupe Mountains National Park Library. Email correspondence with the great granddaughter of Geronimo Segura, Leticia Robles, between 2007 and 2009. Notes and emails in author's possession.
13. Hal K. Rothman, *Promises Beheld and the Limits of Place: A Historic Resource Study of Carlsbad Caverns and Guadalupe Mountains National Parks and Surrounding Areas* (National Park Service, Southwest Regional Office, 1998), 139; From "Williams Ranch, First Draft, 1977," Guadalupe Mountains National Park, vertical file, Guadalupe Mountains National Park Library, Pine Springs, Texas.
14. Chapman, "Visit to nephew of Dolph Williams"; Williams interview.
15. Personal communication with Ruth Segura Padilla (granddaughter of Geronimo Segura) and Leticia Segura Robles (great niece of Geronimo Segura).
16. Chapman, "Visit to nephew of Dolph Williams"; Williams interview.
17. Peggy S. Froeschauer, *Cultural Landscape Report for Frijole Ranch* (Santa Fe: Guadalupe Mountains National Park Service, 1995), 8.
18. Froeschauer, *Cultural Landscape Report*, 8.
19. Froeschauer, *Cultural Landscape Report*, 52; abstract number 5961, file number 133333, section 34, block 65, TSP 1, in Texas State General Land Office, Austin, Texas.
20. Froeschauer, *Cultural Landscape Report*, 79.
21. Frijole Ranch, Smith family reunion, interview June 28, 1992, by Larry Henderson, Guadalupe Mountains National Park Library, Pine Springs, Texas.
22. Frijole Ranch.
23. Frijole Ranch.
24. Rosa Lee Wylie, *History of Van Horn and Culberson County, Texas* (Hereford, TX: Pioneer, 1973), 129.
25. January 12, 1939, *The Van Horn Advocate*, The Center for American History, Special Collections, University of Texas at Austin.

26. Files in the Texas Government Land Office, Austin, Texas; interview with Noel Kincaid, 1983, Guadalupe Mountains National Park Library, Pine Springs, Texas.
27. Kincaid.
28. Files in the Texas Government Land Office.
29. Interview with Noel Kincaid.
30. Kincaid.
31. Kincaid.
32. Froeschauer, *Cultural Landscape Report*, 24.
33. Keith Elliot, "The Treasure of the Guadalupes: An Interview with Wallace E. Pratt," *The Humble Way* (Third Quarter, 1970); Interview with Wallace C. Pratt, Bill Griggs, Tucson, AZ, December 1973, Texas Tech Southwest/Special Collections, Lubbock, Texas; "Memorial," *The American Association of Petroleum Geologists Bulletin* 66, no. 9 (September 1982): 1413.
34. Judith K. Fabry, "Guadalupe Mountains National Park: An Administrative History," Southwest Cultural Resources Center, Professional Papers No. 19, Southwest Region, Division of History, Santa Fe, NM (December 1998), 29; "Memorial," 1414.
35. Interview with Pratt; Fabry, 31.
36. Fabry.
37. Kimberly A. Sawyer, "Cultural Landscapes of McKittrick Canyon, Guadalupe Mountains National Park, Texas" (master's thesis, Texas Tech University, May 2001), 86.
38. Sawyer, 88; Interview with Pratt.
39. Interview with Pratt.
40. Delmar Hayter, "The Crookedest River in the World: Social and Economic Development of the Pecos River Valley" (PhD diss., Texas Tech University, 1998), 115–20.
41. Hayter, "Crookedest River in the World," 146.
42. Hayter, "Early Economic Development," 83.
43. Carl Coke Rister, *Oil! Titan of the Southwest* (Norman: University of Oklahoma Press, 1949).
44. "More Oil in the Salt Flat Region," *El Paso Herald*, July 30, 1901, 5.
45. Hayter, "Early Economic Development," 93.
46. Hayter, 140–45; Rister, *Oil!*; Rinehart Oil News Company, *West Texas-New Mexico Oil* (Tulsa: Rinehart Oil News Company, 1937).
47. Rister; Rinehart Oil News Company.
48. "West Texas Wildcatting Trend Sharp," *El Paso Times*, October 26, 1941, 9.
49. "Many West Texas Wells Pump Oil into Defense Tanks," *El Paso Herald Post*, November 17, 1941.
50. "Oil Firms Join to Drill Second Well," *El Paso Herald Post*, July 23, 1960, 1.
51. Richard White, *"It's Your Misfortune and None of My Own": A New History of the American West* (Norman: The University of Oklahoma Press, 1991), 395.
52. Rothman, *Promises Beheld*, 126.
53. A.W. Shepherd, "$25 Million Expansion in Potash Industry," *El Paso Herald-Post*, April 28, 1956.
54. Rothman, *Promises Beheld*, 169.
55. Rothman, 170; "Potash Plant, $350,000 School Lead Construction," *El Paso Herald Post*, November 11, 1940, 24.
56. Leah Dilworth, *Imagining Indians in the Southwest: Persistent Visions of a Primitive Past* (Smithsonian Institution Scholarly Press, 1997); Hal K. Rothman, ed., *The Culture of Tourism, the Tourism of Culture: Selling the Past to the Present in the American Southwest* (Albuquerque: University of New Mexico Press, 2003).
57. Martin Padget, *Indian Country: Travels in the American Southwest, 1840–1935* (Albuquerque: University of New Mexico Press, 2006); Kathleen L. Howard and Diana F. Pardue, *Inventing the Southwest: The Fred Harvey Company and American Indian Art* (Flagstaff: Northland Publishers, 1996).

58. Rothman, *Culture of Tourism*.
59. David Dorado Romo, *Ringside Seat to a Revolution: An Underground Cultural History of El Paso and Juárez, 1893–1923* (El Paso: Cinco Puntos Press, 2005), 86.
60. Rothman, *Promises Beheld*, 149.
61. Rothman, 150.
62. Rothman, 151.
63. Rothman, 153.
64. Rothman, 155.
65. Rothman, 156.
66. Rothman, 160.
67. Rothman, 160; Neel Baumgardner, "Bordering North America: Constructing Wilderness along the Periphery of Canada, Mexico, and the United States" (PhD diss., University of Texas at Austin, 2013), 45.
68. Ben Gilmore, typescript of personal memories in the vertical files of the Guadalupe Mountains National Park headquarters, Pine Springs, Texas.
69. Richard Melzer, *Coming of Age in the Great Depression: The Civilian Conservation Corps in New Mexico, 1933–1942* (Las Cruces: Yucca Tree Press, 2000).
70. Unpublished report, Eric Dillingham, Civilian Conservation Corps Camps on the Sacramento Ranger District, Lincoln National Forest, and Beyond, 1933–1942.
71. Dillingham.
72. Melzer, *Coming of Age*; Dillingham.
73. Dillingham.
74. Dillingham.
75. Dillingham.
76. Melzer, *Coming of Age*.
77. Gerald D. Nash, *The American West Transformed: The Impact of the Second World War* (Bloomington: Indiana University Press, 1985), 60; Kevin J. Fernlund, ed., *The Cold War American West, 1945–1989* (Albuquerque: University of New Mexico Press, 1998), 7.
78. Michael Walsh, "The Legacy of Containment: The Military-Industrial Complex and the New American West," in Fernlund, ed., *The Cold War American West*, 88.

Chapter Eight: The Creation of Guadalupe Mountains National Park

1. Hal K. Rothman, *Promises Beheld and the Limits of Place: A Historic Resource Study of Carlsbad Caverns and Guadalupe Mountains National Parks and Surrounding Areas*, (National Park Service, Southwest Regional Office, 1998), 219.
2. Alfred Runte, *National Parks: The American Experience*, 3rd ed. (Lincoln: University of Nebraska Press, 1997), 112.
3. Judith K. Fabry, "Guadalupe Mountains National Park: An Administrative History," Southwest Cultural Resources Center, Professional Papers No. 19, Southwest Region, Division of History, Santa Fe, NM (December 1998), 17.
4. Fabry, "Guadalupe Mountains," 17.
5. *Carlsbad Current-Argus*, March 16, 1928, vertical reference file, Guadalupe Mountains National Park, Special/Southwest Collections, Texas Tech University.
6. Fabry, "Guadalupe Mountains," 20.
7. Neel Baumgardner, "Bordering North America: Constructing Wilderness along the Periphery of Canada, Mexico, and the United States" (PhD diss., University of Texas at Austin, 2013), 7.
8. Fabry, "Guadalupe Mountains," 21; Rothman, *Promises Beheld*, 180.
9. Fabry, 18–19.
10. Rothman, *Promises Beheld*, 181.
11. Fabry, "Guadalupe Mountains," 25.

12. D. D. Obert, Assistant Landscape Architect, National Park Service "Narrative Report on McKittrick Canyon, Culberson County, Texas," for Texas State Parks Board, Austin, Glenn Biggs Papers S85.1, box 3, folder 7, Southwest Collection, Texas Tech University.
13. Fabry, "Guadalupe Mountains," 24; Rothman, *Promises Beheld*, 182.
14. Fabry, 26
15. Fabry, 27
16. John Jameson, "The Quest for a National Park in Texas," *West Texas Historical Association Notebook* 50, no. 47 (1974): 48.
17. Runte, *National Parks*, 7.
18. Baumgardner, "Bordering North America," 47.
19. Jameson, "Quest for a National Park," 51.
20. Rothman, *Promises Beheld*, 172.
21. Rothman, 175.
22. Rothman, 195; Runte, *National Parks*, 116.
23. Rothman, 198.
24. Rothman, 189.
25. Ethan Carr, *Mission 66: Modernism and the National Park Dilemma* (Amherst: University of Massachusetts Press, 2007); Rothman, 209.
26. Monte L. Monroe, "Glenn Biggs and the Crusade for a Guadalupe Mountains National Park" (master's thesis, Texas Tech University, 1991), 15.
27. Monroe, 16.
28. Monroe, 18.
29. Monroe, 21.
30. Monroe, 30.
31. Monroe, 32.
32. Monroe, 33.
33. Thomas J. Allen, Regional Director of the National Park Service, Region 3, Santa Fe, NM, August 15, 1962, box 1, folder file 12, Southwest/Special Collections, Texas Tech University.
34. J. C. Hunter Jr. Abilene, TX, to Secretary of the Interior Stewart Udall, August 21, 1962, box 1, folder, file 12, Southwest Special Collections, Texas Tech University.
35. Glenn Biggs to Wallace Pratt, September 6, 1962, Carlsbad, NM, box 1, folder file 12, Southwest Special Collections, Texas Tech University.
36. Wallace Pratt to J. C. Hunter Jr., January 28, 1963, box 1, folder file 12, Southwest Special Collections, Texas Tech University.
37. Monroe, "Glenn Biggs," 48.
38. Monroe, 51.
39. Glenn Biggs to Joe Pool, February 12, 1963, box 1, folder file 12, Southwest Special Collections, Texas Tech University.
40. Letter from El Paso County judge Glenn Woodward to Biggs, May 13, 1963, box 1, folder 13, Southwest Special Collections, Texas Tech University.
41. Letter from Glenn Biggs to Olin Ashley, editor of the *Odessa American*, July 8, 1963, Glenn Biggs Papers S85.1, box 1, folder 13, Southwest Special Collections, Texas Tech University.
42. Henry Wolf Jr., "Guadalupe Area Unspoiled by Man" *Abilene Reporter-News*, May 19, 1963, Glenn Biggs Papers S85.1, box 1, folder 14, Southwest Special Collections, Texas Tech University.
43. Henry Mathews, "Guadalupes Reveal Breath-Taking Wilderness Scenery" *CURRENT-ARGUS*, May 14, 1963, Carlsbad, NM, Glenn Biggs Papers S85.1, box 1, folder 14, Southwest Special Collections, Texas Tech University.
44. Frank X. Tolbert, "Guadalupe Mountains Road Leads to Beauty" *The Dallas Morning*

News, May 19, 1963, Glenn Biggs Papers S85.1, box 1, folder 14, Southwest Special Collections, Texas Tech University.
45. Glenn Biggs to O. C. Fisher (U.S. Representative, Texas 21st District) February 11, 1963, box 1, folder file 12, Southwest Special Collections, Texas Tech University.
46. O. C. Fisher (U.S. Representative, Texas 21st District) to Biggs, February 15, 1963, box 1, folder file 12, Southwest Special Collections, Texas Tech University.
47. Monroe, "Glenn Biggs," 55.
48. Ralph Yarborough to Glenn Biggs, November 8, 1963, Glenn Biggs Papers S85.1, box 1, folder 15, Southwest Special Collections, Texas Tech University.
49. "Governor Due First Hand View of McKittrick Canyon" *Abilene Reporter-News*, August 20, 1963, Glenn Biggs Papers S85.1, box 1, folder 14, Southwest Special Collections, Texas Tech University.
50. Monroe, "Glenn Biggs," 59.
51. Monroe, 60.
52. Ned Curran, "Senator Says Guadalupe Due Official Park Backing" *Abilene Reporter-News*, November 22, 1963, Glenn Biggs Papers S85.1, box 1, folder 14, Southwest Special Collections, Texas Tech University.
53. Monroe, "Glenn Biggs," 65.
54. Glenn Biggs to Tom Diamond, January 7, 1964, Glenn Biggs Papers S 85.1, box 2, file 1, Southwest Special Collections, Texas Tech University.
55. "Udall Asks Senate Passage of Guadalupe Park Bill," *San Angelo Standard-Times*, September 19, 1964, Glenn Biggs Papers S85.1, box 2, folder 2. Southwest Special Collections, Texas Tech University.
56. Monroe, "Glenn Biggs," 68.
57. Adam M. Sowards, *The Environmental Justice: William O. Douglas and American Conservation* (Oregon State University Press, 2009).
58. "A Guadalupe Mountains Tour with Supreme Court Justice William O. Douglas," miscellaneous document, Glenn Biggs Papers S 85.1, box 5, file 1, Southwest Special Collections, Texas Tech University.
59. Randal F. Dickey Jr. (chairman of the Sierra Club Conservation Committee) to Henry H. During (superintendent of Carlsbad Caverns National Park), January 14, 1965, Glenn Biggs Papers S 85.1, box 5, file 1, Southwest Special Collections, Texas Tech University.
60. Houston-area Sierra Club letter to Senator Alan Bible (National Parks Subcommittee, Senate Interior and Insular Affairs Committee), June 30, 1965, Glenn Biggs Papers S 85.1, box 5, file 2, Southwest Special Collections, Texas Tech University.
61. Monroe, "Glenn Biggs," 75–76.
62. "Guadalupe Park Gets LBJ Backing" *Abilene Reporter-News,* February 10, 1965, Glenn Biggs Papers S 85.1, box 2, file 1, Southwest Special Collections, Texas Tech University.
63. Monroe, "Glenn Biggs," 71.
64. Monroe, 72–75.
65. Hearings Before the Subcommittee on Parks and Recreation of the Committee on Interior and Insular Affairs, U.S. Senate, 89th Congress, First and Second Session. July 21, 1965 and August 9, 1966 (Guadalupe Mountains National Park, Statement of Wallace Pratt), 20. Glenn Biggs Papers S 85.1, box 3, file 2, Southwest Special Collections, Texas Tech University.
66. Hearings Before the Subcommittee on Parks and Recreation of the Committee on Interior and Insular Affairs, U.S. Senate, 89th Congress, First and Second Session, July 21, 1965 and August 9, 1966 (Guadalupe Mountains National Park), Statement of the Honorable Ralph W. Yarborough, p. 9, Glenn Biggs Papers S 85.1, box 3, file 2, Southwest Special Collections, Texas Tech University.
67. "Guadalupes Impress Visiting Senators," *San Angelo Standard-Times*, April 14, 1966,

Glenn Biggs Papers S 85.1, box 3, file 2, Southwest Special Collections, Texas Tech University.
68. Guadalupe Mountains National Park, 89th Congress, Second Session, House of Representatives, Report No.1566, HR 698, June 1, 1966, Committee on Interior and Insular Affairs.
69. Statement of Hon. Ralph Yarborough, a U.S. Senator from the State of Texas, Tuesday, August 9, 1966, U.S. Senate, Subcommittee on Parks and Recreation of the Committee on Interior and Insular Affairs, Washington, D.C., Glenn Biggs Papers S 85.1, box 3, file 2, Southwest Special Collections, Texas Tech University.
70. Monroe, "Glenn Biggs," 77.

Chapter Nine: A National Park for the Twenty-First Century

1. Alfred Runte, *National Parks: The American Experience*, 3rd ed. (Lincoln: University of Nebraska Press, 1997), 210–13.
2. U.S. Department of the Interior, Land and Water Conservation Fund, accessed February 3, 2016, https://www.doi.gov/lwcf; Land and Water Conservation Fund Fact Sheet, accessed February 3, 2016, www.lwcfcoalition.org.
3. Runte, *National Parks*, 229.
4. Judith K. Fabry, "Guadalupe Mountains National Park: An Administrative History," Southwest Cultural Resources Center, Professional Papers No. 19, Southwest Region, Division of History, Santa Fe, NM (December 1998), 55.
5. Fabry, "Guadalupe Mountains," 48; Hal K. Rothman, *Promises Beheld and the Limits of Place: A Historic Resource Study of Carlsbad Caverns and Guadalupe Mountains National Parks and Surrounding Areas* (National Park Service, Southwest Regional Office, 1998), 226.
6. Seth Cantor, "War Knocks out Guadalupe Park, No Funds Now for National Tag," *El Paso Herald-Post*, Wednesday, April 17, 1968.
7. Fabry, "Guadalupe Mountains," 50
8. Rothman, *Promises Beheld*, 226–27.
9. Hal K. Rothman, *The Greening of a Nation?: Environmentalism in the United States since 1945* (New York: Harcourt Brace, 1998), 49–50.
10. Rothman, *Promises Beheld*, 229.
11. Rothman, 230.
12. Fabry, "Guadalupe Mountains," 58.
13. Rothman, *Promises Beheld*, 231.
14. Fabry, "Guadalupe Mountains," 58; Rothman, 238.
15. "Guadalupe, Carlsbad Parks to be Discussed at Parleys," *Albuquerque Journal*, September 22, 1971; "Hearings on Wilderness, *The Mesilla Valley Shopper*, September 22, 1971.
16. Fabry, "Guadalupe Mountains," 59; Rothman, *Promises Beheld*, 237.
17. "Julie Dedicates National Park," *Odessa American*, October 1, 1972.
18. Roger Reisch interview, 1983, tape 1, Guadalupe Mountains National Park Library, Pine Springs, Texas.
19. Rothman, *Promises Beheld*, 40.
20. Gordon Zeigler, "Guadalupe Mountain National Park Drawing Crowds, Rancher 'Fed Up' With Tourists, *Lubbock Avalanche-Journal*, May 27, 1973.
21. Zeigler, "Guadalupe Mountain National Park."
22. Fabry, "Guadalupe Mountains"; "Guadalupe Mountains Park has High Solitude—To Spare," *Lubbock-Avalanche Journal*, July 31, 1977, A-7.
23. "McKittrick Canyon Could be Battlefield," *Roswell Daily Record*, November 14, 1980, 20.
24. Runte, *National Parks*, 214, 233.

25. Fabry, "Guadalupe Mountains," 114.
26. Runte, *National Parks*, 227–28.
27. Rothman, *Greening of a Nation?*, 171–72.
28. Runte, *National Parks*, 228–30; Rothman, *Greening of a Nation?*, 174.
29. Rothman, *The Greening of a Nation?*, 175–76.
30. Richard White, *"It's Your Misfortune and None of My Own": A New History of the American West* (Norman: The University of Oklahoma Press, 1991).
31. "McKittrick Canyon."
32. "McKittrick Canyon."
33. Rothman, *Promises Beheld*, 232.
34. Rothman, 233.
35. Rothman, 234.
36. Reisch interview.
37. Reisch interview.
38. Bill Feather, "Mountain Lion Control: State Game Commission overturns regulation aimed at predators," *New Mexican*, September 20, 1987, B-6.
39. National Park Service, "Importance of Carlsbad Caverns and Guadalupe Mountains National Parks to Area Economy Told," News Release, March 19, 1982, Carlsbad Caverns National Park Library.
40. Cathy Elson, "Guadalupes Appeal to Hikers," *Roswell Daily Record*, May 6, 1984.
41. "Parapalegics Return to a Hero's Welcome," Carlsbad, NM, United Press International, July 18, 1982.
42. Tom Kerr, "The Mountain Trek Heard Round the World," September 22, 1997, Advance Healthcare Networks, Occupational Therapy Practitioners. Accessed June 18, 2015. http://occupational-therapy.advanceweb.com/Article/The-Mountain-Trek-Heard-Round-the-World.aspx.
43. "Guadalupe Mountains park begins to get attention," *The Galveston Daily News*, August 5, 1982.
44. Richard West Sellars, *Preserving Nature in the National Parks: A History* (New Haven: Yale University Press, 2009), 267.
45. Sellars, 273.
46. Sellars, 289.
47. Josh Hicks, "National Park Service delayed $11 billion in maintenance last year because of budget challenges" *Washington Post*, March 25, 2015
48. "Guadalupe Mountains a Star Attraction," *The Lethbridge Herald*, November 14, 1994.
49. Peggy Froeschauer, Cultural Landscape Report for the Frijole Ranch, Guadalupe Mountains National Park, Office of the Associate Regional Director, Planning and Professional Services, Southwest Regional Office, Santa Fe, NM, October 1995.
50. Fred Armstrong and Katie Keller Lynn, eds., *The Guadalupe Mountains Symposium: Proceedings from the 25th Anniversary conference on research and resource management in the Guadalupe Mountains National Park*, April 22–25, 1998, National Park Service, Department of the Interior.
51. Eleanor King and Charles Haeker, "The Archeology of Buffalo Soldiers and Apaches in the Southwest" Archeology in the Parks, Research in the Parks, National Park Service, Department of the Interior. Uploaded March 2016, accessed June 28, 2017, https://www.nps.gov/archeology/sites/npSites/guadalupeMts.htm.

Conclusion: A National Park in the Southwest Borderlands

1. Hal K. Rothman, *Promises Beheld and the Limits of Place: A Historic Resource Study of Carlsbad Caverns and Guadalupe Mountains National Parks and Surrounding Areas*, (National Park Service, Southwest Regional Office, 1998), 219.
2. Rothman, 224.

Index

Albright, Horace, 141, 153, 155, 176
Allen, Thomas J., 160
Anasazi, 27
Antiquities Act of 1906, 4, 142
Apaches, leaders: Barranquito, 79, 80, 97; Chinonero, 76; Josecito, 78, 79; Manuelito, 82; Palanco, 79; Santos, 79; Victorio, 98–100
Apache treaty of 1852, 78
Applegarth, Susan M., 22–24
Archaic period, 20–22, 24, 25, 27, 34
Armijo, Manuel, 54, 61
Artesia, 3, 43, 47, 101, 105, 113, 116, 118, 120, 135–37
Avalon Dam, 115–17

Bartlett, John Russell, 70–72
Bartlett-Conde Agreement, 72
Baylor, John R., 70–72
Belcher, Henry, 110, 111, 122
Benavides, Alonso de, 44
Bent, Charles, 62, 82
Big Bend National Park, 43, 153, 155, 157, 163, 170
Biggs, Glenn, 9, 10, 150, 151, 158–66, 168, 169, 199
Blackdom, New Mexico, 84
Blackwater Draw, 20, 22
Boles, Thomas, 143, 156, 157
Bolson de Mapimi, 49
Bosque Redondo, 79, 82, 87
Bourbon Reforms, 49–51
Bowl, the, 2, 4, 9, 10, 18, 32, 147, 150–57, 168, 171, 177, 182, 187, 188, 194
Buffalo Soldiers, 6, 97, 99, 122, 195
Burnett Cave, 23
Butterfield Overland Mail, 6, 47, 74, 75, 162, 188, 195

Caddo, 29, 38, 47
California Column, 81, 88, 91

Calvo López, José Joaquín, 54
Camino Real, 39, 44, 49
Cammerer, Arno B., 142, 153, 155
Carleton, James, 81, 82
Carlsbad, New Mexico, 7, 8, 21, 23, 25, 43, 47, 48, 86, 88, 101, 106–9, 115, 118–20, 122, 123, 125, 133, 134, 137, 138, 142–44, 146, 151, 162, 163, 177–79, 189, 196, 199
Carlsbad Caverns, 8, 10, 12, 141–43, 147, 152–57, 166, 170, 171, 177, 186, 188, 191, 192
Carrizo Mountains, 64, 72
Carson, Kit, 82, 91
Casas Grandes, 29, 32
Chamuscado, Francisco Sánchez, 39
Chandler, Daniel T., 76, 78
Chihuahuan Desert, 1, 2, 11, 15–18, 22, 85, 145, 150, 177, 188, 197, 200
Chihuahuita, 92
Chimayó Rebellion of 1837, 62
Chiricahua, 52
Chisum, John, 87, 88, 104, 107, 110
ciboleros, 42, 91
Ciudad Juarez, 5, 8, 32, 33, 40, 44, 140
Civilian Conservation Corps (CCC), 145–47, 154
Civil War, 6, 58, 75, 80, 81, 83–88, 90–92, 95, 97, 100, 102, 111
Clovis culture, 15, 21, 22
Comanche, 6, 30, 44–49, 51–59, 61, 63, 64, 66, 69, 70, 76, 77, 83, 84, 95, 97, 98, 99, 109, 125, 140, 194
Compromise of 1850, 63
Conde, Garcia, 55, 71, 72
Cornudas, 46, 47, 50, 64, 75, 109
Coronado, Francisco Vázquez de, 38, 39
Cox, Cornelius, 66, 67, 113, 129, 144
Croix, Teodoro de, 51, 52
Cuerno Verde, 52–53

Dark Canyon, 23, 106, 107, 116, 146
Davis Mountains, 5, 17, 24, 31, 37, 41, 43, 54, 66, 76, 77, 82, 96
Dayton, Donald, 177
Diamond, Tom, 164, 166
disease, 4, 24, 36, 37, 56, 83
Dog Canyon, 16, 78, 80, 82, 94, 106, 107, 122, 129, 147, 177, 179, 192
Doniphan, Alexander, 61
Douglas, William O., 10, 151, 165, 169, 199
Drury, Newton, 154, 156
Dunmire, Bill, 189

Eddy, Charles B., 105, 115–17
Eddy Dam. *See* Avalon Dam
Eisenhower, Julie Nixon, 179
El Capitan, 1, 8–12, 14, 19, 65, 71, 75, 123, 125, 128, 136, 140, 148, 150–53, 157, 167, 168, 197, 198
El Paso, Texas, 2, 5, 7, 8, 20–30, 34, 40–49, 52–61, 64–69, 71–81, 88, 89, 95, 97, 98–105, 109–14, 118–24, 129, 135, 136, 140, 141, 151–54, 161, 163–67, 173, 174, 177, 195
El Paso Natural Gas Company, 136
establecimientos de paz, 52, 54, 55
Espejo, Antonio de, 39

Florence, New Mexico. *See* Vaud, New Mexico
Forbes, Jack, 31, 33
Ford, John S. "Rip," 65, 66, 104
Fort Bliss, 69, 73, 77–81, 95, 110, 112, 145, 147, 148, 189
Fort Fillmore, 77, 78, 81
Fort Stanton, 77–82, 87, 91, 95, 96, 102
Fort Sumner, 82, 87, 102
Fort Thorn, 77, 79, 80
Franciscans, 44, 45
Fred Harvey Company, 138, 139, 143
Frijole Ranch, 88, 94, 111–14, 120, 125–30, 144, 162, 179, 180, 193, 194
Fuente, Pedro José de la, 50

Gadsden Purchase (Mesilla Treaty), 72, 73, 75, 90
Garcia Conde, Francisco, 55, 71, 72
genizaros, 42, 55
Gilmore, Ben, 88, 93, 144
Goodnight, Charles, 6, 87–89, 107, 110
Granado Cave, 28, 29, 35
Gray, Andrew B., 71–74

Great Depression, 8, 123, 126–29, 134, 143, 144, 147, 154
Guadalupe Mountains: biological characteristics, 13, 15, 16; early human occupation in, 20–23, 27, 28, 32, 34; establishment of park, 150, 155, 157, 167, 167, 168, 170; geology, 3, 11, 13; Guadalupe Mountains Ranch, 88, 94, 111–14, 120, 125–30, 144, 162, 179, 180, 193, 194
guano, 118, 119

Hagerman, James J., 104, 114–17, 123, 133
Halagueno Ranch, 89, 116
Harrell family, 93
Hartz, Edward L., 15, 174, 198
Hartzog, George J., 174, 198
Hatch, Edward, 77, 95, 98
Hays, John Coffee, 66
Hazen, William B., 80
Hispanos, 6, 8, 53, 54, 62, 84–86, 89, 90–92, 101, 102–5, 139, 141
Holmesley, Tom, 109, 110
Hope, 88, 103–6, 109, 115, 116, 131
Houston, Sam, 65
Howard, Charles H., 100, 101
Howard, E. B., 20–23
Hueco Tanks, 21, 30, 47, 50, 64, 67–69, 71–75, 78–82, 93
Hunter, J. C., 9, 10, 123, 126–33, 144, 148–54, 158–64, 167–69, 173–76, 193, 194, 197–99, 200
Hunter Ranch, 126, 151, 174, 199

irrigation: artisan wells, 7, 8, 72, 73, 102, 113, 114, 117, 118, 134; large scale irrigation, 7, 8, 85, 86, 92, 103–6, 114, 115, 118, 133, 141

Jaffa, Nathan, 123
Jicarilla, 56
Jim Crow, 6, 84, 103, 115
Johnson, Lyndon Baines, 10, 66, 88, 151–53, 161, 166–73, 199, 200
Jornada del Muerto, 63
Jornada Mogollon, 2, 20, 22, 25–31
Jumanos, 28–33, 37–47, 56
Junta de los Rios, 20, 31, 33, 39–43, 47, 56

Kearney, Steven W., 61, 62, 90
Kincaid, Noel, 29, 179, 199

224 Index

Land and Water Conservation Fund Act, 166, 172, 175, 200
Lane, William Carr, 72, 78
Largo, Jose, 56, 82
Las Cruces, 10, 33, 46, 56, 61, 79, 88, 105
Las Placitas, 91, 102
Last Chance Canyon, 15, 16, 20
Leah, Joseph C., 104, 105
Leopold, Aldo, 175
Lincoln, town of, 84, 88–91, 105–9
Lincoln County War, 88, 89, 105, 106
Lincoln National Forest, 107, 109, 140, 145, 146, 153, 157, 177, 180, 181, 185–87
Lipan Apache, 31, 48, 49, 56, 59, 77, 98, 195
Llano Estacado, 13, 17, 30, 38, 40–44, 47, 57, 68, 72, 91, 95
Longstreet, James, 79
Loving, New Mexico. *See* Vaud, New Mexico
Loving, Oliver, 6, 87–89, 107, 110, 116
Luxán, Diego Pérez de, 40–42

Magoffin, James, 81
Malaga, New Mexico, 106, 113, 116
Manso, 29, 32–34, 44–47, 100, 125, 197
Manzanita Spring, 94, 111, 127
Manzano Mountains, 6, 31, 47, 79, 84, 91
Marcy, Randolph B., 6, 47, 65, 66, 69
Maria, José Maria, 54
Mather, Stephen T., 138, 141, 143, 155, 176
McCollaum, Opal Green, 108, 109
McKittrick Canyon, 94, 107, 110, 114, 123, 128, 129, 132, 150, 151–54, 158–65, 173, 179–82, 185, 194
McMillan Dam and Reservoir, 116, 134
Medill, William, 64
Mesa Verde, 20, 27, 139, 155
Mescalero Apache, 8, 18, 31–37, 44, 46, 48–56, 66, 68, 69, 75–83, 87–107, 122, 125, 129, 139, 142, 171, 194–97
Mesilla, 49, 54, 56, 61–63, 72, 76, 77, 81, 89, 99
Mesilla Treaty. *See* Gadsden Purchase
Mexican independence, 53, 54, 58
Middleton, Pearl Cochran, 108
MISSION-66, 157, 177, 197, 198
Monterde, José Mariano, 55, 56
monumentalism, 151, 155, 172, 198, 199

National Environmental Protection Act, 173, 191

National Historic Preservation Act, 173, 177
National Geographic, 142, 152
National Parks and Recreation Act of 1978, 178, 182, 183
National Park Service, 138, 141, 156, 172
National Wilderness Preservation System, 72, 75
Native American Graves Protection and Repatriation Act of 1990, 4, 194
natural gas, 131, 136, 172–74, 180, 184–88, 192
Neighbors, Robert Simpson, 64
Neighbors-Ford expedition, 65
New Deal, 122, 144–48
New Mexico Game and Wildlife Commission, 187
Niza, Marcos de, 38
Nuestra Señora de Guadalupe de los Mansos, 44

O'Connor, Hugh, 51
oil exploration, 131, 135, 144
Ojinaga, 5, 47, 52, 56, 77
Oñate, Juan de, 43
Organ Mountains, 5, 33, 47, 51, 65
Ormsby, Waterman L., 74, 75
Otermin, Antonio de, 33, 45

Paleo-Indians, 14, 19, 34
Paraplegics on Independent Nature Trips (POINT), 188
partido system, 42
Pecos River, 2, 4, 7, 11, 16, 17, 22–32, 37, 38, 40–43, 46–49, 53, 64, 66–69, 73, 86, 91, 98, 103–5, 114, 117, 123, 133, 134, 136
Pecos Valley Irrigation and Improvement Company, 115
Pecos Valley Irrigation and Investment Company (PVIIC), 115
Pecos Valley of Texas Water Users Association, 133
Permian Basin, 9, 133, 136, 137, 157
Pinery Station (The Pinery), 73–75, 162, 180
Pine Springs, 68, 73, 75, 88, 94, 97, 110, 120, 126
Piro, 32, 33, 39, 43–46, 125, 197
Plaza of San Jose, 91, 92, 102
Pleistocene, 13–15, 22, 23, 73
Plowman, John T., 106
Polk, James K., 55, 60
Pool, Joe, 151, 161, 166, 169, 199

Pope, John, 73, 114, 122, 199
potash, 137, 138
Pratt, Wallace C., 9, 10, 123, 128, 131, 144, 150, 151, 158, 160, 162, 166, 181, 185, 195, 197, 198
Presidio, El Paso, 47, 49, 50, 54, 56
Presidio del Norte (Ojinaga), 5, 34, 36, 52, 54, 66, 77
presidios, 5, 36, 39, 38, 50–56
Pueblo Revolt of 1680 (Great Northern Rebellion), 32, 45, 46, 57

Queen, 88, 105–9, 120, 122, 125
Querecheros, 32, 38, 40, 43

railroad, 6–8, 59, 64, 71–75, 81–85, 89, 95, 102, 104, 113, 115, 117, 118, 120, 135; Atchison, Topeka, and Santa Fe Railway (ATSF), 114; Pecos Valley Railway (PVRy), 114, 117; Southern Pacific Railroad, 101, 114
ranching, 7, 86–91, 105, 109, 111, 113, 123, 126, 132, 144, 145
Reagan, Ronald, 171, 183, 184
Reconquista of 1692, 96
Reisch, Roger, 179, 180
Republic of Texas, 5, 58, 59
Rio Grande, 5, 26–33, 38, 43, 46, 48–51, 54, 58–67, 76, 81, 89, 90, 100, 125, 129
Roberts Rockshelter, 24
Rocky Arroyo, 15, 17, 43, 107, 109
Roswell, 2, 7, 84, 86, 88–93, 104–6, 113–15, 118, 120, 123, 137, 140, 152
Rubí, Marqués de, 50

Sabeata, Juan, 47
Sacramento Mountains, 2, 4, 11, 37, 40, 53, 54, 68, 71, 100, 101, 195, 200
Sadler, Jerry, 173
Sagebrush Rebellion, 184
salt beds (salt flats), 2, 4, 11, 16, 43, 65, 69, 71, 100, 101, 195, 197, 200
Salt War of 1877, 95, 100, 101, 140
San Elizario, Texas, 54, 64, 77, 80, 100
Santa Fe, New Mexico, 5, 8, 43–45, 48, 49, 53, 60–68, 77, 78, 82, 90, 101, 139, 141, 164, 171, 173, 193
Scott, Winfield, 63
Segrest, Ruben, 125
Segura, Geronimo, 125
Seven Rivers, 87, 89, 105–9
Shattuck, John S., 107

sheep ranching, 91, 92, 110, 131, 143, 158
Sierra Blanca: mountains, 5, 22, 51, 76, 82, 96, 100; town, 7, 26, 28, 29, 99, 101, 112, 120, 122
Sierra Club, 161, 166, 177, 178, 185, 199
Signal Peak Café, 144
Skyline Drive, 177
Smith, Joe T., 111, 112, 122–27, 130, 140, 193, 194
Sosa, Gaspar Castaño de, 42
Steck, Michael, 79
Steen, Enoch, 76
Suma, 29, 32–34, 45–47, 100, 125

Taos Rebellion (1847), 82
Taylor, Zachary, 60, 63
Texas Rangers, 84, 93
Texas Rebellion, 58
Texas State Parks Board, 152, 153
Teyas, 30, 38, 39
Tiguas, 69, 70, 100, 195
Toll, Roger, 153
Topographical Corps of Engineers, 64, 72
tourism, 98, 123, 133, 140, 141, 145, 151, 152, 175, 176, 178, 188, 192
Treaty of Guadalupe Hidalgo, 52, 62, 63, 70, 71, 75, 76, 100
Treaty of Mesilla. *See* Gadsden Purchase
Tulk, J. W., 106

Udall, Stewart, 10, 151, 160, 163, 199
U.S.-Mexico Boundary Commission, 63, 70–73
U.S.-Mexican War, 47, 56, 58, 73, 75, 100
U.S. Reclamation Service (Bureau of Reclamation), 134, 157

Vaca, Álvar Núñez Cabeza de, 33, 37, 38
Van Horn, 7, 21, 64, 99, 101, 110–13, 120–28, 135, 137, 140, 152, 181
Van Horne, Jefferson, 66, 77, 80, 112
Vaud, New Mexico, 116
Victorio, 63, 70, 71, 73

Warriors Project, 195
Watt, James, 171, 183, 184
White, C. L. "Charlie," 142, 143
White, James Larkin "Jim," 119, 120, 141, 142, 143
White, Richard, 116, 174, 177, 178, 182, 190, 199, 200

White Sands, 100, 147, 148, 152
White's City, 143
Whiting, W. H. C., 66, 76
Wilderness Act of 1964, 172, 175, 176, 182
Wilderness Society, 175
Williams, James Adolphus "Dolph," 123–29, 144
Williams, Tom, 124, 126
Williams Cave, 15
World War II, 9, 119, 122, 136, 143, 147, 150, 151, 154, 169, 175, 198, 199

Yarborough, Ralph, 10, 151, 161–70, 174, 175, 179, 199
Yard, Robert Sterling, 172

www.ingramcontent.com/pod-product-compliance
Lightning Source LLC
LaVergne TN
LVHW040735250326
834688LV00031B/313